EXCHANGES WITHIN

EXCHANGES WITHIN

Questions from Everyday Life

Selected from Gurdjieff Group Meetings

with John Pentland in California

1955–1984

John Pentland

JEREMY P. TARCHER / PENGUIN

a member of Penguin Group (USA) Inc.

New York

Most Tarcher/Penguin books are available at special quantity discounts for bulk purchase for sales promotions, premiums, fund-raising, and educational needs. Special books or book excerpts also can be created to fit specific needs. For details, write Penguin Group (USA) Inc. Special Markets, 375 Hudson Street, New York, NY 10014.

Jeremy P. Tarcher/Penguin
a member of
Penguin Group (USA) Inc.
375 Hudson Street
New York, NY 10014
www.penguin.com
First published in 1997 by the Continuum Publishing Company
First Jeremy P. Tarcher/Penguin edition 2004

Library of Congress Cataloging-in-Publication Data

Pentland, Henry John Sinclair, Baron, 1907–1984.
Exchanges within: questions from everyday life selected from Gurdjieff group meetings with John Pentland in California, 1955–1984 / John Pentland.
p.   cm.
Originally published: New York: Continuum, 1997.
ISBN 1-58542-365-3 (pbk.)
1. Pentland, Henry John Sinclair, Baron, 1907–1984.   2. Gurdjieff, Georges Ivanovitch, 1872–1949.   I. Title.
BP605.G9P46   2004   2004046020
197—dc22

Printed in the United States of America
1   3   5   7   9   10   8   6   4   2

CONTENTS

Part One
1955–1968

CHAPTER 1

CHAPTER 2

CHAPTER 5

CHAPTER 6

CHAPTER 7

CHAPTER 8

Part Two
1961–1977

CHAPTER 9

CHAPTER 10

CHAPTER 15

CHAPTER 16

Part Three
1977–1984

CHAPTER 20

CHAPTER 21

CHAPTER 22

CHAPTER 23

CHAPTER 24

CHAPTER 25

CHAPTER 26

CHAPTER 27

CHAPTER 28

CHAPTER 29

FOREWORD
by Roy Finch

With the publication of *Exchanges Within*, a new contribution has been added to the small number of genuinely valuable modern works of spiritual direction and guidance. This volume takes its place alongside the best writings of such spiritual explorers as Simone Weil, Baron Friedrich von Huegel, D. T. Suzuki, Thomas Merton, Bede Griffiths, Martin Buber and Frithjof Schuon. Its background lies in the Gurdjieff teaching, with all that teacher's special cosmic, mythic and esoteric dimensions.

Exchanges Within, in fact, concentrates on one main question: finding within ourselves what we have (this time almost irretrievably) lost: our reality, wholeness and significance as the human kind of being in the universe. The real human individual (virtually without our having noticed it) is missing, while knowledge and social power grow everywhere out of control. The "unreality" which, like a miasma, has been invading our civilization and our lives at every level, has its ultimate source here.

"What is a human being?" This is the question on which our future depends. For a long time we thought we knew the answer. A human being, we would have said, is an autonomous, freely choosing will, or the combination of such a will and practical intelligence in harmony with the theoretical intellect, which, we believed, knows eternal forms and laws. This classic formulation preserved a relative balance between natural and supernatural, science and religion, reason and revelation.

When modern science, however, with its technological essence, reduced the universe to strictly measurable physical forces without spiritual or ethical content, the human individual was cut off and isolated as a lonely private subject, compensated with illusions of scientific power. Illusions because it is a power we are far from understanding or controlling, while all the time we imagine ourselves to be its "master" or "possessor," unaware that it has long since taken possession of us. From birth to death we are in the grip of suggestion, fashion, habit, greed, fear, opportunism and self-and-group-interest. Where in all this is there room for objective conscience and individual responsibility?

Lord Pentland characterizes this enslavement as our "mechanicalness." It goes deeper than any present dream; it is the prime human illusion. We are not the agents of our own lives, but, it seems, almost always sleepers and dreamers; only the dream varies. Today we are asleep on the edge of a precipice dreaming that we are the masters of great power, which in actuality is destroying us, and leaving us empty shells in a world of unreality.

To begin to wake up requires a whole new shift of orientation from the seemingly so powerful but actually helpless ego-will to the undeveloped capacity to see ourselves objectively at last. This new step has to be the ability to focus our attention on our daily self-deception. With adroitness and subtlety Lord Pentland brings out that we can begin to become fitfully and unexpectedly aware of what we really look like. We can begin to catch tiny glimpses of just how total our fraudulence really is. When it is possible to keep some small amount of attention free from being totally immersed in whatever happens to come along to seize our energies, we will begin to get a taste of what "waking up" feels like, and this is the beginning of genuine development. Not illusory self-willing, but real self-seeing, which is the start of "remembering who we are."

The English writer D. H. Lawrence, who also knew Gurdjieff, once remarked that, as things stand, we have two main ways of dealing with ourselves. There are, first, the "things we tell ourselves" which, even when they are couched as criticisms, are calculated to please us, and, second, the "things which we find out about ourselves" which are unpleasant and sometimes shattering. This difficulty in seeing the truth about ourselves is in fact one of the principle themes of world literature.

Lord Pentland was well aware of the other "ego treachery," of how ego hides behind "spiritual development." How proud we are of our humility or of "seeing through the ego"! But it is one more deception. There is no "I" to be proud or to congratulate itself on such "accomplishments." What is truly seen of these imaginations disappears. It was always a nothing.

How to expose the false self? It cannot be done by introspection, spiritual disciplines or psychological analysis. One doesn't get to *know* oneself in these ways. Nothing can take the place of "direct seeing." We need to catch ourselves with our defenses down, which is never the case with these prepared methods. Direct seeing goes beyond any number of "interpretations" which subtly and secretly distort the truth. Do we need new myths masquerading as destroyers of old ones?

For Lord Pentland, as for most of the religious traditions in their spiritual cores, a self which is not able to undergo radical transformation out of old identifications and attachments is not capable of full development. The more content we are with ourselves and our inherited worlds, the more sound asleep we are. It is only when we have begun to realize that there is something seriously wrong with most of human life, including, in the first instance, ourselves, that we are ready to meet a teacher or guide who will be able to help us find out what to do about it. A wholly sincere wish to awaken will lead to the beginning of an inner separation between the ego-dreaming self and the reality-seeing self. The really good news is that the former can merge into the latter. But, as the ancient Gnostic saying has it: *In order to become wholly one, we must first become two.*

With that marvelous practicality that characterizes the best spiritual directors, Lord Pentland calls attention to the fact that the best time of day for practicing this separation is the early morning when we first wake up and before the "identifications" of the day take over. Insights into our own patterns of behavior may occur to us then, which would not at any other time. But we have to catch hold of them and see what they mean for everything else we are doing.

That the ego is nothing is a religious teaching to be found as much in Sufism, Hinduism, Buddhism and Taoism as in Christianity, in the world's scriptures as well as in the tomes of theologians. Christ's teaching of the necessity to be born again demands the death of the ego and the birth of a new Universal Spirit self. With almost scientific precision St. John of the Cross and St. Theresa of Avila spelled out a "method" of such a change, as did, in their Protestant framework, Jacob Boehme and Henry Suso. In our own century the "naughting of the ego" is the central idea of Simone Weil and Thomas Merton. In regard to this, East and West are in agreement. "The taste of self-remembering is liberating because it is the feeling of reality." At this point we feel that we have at last broken through the webs of illusion and self-deceit that psychology too often provides for us. The same kind of *sublime common sense* that we find in the Gospels, in Laotzu, in the Zen koans, Rumi and the Sufis is here too in Gurdjieff. But of course it is coded differently in each of these. We cannot read any two of them in the same way.

The certitude which arises from all these simple but inexhaustibly mysterious writings goes deeper by far than the certitude which we get from scientific knowledge alone. This is because they speak for our feelings as well as for our minds, for the vast range of human relations, and for the lessons of the daily round. The whole of human life is in them.

There is a widespread belief that science deals with what is most concrete. But in fact the most concrete is the least graspable and most mysterious. What is closest to us and most obvious is what we are least able to see. The scales do not fall from our eyes because we look in the wrong place and in the wrong way.

There is an uncanny beauty in the great religions, often embodied in the supreme figures of culture: St. Francis, Dogen, Milarepa, William Blake, Ramakrishna, Gandhi. These names glow. In the work of Gurdjieff and Lord Pentland there is also such a glow. I am tempted to call it *Gnostic beauty.* It is embedded in the responsibility and faithfulness of Gurdjieff, who asked no favors and expected no consolations. Two sentences from Gnostic sources sum this up.

Though far-off we did not cease to think of Thee. Remember who
you are—sons and daughters of the Most High.

INTRODUCTION

This book offers a glimpse into the dynamics of a living teaching, into the actual process of exchange during which the substantial food of discovering and understanding inner growth is shared. Here an exceptional man, in his role as teacher, meets his pupils within the moment-to-moment experience of discovering the potential for awakening and the forces that stand in its way. These exchanges reflect genuine efforts towards the discovery and practice of meaningful living, in a world that has drained human life of the sacred.

Gurdjieff taught that it is impossible to know what man is without knowing the purpose of his existence. But we cannot know why we exist without first knowing *that* we exist, that we are "here and now." It is this awakening to our own presence that lies at the practical heart of the Gurdjieff teaching, and it is the struggle to awaken and find true values in life that can be sensed in the following pages.

As a direct pupil of Gurdjieff, one of a small circle engaged in the task of transmitting the Gurdjieff work to others, Lord Pentland guided hundreds of men and women in the search for the mysteriously elusive yet direct experience of themselves. Under his guidance the grand order of the universe described by Gurdjieff could at moments become intimately relevant to the episodes and crises of an individual's personal life.

Lord Pentland was born Henry John Sinclair near London in 1907 to Scottish parents. From the ages of 5 to 12, he lived in India while his father was Governor General of Madras. At the age of 18, he inherited his title of Lord Pentland. He studied engineering at Trinity College, Cambridge, and travelled widely, and had begun to take his place in the world of politics and business when he attended P. D. Ouspensky's lectures on Gurdjieff's teachings in 1937 in London. From then on he worked with the Ouspenskys in England and later in America until he met Gurdjieff: "It was after Ouspensky died and I went out to India and on the way back, actually, it became clear to me that even all those years with Ouspensky, I hadn't arrived at anything. I came to nothing. And it was then through Madam Ouspensky's introduction I went to Paris and met Gurdjieff. And it was a short period, only about nine months: but a couple of months after that he died. And the way he left things, it made it perfectly easy for me to have to really enter in a position of responsibility as such. So it made it essentially easy for me to try to understand more deeply what he showed me."

Gurdjieff had appeared in Moscow in 1912 on the eve of the Russian Revolution and the First World War at a time of gathering uncertainty. No one like him and nothing like the ideas he brought had been presented in the modern West. He was not recognizable as a traditional religious teacher, yet the knowledge he represented echoed something of the root and content of the great religions. At the same time, he expressed his ideas in forms and language evoking laws and mathematical precision. He is described by those close to him as a man of astonishing force and compassion, both in his sensitivity to the hidden feelings of his pupils and in his ability impartially to strike at the illusions that prevented them from seeing themselves.

What are these ideas that attracted Lord Pentland and so many others? Man, Gurdjieff taught, is asleep. This is the tragedy of our human condition. War, injustice, meaninglessness, and much of human misery are a result of this sleep. Referring to very ancient sources, Gurdjieff brought a way of self-knowledge that calls us to awaken. For this, the first step is to develop our capacity to see ourselves as we really are, to see our submersion in the automatism of thought, feeling, and instinct. We are not yet authentic individuals; we are a multitude of conflicting selves, none of which can truly say, "I." To free our captive energies, an inner work is necessary.

"I can't help you," Gurdjieff is quoted as saying. "You can only be helped by the conditions I create." Around Gurdjieff conditions changed constantly. He brought a number of forms as conditions for work which continue to be explored. In addition to the group meeting, these include his Movements, also known as Sacred Dances, readings from his written works, crafts, meditation, music, and all kinds of intellectual and physical work. Throughout, Gurdjieff stressed the need to work with others of varying experience. The pupil remains connected to the source of the teaching through a network of exchange between youngest and eldest that enlarges the perspective of the traditional teacher-pupil relationship.

The group meeting was a principal form of this exchange and during Gurdjieff's life such groups formed in many countries. After his death many of his pupils and the groups that worked with them came together under the guidance of Jeanne de Salzmann, with whom Lord Pentland worked for the rest of his life. In New York the Gurdjieff Foundation was established in 1953 with Lord Pentland as its president. In 1955, responding to inquiries from interested people in California, Lord Pentland first visited there; and soon groups formed around him in San Francisco and later in Los Angeles. The material in the present book is drawn from group meetings in California between 1955 and Lord Pentland's death in 1984.

With great personal demand and impartiality, Lord Pentland devoted himself to group work, considering it a central instrument for transmitting the way. Readers who are familiar with Eastern and Western spiritual traditions may feel resonances in this Gurdjieffian mode of exchange; but for most people today the group meeting remains unique.

It may help the reader to be aware that these exchanges take place in a specially sensitive atmosphere, where diverse and differently prepared groups of men and women meet to find and express their own questions. These exchanges do not necessarily lead to definite answers but, on the contrary, encourage deeper questioning and further experience. Through the intensity of his own search, Lord Pentland radiated the help necessary for group members again and again to discover and try to express where they actually are in the process of understanding and in the movement towards being. What will not be found on the printed page is the silence of a group's shared self-confrontation, the extraordinary experience of consciousness.

Part One
1955 – 1968

Part One

one

Ideas and my life are not related . . .

LORD PENTLAND: Have you been able to relate Gurdjieff's ideas to your life? If you have, then we can help each other here by telling what we have found. There are these two things: we are interested in these ideas, but they are not yet related to our lives. We don't often think about our lives. I don't know what picture you have of your life, but if we can be sincere, and if we can forget about the times our vision is clouded by negative emotions, we find that our lives are very full—our families, friends, jobs. We give our attention to what is occupying us without questioning what we are doing. Only when we are tired do we think of Gurdjieff's ideas. We turn from our actual life and concern ourselves with talking to ourselves or others about ideas. Talking.

These ideas are one thing; on the other hand, there is our life. But they are not yet related. We never remember to relate them. Of course some of you have tried to relate them, but it is not simple. Something is missing. If you have tried you have begun to see that it is almost as if we were two different persons, two different natures. One has an ideal, but he dreams about it instead of trying to achieve it. The other has the means to achieve, but on the way he is stopped. He is limited, not free, just a creature of circumstance used by nature for creating a family or a book.

QUESTION: What is it that is missing? I guess it's my own effort to make the two come together.

LORD PENTLAND: It may be.

QUESTIONER: But should I be more consistent?

LORD PENTLAND: Maybe.

QUESTIONER: What would you say?

LORD PENTLAND: I'd say that we have to see the gap. It is not enough to have a picture. One has to see it. It is like zero and infinity. There is no connection between the two persons in us. They never meet. They contradict each other.

QUESTIONER: How are they ever going to get together?

LORD PENTLAND: You see already you speak about how to try to get together. I speak about how to see. We never remember it. You must find your way.

There are two worlds. One world is the world of accident, the earth. We never remember about it. We live in it but never experience it. We may experience a little, and we speak a little about some kind of psychology, but the real fact of our lives on earth we never experience. We only know it by logic. Then there is the higher world. We experience it a little; we can't deny that there is something. If we reason with ourselves and try to deny there is a higher world, we can't. It too is part of our experience. We live all the time in these two worlds and we can never experience both at the same time or either one separately. And yet, it's our situation. So something is missing. I don't know whether you agree or understand how we are trying to approach these ideas. You tell me.

QUESTION: Would you suggest that one select some aim in the morning, some proper method to pursue to accomplish development of essence?

LORD PENTLAND: I don't see how your question relates—making the same old good intention. What is not mechanical about what you say? What can you or I say which can alter something which has to be seen many times? Only for a moment can we behold this terrible situation. What difference does it make? Do you see what I mean?

QUESTIONER: No, I don't.

LORD PENTLAND: Perhaps someone else?

QUESTION: There seems to be no way of getting to the other stream, no way of getting across into sensing that there are two worlds. But in speaking of life as it is today and these ideas as we know and use them, is it not possible to bring them into our experience of today in order to reach a place of understanding? Would that not help us?

LORD PENTLAND: Yes, you may be quite right. Do you see what is missing?

QUESTIONER: Is it knowledge of ourselves that is missing?

LORD PENTLAND: Of course. If we've really seen the gap, we see that we've hardly experienced it. The gap exists because we have no knowledge of ourselves. We really must feel the necessity of bringing the two aspects into relation. Is anyone here really satisfied with the impact of these ideas on his life? Isn't it because we know nothing about ourselves? First of all these ideas are for studying ourselves as we are. They are all a help for that. We can use them because they can help us to study ourselves as we are.

QUESTION: Is it true that we must have someone who knows to teach us?

LORD PENTLAND: Quite true. If I really see the necessity to study myself, I need a teacher. How often have you felt the necessity?

QUESTIONER: Almost ever since I started reading these teachings.

LORD PENTLAND: We come now to the question of sincerity. Until I have understood something about sincerity no teacher can help me. It's quite a different thing to see the necessity of studying oneself in this situation. Am I sure my wish is such that I can demand a teacher? Do you see what I mean?

QUESTIONER: I believe I do.

We study ourselves in relation to sleep and waking . . .

QUESTION: Is it the realization of inadequacies, of self-love, of the lack of development that makes one feel the need of a teacher?

LORD PENTLAND: The need for a teacher arises when a question arises. But one can study oneself out of self-love. It is something we have to speak about. I'm sure almost everyone here has seen that something is missing. What is missing is that I don't know myself. We don't wish to study ourselves. We'd rather achieve, or dream about achieving something.

QUESTIONER: Isn't that just the point? I get very confused as to whether I'm dreaming or self-observing. Isn't there a need for guidance? How does one know one is not going around in a whirlpool? Gurdjieff stresses how little we know about ourselves. I find that true, and I wonder if I'm on the right track. Guidance is necessary for beginners. How do we know we are on the right track?

LORD PENTLAND: Do you see what is the right track?

QUESTIONER: That's what I want to know.

LORD PENTLAND: We have so little capacity to wish to study ourselves. Do you see in relation to what principle we study ourselves?

QUESTIONER: We must attempt understanding in relation to ourselves and in the universe. Our motive would be to increase our being.

LORD PENTLAND: Yes, that would be the motive. But I have to study myself in relation to some principle. I have to study myself in relation to the idea of states of consciousness. We don't study at random. We study ourselves in relation to sleep and waking.

QUESTION: I would like to become more conscious. Is there any particular time to study?

LORD PENTLAND: Now we have left our situation. You see? "I would like to be more conscious. I would like to be a painter." What is the difference? Did you get any result that way? Of course not. Our task is to watch, observe what we are. We study ourselves in relation to states of consciousness. Each time we shall see something different. We study. We are not yet remembering ourselves. You see? We are trying to study ourselves.

QUESTION: I would like to say something in regard to a little experiment I tried. I thought I was observing, but I did not realize until later that my attention was outside.

LORD PENTLAND: Does this help you?

QUESTIONER: I hope so.

LORD PENTLAND: Why should we hope? The taste of an automatic movement is quite recognizable. Perhaps someone saw himself this week as quite mechanical. Why should we hope? It is better to be precise.

QUESTIONER: Well, because we want to strive to be better. How can we be better if we don't strive?

LORD PENTLAND: Now I return to my situation. I need to bring together these contradictory sides of my life. If I wish to try, it is not a bad thing, but for finding out about myself, I must wish to study myself. These other things are not bad, but they are not for this purpose. We mustn't cling to the idea that what is good for us isn't clear. Why can't we be clear? Perhaps you were brought up to believe that all this side of life is emotion, dependent on emotions. We must learn to think.

QUESTION: Suppose you observe one state of consciousness and recognize it is not good. How do you raise it to another? How do you get out of it?

LORD PENTLAND: Yes, this is very important. But we haven't reached this yet. You must be patient.

A better understanding now appears like
a lack of understanding . . .

QUESTION: At first, when I started to read the ideas, I thought I understood what I was reading, but as time went on I found I didn't. Instead of my understanding increasing in relation to the effort I put in, I seem to understand less.

LORD PENTLAND: Can you speak a little more about your actual experience?

QUESTIONER: Well, my position in life seemed fairly certain. I seemed to know where I was with people around me—friends, associates, family—and my ideas about life were not fixed, but I thought I knew their

7

direction. Now all this seems vague and confused. My standards of evaluation seem to be altering, but I can't seem to understand why.

LORD PENTLAND: You see the result was different from what you expected. It has to be so. If you study something new, it has to be a new picture. You see a better understanding now appears like a lack of understanding, a truer understanding appears like a loss of understanding.

In the same way, if you make this attempt to understand yourself in relation to states of consciousness, you will see—if you persevere—you will come to the understanding that you are asleep. This would be the first step. In all sorts of relationships we see we are in a dream. At those times something more central in us is aware. That, of course, is not a continuing experience. So you see it is a long time before we can ask for a new understanding.

Nothing really resulted from attempting too much . . .

QUESTION: The hardest thing for me personally is to believe that I am asleep or mechanical. Will I defeat my purpose in feeling this way?

LORD PENTLAND: The difficulty isn't that. The difficulty is in working. I spoke just now of the result of a process. It is not the result of one effort. It is the result of many attempts.

But we must start. You have the opportunity of starting and, if you study, you'll see what stands in your way, for instance, that we always attempt too much, take too big an aim. To start, you have to take some small habit and make a start from that. If you look back, you will see one has never taken a small enough aim. You will see how difficult it is even with something small. If you look back at your attempts, you see that nothing really resulted from attempting too much. Maybe someone understands what I mean?

This energy that goes into useless talking is all that we have for working on ourselves . . .

QUESTION: If while one is talking mechanically one is aware of it, does that awareness mean anything?

LORD PENTLAND: It's so difficult, isn't it, to be aware of more than one thing. For instance, if anyone here has really made the effort to control talking, you can see that it is impossible unless you can remember why, unless you can see that this energy which goes into useless talking is all that we have for working on ourselves.

You see we forget to look at our actual lives. As soon as we come to a particular means of understanding ourselves, we forget the real situation of our lives. We forget there are the two ways of looking—the automatic, where we justify what is happening and follow behind, always trying to catch up with ourselves, and the other way, quite different, which is the small idea that we can wish to change ourselves. Gurdjieff said, "If you wish, you can."

QUESTION: The terms self-observation and self-remembering, the distinction between them is not clear to me. What is the distinction? Or are they the same?

LORD PENTLAND: Of course we speak of something we know very little about. What is self-remembering? Something I cannot approach directly. I can only say it is a state of consciousness which is my right and within my possibility, but I cannot achieve it. But self-observation is an action. It is something one can do in that state. Do you see?

QUESTIONER: Not synonymous, then?

LORD PENTLAND: Not synonymous. You have made a better answer than mine.

QUESTION: Don't you need to go along with self-remembering?

LORD PENTLAND: What do you mean, "go along"?

QUESTIONER: Not identify with something. Try to feel detached and sort of small and yet try to hold on to what is stable.

LORD PENTLAND: But what is stable?

QUESTIONER: I don't feel it is myself.

LORD PENTLAND: What can we hold on to then? We try not to identify, so what is stable?

QUESTIONER: I try to feel it.

LORD PENTLAND: It is your imagination. Your fear. Do you see what I mean? Do you see what we mean by the feeling of not remembering one-self, the feeling that there is nowhere to stay? This is the beginning. In order to come to this we must work against some very definite obstacles; otherwise we imagine everything, and our lives will become very narrow. I don't know whether you understand, but I believe that we all feel that in Gurdjieff's ideas there is something we can work on—reasonable and sound—and not take our feet off the ground. Let's not get off into something fantastic. It becomes more difficult.

QUESTION: How does one approach these things without words? I'm constantly involved in inner talking.

LORD PENTLAND: Yes. You've read that talking is an obstacle?

QUESTIONER: Yes. Outer talking. But this inner talking. . . .

LORD PENTLAND: But you never saw it as an obstacle before?

QUESTIONER: I do now.

LORD PENTLAND: It's very good that you see this. You will see a new reason to study. It's how we are. You will see a need, a reason to study. Before it was theory, but now you have seen what stands in your way.

QUESTIONER: Yes, if I could somehow get away from talking.

LORD PENTLAND: It's not the talking itself. It's that we identify with it. We lose our energy in those words. And what is energy? We put all our attention in those words and lose all our energy. Just as it has happened millions of times this way, so it will take millions and millions of little efforts to change it.

QUESTIONER: Even with all the words I can't express myself.

LORD PENTLAND: Yes, you express yourself very well. These words you speak take away the little energy you have. From long habit one's attention is distracted outwards. Where is my attention? Scattered in many places. You must see it as a force that can be controlled a little. You have some possibility of seeing how it goes, by trying to turn it the other way.

Each morning, remember Gurdjieff saying that the only preparation we can make is trying to keep a little attention on ourselves. Instead of rushing at once into all I will do, there is a possibility just then of remembering about not allowing attention and energies to be drawn in all directions.

QUESTIONER: If I could do it without talking . . . .

LORD PENTLAND: Well, you start doing it now.

*My possibility for change is only now when I realize
my mechanicalness . . .*

QUESTION: If we are mechanical, then we can't change, can we? We're under mechanical laws.

LORD PENTLAND: Yes, it's quite true. Yet if I were to say to you that there is no possibility of change, would you agree to it?

QUESTIONER: No, I resist that.

LORD PENTLAND: My possibility for change is only now, when I realize my mechanicalness. And I can speak about my possibility of change, of evolution, but it's then I experience the hopelessness of my dreams, then I can wake up. When I'm driven to a dead end where I see the total meaninglessness of my life, my plans, my hopes—it's exactly then that the possibility of change is real. But afterwards I speak about changing myself— what I want to change from—but it hasn't the same meaning as when I see it, and when I'm aware of my total mechanicalness.

It's a great help to read the chapters on the cosmological ideas in the books of Gurdjieff and Ouspensky. It's not easy. But if you've led a normal life, an appreciation of the big world around us can help us find our place.

Gurdjieff says that everything in the universe is material and consists of vibrations, everything physical and psychical. Everything that exists can be expressed as vibrations of a certain order. He explains the law, which represents the process by which one material is transformed into another, so we have a table of the vibrations that exist in the universe. We have the Law of Three Forces, one of which is active in relation to the others, and one of which is passive or denying, and the other, the neutralizing.

Gurdjieff arranges the whole universe into what he calls the Ray of Creation, the ray that goes through the earth on which we live, and he shows that this series of worlds from the Absolute to the moon is arranged in a descending octave, that is to say, a process that proceeds from the Absolute, through all worlds, all suns—that is, the Milky Way—our sun, the planets, and from the earth, to the moon. And there is a discontinuity in the scale between *do* and *si* and *fa* and *mi*.

You see, we can even take a diagram like this quite literally. We may be able to experience some of these meanings later. And when we look around and look at our place in the universe, we can't any longer feel quite the same about all our plans.

It's important to our understanding to think of our mechanicalness as the force that moves downward through the earth to the moon. Sometimes we recognize that it's not our force that passes through us—our violence or ingenuity. In any case, a force passes downward which we call the involutionary. This is the force by which everything reproduces, lives, and dies on this earth.

It's an accident that we take up this or that career, and we never notice that at some moment we disappear in our plans. But in that process big things are done—bridges are built, and so on—through the force that feeds the moon, something far beyond our power.

Then there is another so-called evolutionary force by which our energies are renewed, by which things sometimes come together in a moment of coincidence. We are very little conscious of the action of this force, too.

To change our situation would be hopeless, but if you read carefully you will see that Gurdjieff says there is a third force created by conscious men on earth. It's almost impossible to believe—that through these men, through the existence of schools—influences can be brought to bear to help us be aware of these other forces, that it is possible for a few people to come into such a relation with this conscious circle that they are able to make actual changes in their lives.

Seeing mechanicalness as a force . . .

QUESTION: It is said in the books that when we study ourselves and see something we do not like, we cannot change it. Well, if we see something and know we cannot change it, do we just go on and observe it?

LORD PENTLAND: Yes. But can you see this?

QUESTIONER: Yes, I have sometimes. And I've attempted not to analyze, but I repeatedly see myself doing things that I don't like to do.

LORD PENTLAND: Some of us here have seen this mechanicalness as a force. And if we have seen this mechanicalness as a force that passes through us, we have appreciated a truth from which there is no going back. When we see this, colored with distaste for my laziness or my greediness, we know it is something to struggle with—but not with logic. In the moment when I see this mechanicalness as a force, I am in touch with something stronger than logic. It's very difficult to see this not colored with feelings about my various shortcomings. Still, I shall try to see myself as I am, a creature at the mercy of mechanical forces so big, so huge, so powerful, they are out of scale altogether with these little feelings of distaste.

QUESTION: You say force, but I don't see any force. I don't know what you are talking about, "mechanical force." I do something with a certain amount of awareness some of the time. But when you say a force passes through, what do you mean?

LORD PENTLAND: I expect you've seen it, but maybe you didn't understand me. Perhaps you've seen your arm move? What moves it? Sometimes you've seen yourself light a cigarette. Who lighted it? Not your force—you weren't there. You see, we are asleep. We are blind. We don't see what is going on in us. Have you any feeling of agreement with this?

QUESTIONER: Yes.

LORD PENTLAND: Then you know that you just see through the chinks. Some force is acting through you. In order to appreciate this, we have to resist this force. It sounds ridiculous that we, with no force, should try to resist these big forces. But if we try—for instance, if you listen now and try to understand what I am going to say—we may be able to see something.

All the time these forces are leaving us. These vibrations are passing through us all day. Most of the time we are quite asleep to this. Tonight we renew; tomorrow it leaves us again. It would be useful if you would try sometimes to retrieve these vibrations that are leaving you all the time. Sit as quietly as you can and feel this energy as if it were leaving you, and you try and be a little magnet and draw it back. Maybe a few minutes of this every day and you would begin to realize that there are big forces at work. Is something not clear about this?

Because we have a picture, we neglect to experience . . .

QUESTION: Suppose that, to a certain extent, we stop this energy flowing out, will it be like a dam in a river? Will it give us more energy if we dam it up?

LORD PENTLAND: Now we come to a difficult thing. All our attempts to understand ourselves are spoiled by pictures. I don't know if you've seen that. But it's the most mechanical thing. Because we have a picture, we neglect to experience these things. Of course what you say is true. We could make little dams. And they would be like little earth dams, easily swept away, but would give us moments in which we could remember ourselves more than we ordinarily do. Now you could try this, as I said, and without pictures. Next time think before you try to imagine about something, about an experience you haven't tried.

QUESTIONER: Well, I hear constantly about this energy flowing out.

LORD PENTLAND: Yes. But you need first to experience what I have told you about.

QUESTIONER: I remember that Gurdjieff says we cannot do anything, but maybe we can try plugging up some of the leaks.

LORD PENTLAND: Very often when I ask a question, I get an answer that comes a little bit from the side. I must try to listen and get away from my own point of view. There is no reason to think it is better. I must look out for hints of a new point of view. For you, it would be particularly helpful to be on the lookout for a new point of view.

QUESTIONER: Yes. But we must have some aim.

LORD PENTLAND: Perhaps all we can hope to accomplish is to find what our aim is. Perhaps by understanding these forces, we shall understand better where to go.

*We don't value enough this state of being able
to see inner confusion . . .*

QUESTION: The other night I sat down and decided to work. Someone rang up on the phone and invited us out on a boat, and we had a wonderful evening. When we got back, I felt something unfinished. I had a feeling I should have been working instead of boating. It seems that part of me is tremendously interested in these ideas and part of me is not.

LORD PENTLAND: When you are in a state where you realize there are parts that value this work and parts that do not, this first contact exposes the inner confusion in myself. I'm sure you will agree that there is a little quality of light about it that is new. Are you sure that seeing this inner confusion is what you want? It takes a long time to understand how to even begin to take the first step. It's because we don't value enough this state of being able to see this inner confusion.

We're always losing ourselves in life. So how to begin. Something reminds me of Gurdjieff's work. I remember about the ideas. There is something missing, something which I am not able to bring into my life. My life is not exactly unsatisfactory. I do what I can to understand ordinary, decent behavior, but I feel something is missing. It's the idea of mechanicalness I remember here.

What does it mean to you? Perhaps you've heard that man is a machine; you've read that man is a machine, and there's the ordinary idea that man works according to certain scientific laws. But you cannot make the connections. We never remember that we are mechanical. The whole idea of Gurdjieff is the total and complete mechanicalness of man. It's something I'm able to appreciate after a long day—I see that I never acted from myself. I see afterwards that it was just reactions that corresponded to the inner situations I came in contact with. Perhaps it will help to remember that mechanicalness is inner passivity. We think we choose but actually we are chosen.

One of Gurdjieff's closest pupils has often said that she recognized, at even a very early age, that she was a puppet, and her whole interest was to find out who pulled the strings. But there are few of us who could say the same.

Take my relation to somebody else, for instance my relation to friends or family. Again and again I may decide in advance that I will be a certain way—to be sympathetic or to get something from them, perhaps—but again and again I find that something else happens. Even quite practical business experiences are the same. I may think for a time that I've been able to take into account the whole field in which my business works and that I will be able to arrange for things to happen in a certain way. But the time comes when I see that it was just part of a process, like waves coming from waves, and I find myself on top of the wave and then down in the trough of the wave.

There are no spheres in which you cannot see the passiveness. We have to look into the dark sides of ourselves and see that the same thing happens there.

The next step is to see the lack of unity in ourselves. I don't mean the little changes—today I say one thing, tomorrow another. I mean the real changes in my whole person which take place all the time, without my knowing it. We are hardly ever aware of our feelings, only the manifestations afterwards.

Coming here in a taxi I was trying not to be altogether lost in the beauty of the surroundings and suddenly the taxi driver, who had been driving safely and sanely, became a dangerous man in a matter of seconds. Of course, it's only too easy to see this in other people, but it is very difficult to see it in ourselves. We don't even know what real emotions are and, when we have them, they last a much shorter time than we think because, as we are, we identify all the time with what is going on in our heads. I am what I think. If I deny what you think, I deny what you are and you can't bear it. It's what makes conversations and discussions impossible.

Actually, Gurdjieff has explained that this big brain is not meant for what we use it for. It is the secretary with the connections and files, the secretary who can answer yes or no. But we use this part to make decisions with—from conversations overheard by the secretary.

We are aware, a little, of thoughts, but we identify with them. Our bodies are less spoiled than our minds and our feelings. It's very rare that we take any notice of our bodies. We awake to find we have dropped something or are carrying something, so perhaps we see that our bodies live in a different world.

All our attention is centered in our heads. We have no possibility of unity. So what to do? Perhaps we have to begin by saying this: "I see that something is missing, that all the time I change. Part of me wishes to be able to be a man, able to be unified, and part of me doesn't wish." And work begins when something wishes to see this conflict.

Of course, it's very difficult, so I advise you that you try to prepare before you start your day. You understood what I suggested during the day, but it didn't penetrate very deeply. For the next day or two you try to establish contact with your body. Sit for ten or twelve minutes and try to feel your body. Try to sense your body and try to realize it plays a very important part in your life. You take your attention away from your thoughts and try to be aware of sensation, something higher than thought. I won't explain more, but I would like to ask you not to speak about it. If you value it, I can assure you that it will help not to speak about it.

The effort is now, to see . . .

QUESTION: I see that I live in life and everything passes me by. I wish now to see my aim in a new way, in a fresh way. Would you speak about this and show me something that will help?

LORD PENTLAND: It's a very useful question. It's a very difficult thing to make a new beginning. The most difficult. And it's very useful to face oneself with that necessity because we have, in fact, all the time to be coming to a new beginning. It's very difficult because even this concept of a new beginning takes me away from my own situation. The effort is now, to see. Where am I? If even for a moment to see myself—occasionally with the idea of a new beginning—I come back with something more essential, a little degree of my presence. Maybe I need to give up this idea of a new beginning in order to begin. And there I'm faced with the fact I cannot come to that without help, something given.

In making this effort to look, at certain moments, a time will come, and maybe soon, when something will be given so that I see the beginning of the old idea, but in an entirely inconceivable way. Do you understand?

QUESTIONER: You are telling me something that I don't understand with my head, but I feel.

LORD PENTLAND: Yes.

There are different qualities of attention . . .

QUESTION: I sometimes believe that I try just too hard. One of my efforts has been to try to keep from expressing negative emotions in the ordinary work day. I remember these meetings and I start talking to myself, little Pollyannaish talks, and I try to remember what you tell me. I believe that I try too hard instead of just observing as things happen. But I see so many years of my life that were not constructive and not positive. I get this feeling of wanting to make up for lost time. Am I trying too hard?

LORD PENTLAND: Of course I wouldn't be able to say. But if you would find yourself interested in trying a little less hard, it might be good. Why not relax? Your trying hard about not trying hard is what mechanicalness means. It's our prison. We don't realize it, but it's a vicious circle. In that way, there is no way out. The only way is to stop something.

Why am I here? Why am I doing these things? You find yourself carrying on conversations with yourself. You see this and it means you have to stop and ask yourself, "Why am I sucking my pen? I meant to write a letter," or, "Why am I holding this book? I'm not reading." Why not just stop? It's all a part of never resting.

I'm sorry if I make it sound ordinary. It isn't ordinary. It comes from little moments when I remember the work. Instead of letting that moment go into associations, try to remember to ask "Why?" and see what answer you get. It will be an answer from somewhere more than just your head. Yes?

QUESTION: I start the day out with the intention of observing one particular thing—negative emotions, for example. But within a short time, I'm observing all sorts of things—inner talking, imagination and so forth.

How can I concentrate on one thing and not scatter my forces, not let the other things come in?

LORD PENTLAND: I didn't understand. Would you please say more?

QUESTIONER: Well, I haven't advanced to the stage where I can remember myself, so I've just been concentrating on observing. And I feel that I'm not making as good progress as I could if I could just observe one thing at a time instead of a lot of different things. Perhaps I'm just making my work mechanical.

LORD PENTLAND: Yes. My work. It means that at least for a period during the day you have what you call the possibility of working—of seeing something—some free attention, some attention that is able to see what is going on and hasn't been taken away. Other times, perhaps closest of all, you see yourself negative or about to be negative. It's not wrong that you should wish to observe precisely about these situations. But you see how closely related they are?

Now maybe you can understand that everything depends on this little free attention you have. It's with that that you see. Do you understand what I mean? Now, you wish to be more precise but, first of all, the point is what attention is free? You think that any free attention will do for observing yourself, but it has to be a special kind of attention. That's the reason your work appears to be disconnected.

You need a higher attention. But your higher attention is taken when you are negative. Begin to be interested that there are different qualities of attention—with one you can cook, with another you are not able to paint a picture. We need to have a scale. Do you understand?

QUESTIONER: Are you referring to centers and their work?

LORD PENTLAND: It's connected, but we don't need the idea of centers now. It's my attention. If someone starts to read, I can give it some attention, but in order to observe some of these situations in which I am closest to my associations, I need a very high quality of attention. Do you see what I mean?

Only, perhaps I should say, try not to fall into this situation just spoken about. Try to limit yourself to efforts of short duration, but it's not to be a fixed time. I mustn't be putting obstacles in my path by saying, "There goes my attention." Take little periods when you use some small practical task more for the sake of watching your attention than for doing the task, but do it as well as you can. You may begin with one quality and come to a better one—and come to even a better one at the end.

QUESTIONER: Then all these other things that seem to be prodding me, shall I just . . .

LORD PENTLAND: Continue as I say. What you need is the under-standing of attention—but not quite in the way that you've tried—an understanding of the different possibilities I have in relation to attention: the extent to which I am free and the extent to which I am not free, and all the different qualities of attention. You see this is now for you to study.

two

How to remember myself . . .

QUESTION: Would you discuss the idea of self-remembering? How does one go about remembering oneself?

LORD PENTLAND: There are two ways. How do I know how to remember myself? How do I know anything? Either someone forces me to know it or I myself come to know it. How do you know that I am here? Either I force you to know it or you yourself come to know it. Either the idea attracted you to it or you yourself come to know it. There are two ways. But with what do you come to know yourself?

QUESTIONER: If I'm asleep, how can I remember? I have to be awake.

LORD PENTLAND: How do you remember yourself? You tell me.

QUESTIONER: Either I have to come to it by myself or someone forces me, as you said.

LORD PENTLAND: How do you do it?

QUESTIONER: I just feel I am here or know that I am myself. Otherwise I am in a fog.

LORD PENTLAND: Some condition in you attracted you to yourself. That is one way.

QUESTIONER: I think so.

LORD PENTLAND: Yes? If that is the only way then there is no need for this work together, for effort. I wait, and in certain conditions I am forced to know I am here. If my attention is attracted by myself, you don't need this work here. If there were no other way than that, we would have no need to study or make efforts.

QUESTIONER: Is self-remembering self-observation?

LORD PENTLAND: You understood my answer to your question, did you?

QUESTIONER: I think so.

LORD PENTLAND: What's the use of all the system about self-observation and so on if there is only this one way—by being forced to know we are there because our attention is attracted to something in ourselves? If that is the only way, what is the use of working together? What's the use of the group? But you know there is another way. You know that by yourself you can find something out. Against the pull of all sorts of attractions, you yourself have searched something out. With what did you search? How were you able to turn away from these attractions?

QUESTIONER: I can't think of a specific case right now.

You need to observe your attention . . .

QUESTION: At times I have thought it was I who was searching to remember myself, and then it seemed I was merely being forced. I can't tell the difference between these two. I find myself thinking I am doing the one and finding I am merely doing the other.

LORD PENTLAND: This is a good question. You think you make efforts, but as you go along you see that even in that very moment when you wish something, immediately after that it goes by itself, and you are not present. You are attracted. So even your efforts seem to be mechanical. Even your work seems to be in sleep. It brings you to the necessity for observing. Try to discriminate about what is more yourself, what is connected with the feeling of you and what is mechanical. You need to observe your attention. Hold your attention. Watch all the different parts of you from which this attention originates.

QUESTIONER: The different parts?

LORD PENTLAND: We have more than one part. Only we have very little attention that is available to ourselves for taking some initiative because all of it is enslaved in these different parts. So we take two principal means of working. First of all, placing ourselves in the best conditions where there are the least possible attractions of life, we study how to make more attention possible. Then, secondly, in life we don't try to remember ourselves; we try to watch to see in which parts our attention is enslaved. For instance, I sit next to somebody and I notice that with my body I dislike this person. I am not able to be so free as I am at home with my family. My ability to function is constantly interfered with by the feeling of this person.

The likes of the body are very important. In a way it is just that body attention that brings us to the most real struggle and friction. So in life we try to watch where our force or attention is enslaved. You understand?

QUESTIONER: I am not sure. Do you mean that if I observe and I find my body enslaved and try to direct the attention of my body, then this problem of self-remembering might be directed rather than forced or attracted?

LORD PENTLAND: No. But for the time being we should only try to direct our attention where there is the least possibility of its being attracted. When we are sitting by ourselves, then perhaps we can begin to direct our attention.

In life all we should try to do is observe the different qualities of attention, observe the energy as it leaves us. Observe from which part the energy comes and where it is enslaved. It is something that only has real value when you can do it at the time. But it is of some value to do it afterwards, to go back over one's day, to remember a certain incident and say to oneself, "Now it's just because I was so taken with her face that I liked her," or "I was so taken with the discomfort of the heat that I was lazy like that."

We can remember this mechanical person as ourselves . . .

QUESTION: Could you comment on the part played by the voice? I find my voice is way ahead of me and difficult to control, even if I am trying to do so.

LORD PENTLAND: Yes, the voice is a very important function and one that is very sensitive to the general functioning. But when you have seen that, don't you think one is too easily taken by this idea? One forgets about the real difficulty of becoming more conscious.

It would be true that a conscious man would have such a voice that could really remind himself, and remind others, how to be a conscious man. It is too much to just wish it, as if one could be there in one jump.

What does it mean that we function in different states of consciousness? All the time we are losing energy, putting our energy into a certain form. Our energy is unformed and all the time our functions are taking it in order to make certain sounds or certain actions. Now what would be the first step toward consciousness? It would be to know that, to accept that my functions are always taking my energy. I am far from having a center of initiative. The first step would be to be conscious of that. When I observe that, I see how mechanical I am. The next step is to see that this is my own energy going, not someone else's.

If I could feel that voice as being mine—not only mechanical—then I could accomplish something. Mostly we just see this voice, or automaton, stupidly acting. But sometimes we can see it as me, my energy being wasted, my voice. When we feel that, we get an impression of ourselves. It is only then, when we can remember this mechanical person as ourselves, that this impression is digested and can actually feed the inner part of me. It can start to create a part which could be a center of initiative.

Now you see how dependent I am on this mechanical part of me—dependent in general, of course, but also dependent in this way, that I need it in order to feed this new part of me, and I need it to know that.

QUESTION: I have been looking at the various segments of myself and some I don't like and I see are incompatible with consciousness—these constant negative attitudes, laziness. I would like to be able to get more force when I am in a higher state so that these mechanical things will not swallow me. I hear about self-remembering and sometimes I do it, but these intellectual considerations do not seem to really work.

LORD PENTLAND: Consciousness is a very big thing. To be conscious of all the presences within ourselves—it is something which we couldn't even bear. To be able to do—to will—is the same as consciousness. To be able to will would be to have that kind of consciousness. Even in our efforts to be conscious, we must remember the affinity between consciousness and will. For instance, it makes a lot of difference whether I am attracted or whether at the very beginning I do this thing by myself, for myself. It makes a lot of difference if, as I was attracted in the first place, I am able to finish. It gives me a certain force to finish the day and say, "Well, at least I finished this or that." I am speaking of small external things.

QUESTIONER: Would making a list be helpful?

LORD PENTLAND: Making a list of things is one thing, but finishing is another. I do not mean finishing a list. You always try something so difficult that you were able to say at the end of the day, "It was too difficult." Better try something simpler.

Conscience is not a relative idea . . .

QUESTION: What did Gurdjieff mean in what he said about "coming to conscience"? How can I relate that to myself? What does it mean?

LORD PENTLAND: Of course I think you'll really agree with me that his words on that are a help, but all other words get in the way. It's like "being." But to come to it through words is very difficult. In a sense we already understand. But it's one of the words, perhaps the only one, that is not a relative idea. Perhaps that's why it's so difficult to speak about. "Understanding," "being," "knowledge," all these we speak about on different levels. But conscience—and perhaps this is why it interests you—is there or it isn't. We can't speak of it relatively. Do you see?

We could at least say that if we only have flashes of it, it would be because our feelings aren't properly prepared. I think the first step towards conscience would be the study of the degrees of feeling—really to know what's a truer feeling or a less true, more colorful one. The truer feeling is very quiet, isn't it? It is very often forgotten by us because it speaks so quietly. We can hardly bear to live without a certain contact with the less valuable, more colorful feelings. So the way towards conscience would be through the different levels of feeling.

QUESTIONER: Yes. I've recognized in my body sometimes a thing that I've called a feeling but I know that really isn't it. . . .

LORD PENTLAND: In any case, it is necessary for you to understand that one can't understand about feeling until one has understood feelings, and that's only possible when we have a certain command over our attention. That depends on a certain ability to relax, to maintain an inner activity.

So we must return and say that really all our work is for coming towards conscience. I wish particularly that we could understand that together. Gurdjieff says that in a sense our work begins from conscience. In my own work I can't remain conscious of my own possibility, and relate it to others', if there is any part of a fixed idea in me. The only danger of beginning from conscience could be that maybe we have a fixed idea. Do you see that?

How do I react to experiences of a higher kind?. . .

QUESTION: In asking myself the question of who I am, it was as though I saw some symbolic representations through glass, having the feeling I am power, I am will.

LORD PENTLAND: Not wrong. But not satisfactory. We all have experiences we can call of a higher kind—the question is how do I act towards such experiences? It is what Gurdjieff's teaching is all about. These pose a question. What is the meaning of such experience in my life? Most of us don't face this question. We collect experiences like butterflies and pin them in a book and at the end have only a book of dead insects.

Gurdjieff says man could be able to feel a relationship with everything around him, could actually be a part, play a part, of the surroundings. We see in respect to such experiences that we try to catch them, prize them. After a time, there is a satisfaction in having experiences—getting, then not understanding them—because experiences prove we are linked with something higher. We must understand our ordinary functions, which lead us to catching these experiences and pinning them in a book.

Through what forms can I come to emptiness?. . .

QUESTION: Is the prayer of Jesus a possible means for helping us to see something other than the usual thoughts and personal things that go on?

LORD PENTLAND: What do you find? I must say I have never been in an Orthodox Russian monastery. I have never had experience of that. The only book I have read is the one about the pilgrim, where it is made clear that it is an experience to be attempted only under a *starets*, so I never attempted it.

Through what forms can I come to emptiness? Through what exercises? One is speaking about using a technique, a form, in order to go beyond form. One wants to have a direct experience of something, that is to say, to be in touch with something higher than form. In order to be in touch with the higher, one uses the lower. How to come to the higher through the lower? How to go beyond form through the use of form? Well, how can one?

I think it means that there are certain particular forms which lend themselves—to those who understand what it means to be aware or to listen—which lend themselves to creating echoes or reflections of the higher. For instance, if you repeat, "Have mercy on me," just with your ordinary thought, maybe it produces an echo, as it were, of something higher perhaps, more formally. So there are certain exercises that Gurdjieff gave me which give me a certain understanding of what you have been trying.

But we really opened this house for the study of Gurdjieff's way. At a later stage it is useful to have comparative study of other traditions, but it is a pity, out of impatience, to go to other traditions here when most of them have representatives in the city. Here we try not to hurry bringing such exercises as "Lord have mercy." This is not intended to be in a narrow sense a study of Gurdjieff's ideas. Still we are not intended to be without some of the lessons that he passed on. In other words, this house can't simply be showering down mercy and answering questions. There has to be some severity. There has to be reflected here a feeling of a certain line of study, of knowledge.

Well, of the ninety-nine, if one sheep goes off to the Russian Orthodox Church, don't expect me to come running off after you. There is a certain severity which is part of what I understand from Gurdjieff. It is up to you if you come here, but if you come here, you come for this.

Generally one understands enough to not be impatient. This picking something out of a book comes from impatience. There is a sort of impatience to study oneself. So in oneself one picks a certain impression, comes to a quick conclusion, "I am that sort of person," or out of a meeting one picks this or that. You have to try to understand, through a work of listening, that we have a tendency to grasp at something and then not listen. This is interesting. This is one of the obstacles to consciousness, obviously. Why it should be so, I don't know. But I have found, myself, that when there is that type of movement—grasping at something referring to someone else—that one always seems to be asleep when things that apply to oneself are said. One grasps at things applied to other people. Just when something really interesting to oneself is to be heard at the weekly meeting, you grasp something which makes you deaf.

The wish is your only initiative . . .

QUESTION: I'm wondering if the time is approaching when we could be told, almost brutally if necessary, what is our chief feature. I've had glimpses lately of an entirely different feeling that I've never had before, of believing that I was a little more present. I almost believe I'm ready to begin to work. I realize how much help I need, and I wondered if I were brutally told what my chief features are, could I grasp them or would I rush off and not want to face them?

LORD PENTLAND: If I told you what your chief feature was, would you believe me?

QUESTIONER: Yes, I would.

LORD PENTLAND: It shows you're not ready. We work for guidance, not for belief. All your work is based on a very small thing, which connects you with the line of great teachers including Gurdjieff—the wish to understand yourself in relation to your situation in the work. And the wish is your only initiative.

There's very little light, but occasionally you get an inkling. Everything is against you. Your chief feature is the focus of all your mechanicalness. It represents all that keeps you in darkness. Until you can see all that, you cannot know your chief feature.

Don't believe anyone who tells you your chief feature. You work. A great teacher can give you guidance, but he can't do the work for you. The best step for you is to try to come to a more deep separation, something which is under all this talk about chief feature. This teaching is mostly in our feelings, but we wish to come to something separate from our feelings.

All negativeness is based on the idea that
machines should be conscious . . .

QUESTION: The latter part of the vacation I tried to see myself without thinking too much about the work and within the last ten days it seems the relationships in which I live are all different. Everything is the same, but it seems different. In places where there was friction, there is no friction. In places that would bring forth a negative quality, it doesn't seem to happen anymore. It's just very different. Things I always took as something to wake me up, such as negative reactions and so forth, just don't seem to happen. It's just very different and I don't know about it.

LORD PENTLAND: Do you feel uncomfortable?

QUESTIONER: No.

LORD PENTLAND: But you feel something is missing?

QUESTIONER: It feels like everything just is.

LORD PENTLAND: But you feel something is missing?

QUESTIONER: Well, friction is missing.

LORD PENTLAND: Purpose?

QUESTIONER: No. Friction.

LORD PENTLAND: Well, what is purpose for you now—not yesterday, but for today? Had you a purpose for today?

QUESTIONER: Yes, to come here.

LORD PENTLAND: Was it very difficult?

QUESTIONER: No, it wasn't at all.

LORD PENTLAND: Then it was no purpose. I'm trying to tell you that we lose a lot of time if we wait at this resting place. I'm quite sure you need to find something.

QUESTIONER: Well, my aim was to see myself.

LORD PENTLAND: Yes. But you feel something is missing. You feel too comfortable. We live in our machines. My machine. Your machine. A loco-motive. Let's suppose that there are other locomotives going in all direc-tions. We have to jump out of their way. We're all living in this mar-shalling yard. There are big collisions and I always blame the other locomo-tives. But it's my place to keep out of the way of the others. I shall always have to give some attention to keeping out of the way of other locomotives.

QUESTIONER: It isn't that I'm indifferent. It's just that everything's dif-ferent.

LORD PENTLAND: It's good practice to jump out of the way of other locomotives. One thinks the other locomotives should get out of the way. To some extent I'm a man in this situation and I can't help it. And I've got to be practical, finding out what is negative emotion. Why blame the other locomotive, instead of jumping out of the way?

QUESTIONER: Is that what I was talking about?

LORD PENTLAND: It will be soon.

QUESTIONER: Evidently I don't know what it means to be negative.

LORD PENTLAND: When one is negative, one forgets about mechanical-ness. All negativeness is based on the idea that machines should be conscious. But machines are machines. And you'll find that in these situations, which are quite common, when one feels in a good situation, something is missing. Friction is missing. Negative emotion is one state which can be studied.

Would you care, each of you, to make a written record of what you feel you really understand about the idea of awakening from sleep? We can work at that together. Try that in writing. It is not the same as the effort one makes in a meeting, but it can be done honestly, not as though you were looking it up, but as if suddenly you were stranded on an island and you wish to make a record about what you understand about this idea.

QUESTIONER: How did you define the question?

LORD PENTLAND: Awakening from sleep, just to know what is yours of the things that have been said, what belongs more to you, what you will never forget in a way—knowing you will forget, but that it will come up again at times.

A wish to awake and a wish to sleep . . .

QUESTION: I am not sure how to make a question out of this, but I was very impressed by what you said last night about how we become disconnected at night while we are asleep. After I got home—usually I can't go to sleep after something like that—but last night I got home and it was as though I was able to reach way down deep inside myself somewhere, and it was almost like turning off a key. Everything turned off, and I must have fallen asleep.

It seemed almost like self-remembering, only the reverse in a way. I didn't become more collected, but more disconnected. It seemed very much like the same place I try to reach when I remember myself.

LORD PENTLAND: Yes, this probably is a new idea for you. In a way it meets our hunger for something, like finding something you needed. But perhaps you are not ready for this, not ready to use this. New knowledge has to be assimilated, you can't use it now.

QUESTION: I'm not sure why this would apply to the concept of ordinary sleep.

LORD PENTLAND: The point is that it meets a particular need for knowledge, a new idea. With another person, it may be another idea. But we have to be able to look at these accidental gifts—and her experience was accidental—without having them take us out of our way.

We must try to find the wish to see ourselves—and know that sometimes the wish for knowledge comes from an ordinary place. The important thing is how to understand this awakening.

QUESTION: What resistances do I look for?

LORD PENTLAND: The wish to hide. How can you see these better?

QUESTIONER: I have to work again.

LORD PENTLAND: First you have to awake. How can you work again if you are not there? You are asleep. First to awaken—to wish to see. Suppose you see more or less, but what is it you see? That there is an adversary.

QUESTIONER 1: I see it as a wish to sleep.

LORD PENTLAND: What excuses that? There is a wish to awake and a wish to sleep. Something has to justify the wish to sleep. How is that justified?

QUESTIONER 2: Responsibilities, life, my job.

QUESTIONER 3: The sense of my own mechanicalness, the way I am.

LORD PENTLAND: It is my picture of me, my burden, my responsibilities.

QUESTION: I find that most of the time I don't see anything that wants to sleep, but only something that thinks it wants to awake.

LORD PENTLAND: Don't reason in this way. Work like this takes a long time. One has to try to turn oneself towards the possibility of awakening. We have to find the wish to awake—to see.

QUESTIONER: How?

LORD PENTLAND: When you work quietly in the morning. I have seen that I can somehow get underneath this sleep and wish to see. I appear to work with a confidence that is possible. I lose it, but then I return, because I work with a sort of confidence. If I have the wish to see, I can go on. If I haven't, I can't. The wish is different to everybody.

QUESTIONER: To me, the wish somehow seems like something mechanical—like desires—tied into myself somehow, this wishing.

LORD PENTLAND: Think of it as awakening. Every effort we make in life we expect to be paid for. All that is different in this work. This effort is for yourself—there is no reward—just so that you can be awake. Go on working at this. There will be times when you really do wish, when you really have a wish to awake. You may see to some extent. What will you see? Resistances, adversaries—it takes the form of myself as I picture myself to be—I see I am too young, too ill, too busy to understand. It takes many different forms.

What I really want to say is that you have to see more after you have seen. When you awake, you have to awaken again. You try to understand this adversary. Make an effort, not struggle with him, but see what he is made of—not resist, but see beneath, how false he is. Try to realize when you are asleep more deeply. See the face of the false man—not try to rout him out or trace back where he came from. Instead, try to see what he is made of, what lies he tells, what insincerity.

QUESTIONER: This insincere person that you see, is this the person you are trying to cope with?

LORD PENTLAND: You can't rout him out. You have to understand and try to see how he has power over you. You need more moments of seeing. Wish to see him more, how he is connected within you, what wrong connections are. Some wrong connections all come together. This is the idea of chief feature, the underlying source of my adversary. All you see is the form it takes. You have to try to see what is underneath it.

As long as I wish to awaken, I see this adversary as an adversary. But soon he begins to have power over me. He is the one who answers to everything. He is the one who is there and who answers. I need to know this man in me. He takes up all of the room in me. Do you understand? I can't engage with him in sleep or by reading about him in books. I must awake first. It is he who is reading, he who is there. This is what is meant by being displaced.

If the method becomes fixed, it can't help . . .

QUESTION: When I sit quietly and say that I wish to remember myself, and if I am able sometimes to keep that, and if the desire starts to drift away and I seem to catch it and bring it back, is it imagination or the beginning of self-remembering?

LORD PENTLAND: It is the beginning if you go on.

QUESTIONER: It goes away, but I get the wish back if I sit quietly.

LORD PENTLAND: Yes, it is very difficult. Perhaps when you speak together you don't make allowances for how difficult this effort is. There isn't any blueprint. If the method becomes fixed it can't help. What helps me learn is the knowledge that this is different—an effort that we don't ordinarily give. This is an effort we don't understand, but it is possible because I can have moments, can come to this if I go farther.

It is possible to begin, but it always peters out quickly. I need to prepare myself. I need to know that there are scales of self-remembering far beyond what I have experienced—they may be possible for me—but it requires a particular effort I don't understand. If I prepare myself enough in that way, I may be much more alive inwardly and hear that note in time to remember myself and, when it is time to stop, to be able to follow the changing situation inside and penetrate deeper. There are forces inside that reach out to me, but I can't find them because I am cut in two. But it is waiting there to attract you, even.

Nothing can be formulated finally—it is a mystery—we don't understand. However much you remember of the method, begin always with the idea that you don't know and wish to understand.

There is a second part of the exercise you are doing. It is very simple. Some of you have tried it. Make a walk after the first part of the exercise, a voluntary walk, to see how much you can remember of yourself. It needn't be long. Remember when you start that you are asleep, but that part you reached in the morning, that part is still there. You ask yourself, "Am I cut off from it?" and make your walk and don't expect too much. There may be moments when you awaken and you see this false person.

This is not an exercise given by Gurdjieff, but I have found it very good, besides being good for your health. Try that for a short time, until I come again. I have found it very useful in other groups; it brings the work very close to people. How much of work is mostly invention. How different just to be present to myself taking a walk.

There are two parts to the exercise—in the morning while you are alone and not to be disturbed; then later make a walk voluntarily, for this purpose.

QUESTION: What we do during the walk is to see how well we can remember ourselves during the walk?

LORD PENTLAND: Yes, do you all understand?

QUESTIONER: You might find this part in you which could glimpse this false part?

LORD PENTLAND: It is the beginning of remembering oneself. Awakening is the beginning of remembering oneself. We spoke last night about what is awakened. But what does one awaken to? What does one see when one is awake? One sees this adversary, sees this person if it is long enough. All this may fall away and you see just an ordinary person walking down an ordinary street, suddenly just a little microbe. It is the beginning of seeing oneself.

QUESTION: The thing that bothers me is that you keep talking about self-remembering. What is it? I am not understanding it. I say, "What am I?" and I see what I am doing, but it seems like only observation.

LORD PENTLAND: You have to understand what I mean by awakening or sleeping, have to see wrong connections, this state I am in, understand about the wish to awake and the wish to hide. You know enough, but you keep this question—what is self-remembering? It is a good question. You keep this and one day you will have the experience and know it. All you can say is that at the moment nothing you experience is really self-remembering. You have to keep the name but suppose that you haven't had it yet. You can say it when you can say, "I am." Who is "I"? Not this false person.

You keep this word as if one day you will experience it, and it will be right. You will feel yourself as yourself. People who have experienced it can speak of self-remembering. It is a very rare thing to feel "I am here." You have to awaken first. Don't strive for it. Strive for the wish to awake. See more of what opposes it and then nothing can prevent you from coming to moments of self-remembering.

QUESTION: I have tried holding something present in myself, but as soon as I feel my body being here, everything goes blank, emotions, everything.

LORD PENTLAND: It is because you are at the very beginning. We only hear the voices of our very false, very ordinary emotions. Do the work you can do instead of imagining things that stop you. Be there more often, come back again and again. Later you will have enough knowledge to separate from emotions and study them. You have some understanding to see that what you want flies away. Do this more often—after the interest has vanished, after the false dreams have gone. Don't be worried by the rubbish that comes, the advice about upsetting other people, gallantry, and so forth. Resist this.

QUESTIONER: How?

LORD PENTLAND: Think before you ask me to mention ways. Try yourself first.

The beginning of evolution in oneself is sincerity . . .

QUESTION: I have been trying to tell the difference between really working or imagining I am working. And I don't know. Maybe I am asking for a pill of some kind, but is there some possible clue which might tell me that I am remembering?

LORD PENTLAND: I'm glad you spoke about it. Give me an example.

QUESTIONER: I am trying to remember myself. I feel my body and sometimes I might go so far as to see myself start worrying about something, an exam, and then I stop it and I think that I am doing something. Sometimes when this happens I think back, and I think that the person who felt this isn't being very honest.

LORD PENTLAND: The answer is simple. The point is that my inner posture is always changing. The possibility arises that my worrying will turn against me towards passivity later, if I stop it. The effort is useful now, but you might need to think more about the exams later. Try to do what you honestly think is right. Don't question the very first idea to come to you after you sincerely ask yourself the question. If the answer is to worry more, then worry more. Or if it is to not worry, don't. Or if you try and you really don't know, then don't worry more or less, don't allow it.

If you question yourself with sufficient force, some answer comes to all normal people. It is very important, the beginning of feeling. The beginning of evolution in oneself is sincerity. What is there when I really ask a question? The answer may be wrong, but if I do it, it will lead more to a right thing.

QUESTIONER: If I do start to worry, it takes everything out of me.

LORD PENTLAND: But it will lead in a right direction. The answer says you will be wrong, too much worry, but you will see that later. Or you will see it in those moments when you are in touch, while you are quiet.

QUESTION: Being present there to yourself, does this mean putting all our awareness into whatever we are trying to do?

LORD PENTLAND: Yes. It means that there are these two different natures living together in us, the animal nature and the psychic nature. They are in relation together, but one is asleep, the tempo is different. Our actions are an expression of both, but we are aware only of the animal nature except at certain times. We more and more feel that to be present means to be present to my two natures. To be present means to see yourself entirely in negative emotions, cut off from the higher, or more in the higher yet aware of the adversary, the result of wrong connections, which are against awakening—aware of myself as consisting of two natures.

QUESTION: Last night I was struck by what you said about our parents, that we can't love God if we don't love our parents. Today I tried to look at my parents one at a time. I found at first lots of isolated feelings, times when I cared for them or hated them—first with my mother, then I did the same with my father. I tried to bring as much of my whole self to it as I could. Afterwards, what struck me was that these times that I remembered were when I must have been a little more awake. I saw that most of the time I didn't even think of them. It made me feel how tiny my caring or even noticing my parents was. I don't understand how I feel about it. I felt somehow a higher sort of feeling about my parents after this, or while I was doing it.

LORD PENTLAND: Even what you were able to do brought you something. You weren't able even to begin to do what was asked, to have all the feelings together. But even trying brought you much, even seeing one at a time was good. What was asked was to see the whole of it. It has almost unlimited possibilities for genuine being efforts, but you were not able even to approach the fringe of it, of what was asked.

three

The idea of active and passive . . .

QUESTION: I don't know which of two efforts to make when I sit, whether to get a sensation of the body or to try to include other things.

LORD PENTLAND: There is an inner activity, a very subtle thing, a very delicate effort. I have to discriminate between what is more active and what is more passive, see what it is to be more attracted, what it is to be more active. It is a very delicate thing. I search for an attention that will connect me with all my different parts without being drowned—something active and finer and wider. It is only by a sort of taste that I can find my way. My attraction into outer things is a passivity, a lowering of my effort.

You have to find your own way. It depends on you—whether you wish enough. The idea of active and passive might help. You must ask yourself why you do the exercise. Do you wish this attention? The exercise is only successful if you glimpse what your life is made up of. Notice how you spoil everything in life by laziness, selfishness, indecision.

QUESTIONER: I see somewhat. I don't think I see at the moment how I am messing up my life.

LORD PENTLAND: You feel that you exist? You are alive?

QUESTIONER: Sometimes.

LORD PENTLAND: I am alive, on earth. What do you see you have done with that gift? What have you done with that energy, that life that I am sometimes aware of? What have you done with it? How have you used it? Look around—at your family, your day, your friends. Do you know what you have done with it?

QUESTIONER: I have tried to get along better in my work, my studies, with other people.

LORD PENTLAND: Then the exercise has no sense for you. If you are satisfied in how you have spent that energy, there is no sense in studying.

QUESTIONER: I don't see what you mean about satisfied. I'm not.

LORD PENTLAND: It has to make a connection with actual life. Otherwise the exercise is just a trick. Look around at the whole of your life up to now. Is it true that you exist? Maybe you don't exist. Everything happens, nothing works out. You take credit for an accident, but nothing works out, and yet you say that you exist. You have had some moment when you felt aware of life in you. But you have to be watchful. You can't say you exist. I exist and I don't exist. If you really feel that, then you have a need to do the exercise.

Where can I turn? To myself. Only there can I find the answers. Begin by seeing what stares us in the face. Everything comes to nothing. I can't do. I don't exist. I have to penetrate through the defenses personality puts up before there is any sense in doing the exercise.

An obligation to wake up . . .

QUESTION: Gurdjieff referred to effort and intentional suffering. What does this mean? I find that in this quietness I am more aware of my obligations to other people. I don't want these obligations but they are there. I wonder if intentional suffering fits in here.

LORD PENTLAND: Maybe it can come to that. But the first obligation—what obligation is most important?—it is to oneself, really, that I have a duty to remember. If I look, I see how responsibilities, the idea of duty, brings the machine into action all the time. The idea of an obligation to wake up is very, very difficult to remember about. It is, so to speak, a function which we never use. We have to start, if we speak about intentional suffering, where we are. We regard the moment of self-observation as a miracle, and to such an extent it is true.

QUESTIONER: It seems like panic sometimes.

LORD PENTLAND: Try to understand what it would mean that this miracle is necessary for me, an obligation, a miracle and a need, an obligation. We think of a miracle as a luxury, something wonderful which is added. I never realized that this gift is necessary for me, a necessity for man. We think of responsibilities, politeness, duties—it is all right—but the idea of obligation is towards seeing oneself. Waking up. It is difficult to remember that this is necessary for my life. We are not properly balanced without that. I don't receive the food I need without this miracle. We have to give up suffering about our responsibilities. It is that miracle that is necessary.

We substitute for work this introspective thinking . . .

QUESTION: Something in me seems to tell me to go against little everyday comforts. They have no relation to the work—going to a movie, sitting around, wasting time—things that I like very much and are very hard for me not to do. I am wondering whether what tells me to go against them is real.

LORD PENTLAND: That is a very good question, if only you could keep it. You know that nothing but experience really can answer it. We don't have such a clear view that we can say this or that is true. We have to try to peer into ourselves. And mostly we see nothing. But there comes a moment when through wishing for it, and also through carrying out the work, we come to where we do see something clearly. There comes a moment when I do see something real—and what is false. We do get a moment sometimes when we see all that. The answer is the result of many of those moments.

Do you understand? It is only in a certain moment when we are perhaps more awake that we do see our inner life more clearly and we do see what is more true. And it is no use reasoning as to those moments. If we have a moment like that, the best thing to do is to try to have another one. Don't take it that in one moment you can see everything. What is good is to have more moments so that you can see really deep down. You need to see these impulses many times before you can really see deep down. Some may be quite real, but it is the moment of realizing—experiencing—the truth that matters.

QUESTIONER: What should I do?

LORD PENTLAND: Try to stop thinking about it. That is the first thing. It is one thing which is a real indulgence. We substitute for work this introspective thinking. If you have a moment when you really feel clearly that you are being swept down or that you are liking or giving in to egoism or negative emotions, if you have a moment when you see, it is a moment when you are more awake. Then you immediately go to sleep again, and there is no sense in reasoning about the awakened state when you are asleep. The only thing is to try to awaken again.

You know with some people, if you resist them, you never get rid of them. If you resist them, they come back. With some people, if you say just one word, they disappear. Some you can't control by resisting. Some you have to resist all the time or they eat you up.

One thing, you can't get what you want by refusing. You can't work entirely by not doing things. There are different people in you. And some of them you have to control by loving. Some you have to be very strong with and push them away. You have got to live with them all. For example, how have you been trying? You told me you find it difficult to do the exercise. How has that been going?

QUESTIONER: I measure my success in the exercise by whether or not over a period of time I see something new that I hadn't seen before, by having some experience that I haven't had before. And I don't feel I have been getting any further.

LORD PENTLAND: You see when you do the exercise you place yourself alone because you wish to make acquaintance with yourself, with what is there at the time when you begin. So you see you mustn't push yourself away before you begin. We sometimes push ourselves away and then begin. When you sit down to do that work, sometimes you make a complete cut between that moment and the moment before, when you were eating or brushing your hair or whatever. You turn completely away from before.

QUESTIONER: I try to.

LORD PENTLAND: Don't throw yourself away with everything else. Now you sit down. You are asleep. Nothing to get rid of. You wish to awaken. You are already starting to get rid of something without knowing that what you wish to do is awaken—then you will know what is to be gotten rid of.

You will see tomorrow. Don't be so hard on yourself. Just sit down as you are, right in the current of your life, and then start to awaken what you are.

QUESTIONER: While you are talking to me something wants to ask what effort is he telling me to make?

LORD PENTLAND: And something in you understands very well. You hear me. You may be too violent with yourself. All you are doing is to sit down to awaken, to simply stay in the same current you sat down in and try to look for another current.

It is quality of work we need more than anything . . .

QUESTION: I felt I was getting along all right until I started having a lot of papers and tests that I had to work on. And I don't know what to do. I get to feeling I lose what is important. I feel the work is important, but this other thing drives me. I can only work when things are easy. But when things get difficult I sort of collapse. I feel rather badly, and I don't know what to do.

LORD PENTLAND: It is the same with all of us. We can only work when it is easy, when it is useless. It needn't be so. You must try to go on and find enough experience. It is the quality of work we need more than anything; we need good moments. It is really only the moments of good quality that give us any indication. These difficulties that come can be a great help towards work of good quality. I may be able to get one moment when I am not identified. Maybe I am so weak that I can have only one moment; but just because that moment is there, I am able to face my situation.

If you work like that even only once a day, then the rest of the day you become worried and identified, but you don't really believe in that because of what took place in you when you worked. So don't look for difficulties in your life. Don't get into more difficulties than you need to, but don't have too negative an attitude toward difficulties when they come. Try to see if you can't make use of them in that way when they come.

Never let anything become more important than your work. Never let anything prey on you. Fit it in some way—so that you make use of these life difficulties—so that it fits in with a possibility of work.

I am my search . . .

QUESTION: It has been my experience a number of times that when I try to remember a question or follow a line of thought, that something goes on so I perhaps can see various thoughts come up, and I discriminate between them. Can one really do that?

LORD PENTLAND: I don't think it is real discrimination. One is doing it by one's thought, so it is thought looking at thought.

QUESTIONER: This goes on—the thought and the picking of the thought—and sometimes it leads the way, in a technical problem, to real solutions. But this is going on. What can I do? What is it really that I can do?

LORD PENTLAND: I can study the process of thinking. That is what you tried to do. You saw that it is a sort of creation—that one thought leads to another thought. Perhaps you don't see that behind all that there is a very deeply rooted desire for a result, and this goes on for some time until you feel that you have gotten a result. It is not a real result. Behind this, one's thought is never satisfied until a result is reached, and by that time one's position is different. Perhaps one's energy has run out and so one takes any thought that happens to correspond to one's feelings. One says, "I have an answer," and one writes it down and tells somebody and is very surprised that they don't agree. That is what we have to study.

You wish to study. You say, "What is I?" You must find that. For the moment all I can say is, "I am my search." It never can be an answer because I am also that and that. Whatever level one comes to, there always seems to be another level. Who am I? There is no looking for a result here. And it is on that basis that we can find agreement with each other. It is in that search that we can find companions.

But in this other thing, looking for the answer, we only create divergences. Do you expect to collect a group of friends around the answer to a question? Have you ever tried to get some people to agree to a formulation? Don't think you can get all these people in yourself to follow a thought. You never can get them to integrate. But around a question, a search, yes, they will follow. When they hear the right note, they will follow. That is what it means to control, to be master.

I have no right to give all my attention to
looking at my behavior . . .

QUESTION: Through some of my work efforts, I've come to really see myself. I've found I'm without charity. There is an empty place in myself. It is so empty, and I don't know what to do about it.

One day I wasn't in a good frame of mind so I went for a walk during the noon hour. I thought of the way I am, and I thought of the Lord's Prayer. I see I'm never free from taking sides. I'm not impartial with people. There are some people I like very much and others I don't like at all. Outside the group I'm sort of like a shadow. I'll be nice externally, but my heart isn't in it. I don't want other people to touch me.

LORD PENTLAND: Yes. You have a little will with which to begin. So, one begins, and there is only one possible way—to begin to look for something other than my behavior. As long as I am judging my behavior or thinking about changing my behavior, I can do nothing, because there is a part of me that isn't there. I have no right to give all my attention to looking at my behavior.

45

So the question is how can I be a little more free of this concern about my behavior? And I look to see what is behind, what is the sense of my behavior. What animates my feeling? I look and there is nothing there. But I'm looking for something behind, a looking towards life while I'm functioning; it's just that that is missing. I have an impression of liking him and not her and I believe in that most of the time. What is missing is that there is no impartiality—no universality. Impartiality is not to believe so much.

QUESTIONER: I don't know how to love God. When I'm faced with that I just don't know what to do.

LORD PENTLAND: That is exactly what I'm trying to speak about. You think of God in terms of behavior. God isn't behavior. God is life. In looking for God, you look for life. You have various scales of life in yourself—the taste of feeling, thinking, sex, and the search—something quite different than functioning. So the whole thing is perhaps to experience really the taste of searching again—but for itself, not connected with the fact that it helps you to control yourself when you see yourself. The most important thing is that it is a renewing of your energy.

QUESTIONER: I think I understand.

LORD PENTLAND: A little bit.

*I have to find a new part of me and
a new method of thinking . . .*

QUESTION: I have had a very strong feeling for the last three days about the attention I try to hold within myself, without letting it go or be pulled away—and the possibility also of making a small physical movement and not losing myself.

In doing the exercise, I found that there seemed to be the life that goes on every day—duties, and so forth—and at the same time, something else—something I would come to when I sit quietly—that didn't seem to be related to that. Somewhere, between this inner sense and the action of doing something, somewhere there must be a moment when I have to be there, in between, to keep the two things. I couldn't find it before, but now for the first time I understood the possibility of how to try. But how to try harder?

LORD PENTLAND: It is a question for everybody, after the struggle you made. I have to find a new part of me and a new method of thinking and find a possible aim. And after the strong experience that you have had, you see a little better your situation. You see that you don't know what is possible, do not know how to bring it about. The purpose is to have a new point of view. If I could be in between, I would have a new point of view— but I don't know if it is possible. I may have had it accidentally but when I try intentionally it escapes me. The question is how to take advantage of the point where we are. When we are in this better part of us, we have more energy or better understanding. How to go further in the way of those possibilities?

I will try to answer in two ways, because it is interesting for all of us. First, to keep to some extent this new point of view is very difficult. We do not recognize enough the strength of the ordinary point of view—which also is still there in myself.

We don't give anything like enough place in our study on ourselves to the effect ideas have. You see that this idea of yours, that you have to be there and look—and in order for you to be there, you have to be in some way related to this presence in yourself and also related to what you are doing, functioning—is really quite new, and that another idea—the idea that to be we must be doing something, must accomplish something—is very strong in you. The ordinary understanding of "I" is always in relation to doing—"I" must do it.

When you finish your work and go into life, you find within you a point of view which clashes with the one you left behind. It manifests in the street and office. You are not alone in regard to this, but the ordinary way is just contrary to the new point of view you are coming to. You wish to concentrate your energy, but everything else depends on distractions which are there to catch you. So that, quite apart from making "an effort which corresponds," it is just to feel the fact that you have your attention to some extent in your control. This attention is the only thing you have which represents you. And to feel it has to be placed in some way is the opposite of the idea which makes the world go around. You know one of these ideas is higher; one is lower. Both are there, part of organic life, one higher, one lower. And you see the degree of your conviction more if you try to maintain this new point of view in life; you will see you need to know all the ideas which actuate ordinary life and all the ideas of higher things spoken of in our meetings. Then you see what is possible.

I think we will begin a new work. I think it would be useful to try for a time with reading. You finish the exercise and still keep some time. Take a book, and try to feel this presence in you. Take different kinds of books—lighter, more serious—and you see to what extent you can maintain yourself reading. I think we are inclined to choose something much too difficult—or nothing.

Perhaps a trace of the idea that man can do was in your question. We can't do, but we can study. So begin with a book in front of you. Study how it is possible to maintain this presence in front of reading.

QUESTIONER: Could you suggest an amount of time?

LORD PENTLAND: Ten minutes. Until you have tried it, you will not see that it is very difficult. Try as sincerely as you can to understand something about the point of view that is more connected to your question. It is a study we need. You see that this situation which you have glimpsed is to be studied. To see what is possible, we have to find a possible aim, have to try to keep this new point of view. Each week we need to be reminded, through the connections we have made, in order to have higher ideas, so that this new point of view maintains itself, connected with this new world of new ideas.

To sincerely question myself is a possible act of will . . .

QUESTION: In trying to do the exercise that was given, I found that I was not able to control attention. A great deal of energy was spent in dreaming, talking, external activity. I realize a great deal more energy is needed. I need to find a way not to waste so much energy.

LORD PENTLAND: You speak of not being able to control. The only thing that we, as we are, could control is our attention. You touch on something very important there, but when you say you feel that more energy would be the answer, you are just feeling your way, aren't you?

QUESTIONER: Perhaps. Undoubtedly.

LORD PENTLAND: It really raises the whole question of will. And that question has to be raised at the very beginning of our work. Control. What can be, for us, an act of will?

QUESTIONER: Are you asking me that question? I have no control over my attention. It goes away and I can't keep it.

LORD PENTLAND: It is very good that you have been able to see that. Our reason for coming together is to speak of what we see, and you see you can't control. But we also come together in the name of Gurdjieff's ideas, the knowledge that is being brought, and this is a knowledge that has to do with doing. We have got to bring that together with our experience somehow.

QUESTIONER: There is another thing. I find that all the tasks I do are very mechanical. I can't bring my attention to them when I want to. When I'm in a thinking state, or in an emotional state, there is no connection.

LORD PENTLAND: Yes. And most of all, there is no way to connect them with Gurdjieff's ideas. It is just in the idea of control, the idea of will, that we have to find a connection.

Everybody understands that there are different kinds of knowledge. The knowledge that I am interested in as a young man is different from the knowledge I am interested in as a school boy. And as I get older, perhaps I become interested in a special knowledge. My interest leads me to accumulate knowledge about some particular thing. We do recognize one particular scale of knowledge. But we don't see that the highest scale of knowledge, like Gurdjieff's ideas, is connected with knowledge of how to do, how to bring will into my life. Ordinarily the knowledge that is higher for us is less and less connected with doing. We study certain kinds of art or history, but without any real hope of being able to recreate that knowledge in our own lives.

And you know these ideas. You know that we are told that there is a scale of being. It is something that we hardly recognize at all when we mix with people, when we think of people. There is an actual scale of people according to their being. And if we do recognize it, we are very modern about how we estimate people. We say a rich man isn't actually better than a poor man, a man well born isn't necessarily better than a man born of a common, unknown line of heredity.

How do I estimate people? It is a question I can put to myself. Do I think, for example, that people who are more considerate are better? Often one estimates people by their insight—he is interesting because he sees the future. That is not Gurdjieff's way of looking at being. He says that just as what makes an animal different from a plant is that an animal can move, what makes a man different from an animal is that a man can do—exercise will.

How often do you look at people and see he is a very special person—he carries out what he says he will carry out. We don't have close to us that idea of being, as you will find when you look at yourself. You will find you can't even control your attention.

You know by now it is no use accumulating more knowledge. It is really, particularly, what has made our living so complex. We have got a good deal of knowledge about a great many different things. We feel bound to follow a great many different interests. We have even found the most difficult knowledge to get. You hear about it and, to a certain extent, master it. It makes you proud of having the knowledge, but it doesn't affect your weekly living.

We don't want to be proud. We want to be happy. This means to do what I intend to do. The one thing that makes me unhappy is to do something I don't intend to do. Then, to face it, you have to justify and rationalize, "Really it has worked out for the best." In a way it is out of this that all the muddle and confusion has arisen.

The question really is how to introduce some element of the idea of will—of intention—into my life. You are right, I can't control my attention. But, unless every day I can come to an experience of carrying out my intention, I shan't be able to work with hope, because this knowledge is knowledge about how to do, because work on being means work on doing. That is what it means to be a man—to be able to do.

So I come back to my experience again and again. What can be, for me, an act of will? It would have to be something very small because I can't even control my attention. Maybe even to be able to not miss the meetings is something. Even those of us who have just started see how things get in the way. You have to give up some of your interests, even for one hour a week. Maybe just to do the work, the exercise that is given, is a sort of act of will. But, it doesn't really satisfy me because I see I may sit down to do this work but I don't really do it. I can't control my attention. So what, for me, can be, within my possibility, an act of will? This is very difficult.

Perhaps I could give a hint of how I look at that for myself. Really to sincerely search, to sincerely question myself—we can say that is a possible act of will for us. And trying again and again, freely to put a question to myself—to try to not go with my attractions or repulsions or all these different influences and freely to question myself and my life—to do that in a place, at a time, that I wish to do it would be for us an act of will. It is one that is not impossible for us—a moment in which I control my attention, a little moment out of fifteen minutes, in which my attention is my attention. Do you see?

four

Contradiction is the appearance of life . . .

QUESTION: I continue to be in great confusion about the continuity of life and I feel close to panic over what seem to be contradictions in the ideas. You have told me to think about these contradictions, and I know I need to understand, but I don't know how to wish to understand. This is a desperate situation with me.

LORD PENTLAND: In that case help may be nearer. Life is contradiction. Contradiction is the appearance of life, is all life. Life is a result of the struggle of forces that oppose. If Gurdjieff's system is alive, it is full of contradictions. The whole problem is how to feel more contradictions. There are buffers between contradictions. We say one thing now, next time another, and we don't see. We read and hear, but next week we hear the opposite.

What is new is that you've begun to hear contradictions. What could join the contradictions? Only my ability to be there between them. The whole question of life, my life, doesn't remove the contradictions. But can the buffers be removed so I am there between the contradictions?

I have to understand the relativity. How to move about on the scale—to understand the small and trivial contradictions and also very big contradictions? We can't follow through, we get more interested in one than in another. I have to move about on that scale, to be present in a complete way, also in a very small way. The small parts of myself are almost impossible to know. Take any given day, we fall off this scale. If we can know the contradictions in a day, we can know the contradictions in a larger scale, the understanding of relativity.

Energy is relative. Life is relative. Sometimes there is more life in me, sometimes less. In order to relate to it, I have to be present. It comes back to the question about my wish to understand—if I could be connected to my wish—but it is very hidden. If I could understand, then there would be the possibility I'd be able to stand in front of contradictions without getting frustrated, without escaping into an answer.

We need to return to the idea of the world as a world of forces . . .

QUESTION: It seems that the result of all the work is that I see more frequently there simply isn't anything in me to depend upon. This doesn't disturb me so much, but I see along with this a kind of apprehension. It creates a rather unusual state. Does one have to rummage through the whole box and find all the gems?

LORD PENTLAND: In a way we're not so completely without help now because we know many things, but the question is why don't we remember them at the right time. We know the answer from the head. There is always a starting point. Even if we know why from the head, it represents a challenge, a starting point, but we don't seem to find it at the right time.

The starting point to which we need to return is the idea of the world as a world of forces—that I am nothing but a machine, or combination of machines, in a field of forces. It is possible, by reason of the fact that we are forced to look upon ourselves, that when we work alone we have an organic feeling of the world of forces which will return to us without our trying. It's from this idea, at the basis of a new point of view, that I look on your question.

Of course one can't be depended upon. But what can be depended upon? Situations, external and internal, produce similar results. In such and such a situation, no matter how good my intention, I will always behave in such a way. I begin to face the world with this thought, that the world is a world of forces. I begin to depend not on myself but on the reality of these forces. I'm not so much interested now in the old idea that I could bring something to situations. I'm interested in knowing in advance that certain situations will include certain forces—and I need to be there. I'm not struggling with nature any more. I'm trying to be conscious of myself within nature. It means a big blow to the part that wished to transcend myself and it reminds me that my wish is hidden—the wish I wear on my sleeve is a very different one than the wish that has an attracting force upward. But that is something I can't remember all the time, it's not part of my everyday experience.

I can remember that I'm a creature of circumstances—I shall be according to the situation. The point of view can include more or less, but it isn't impossible for me to have a hold of the beginning of it. So at this point, where I have to be lost, I do have that to depend on.

You speak as if you were all the time existing . . .

QUESTION: I keep thinking that I shouldn't be as careless as I am. This carelessness seems to be something I'm seeing in myself more. I think this is a terrible way to live my life. But then I say, why not be careless? I see this part that doesn't take myself seriously. I think there's some deeper part that knows taking myself seriously is important.

LORD PENTLAND: It's a good observation, but don't mix up the observation with the structural idea you have. The idea of observing comes from Gurdjieff, but your structural psychology comes from Psychology 101.

QUESTIONER: Can you say more?

LORD PENTLAND: I can question whether I exist. You speak as if you were all the time existing, but you change from somebody who is careless to somebody who is careful. You don't have any free, independent existence, an existence independent of influences that are bearing on you at the time. You are careless because you are thinking about what you are going to do next, not what you are doing now. Have you noticed that?

QUESTIONER: Yes.

LORD PENTLAND: What are you going to do next? What are you going to do after the meeting?

QUESTIONER: I'm going to go to dinner.

LORD PENTLAND: With somebody? Yes, well, after one more question you will stop listening and will think about how to be at dinner. Or had you started already? What will you do after that?

QUESTIONER: Go home.

LORD PENTLAND: So at dinner, unless you are very lucky, when you will be two-thirds through you will begin thinking about how to face difficulties at home. This is what makes you careless. There are certain things that can only be done with care.

When we stay with something to the end, then we have much energy and we face the next thing. But then, in-between things, the meeting and your dinner, you have to be strong in yourself, or you will waste all the energy. To do one thing and finish and do the next thing produces energy, but the energy gets dropped in-between things. If you go back to living in a more simple way instead of trying to keep ahead of yourself, you will find you have more energy in-between things. Then you have a burden to carry. You have to ride yourself with a short rein in-between things.

So, mainly it's a mistake to say I'm careless. I don't exist, so there is no "I." It's simply that I live in the thing that I'm going to do next. When I wash the dishes, I'm so interested in what I will do next that I think, "I'll just stuff these in the back," not because you are careless but because you are not living through what you are doing now. To call that careless is Psychology 101. You see what I mean—not to mix that up with the idea that we are many, that we don't pay attention. If you want more Psychology 101, go back to school. And if you want more here, try to be consistent. Find your way without mixing the Gurdjieff ideas with the ideas that are not Gurdjieff.

We don't have enough to occupy us. The interest in what I'm doing is so superficial that I'm easily distracted from it. We think that somehow a day will come when we meet somebody who will create a kind of deep thing in us. But it will never come. The wish to have something deeper—you spoke of something deeper—what do you mean by that?

QUESTIONER: I guess an awareness of myself, a kind of attention and knowledge.

LORD PENTLAND: In these quiet conditions you have to acknowledge that's worth more than anything else. But you don't go for it with any conviction, any passion. You can agree but you don't really go for it. So what do you expect?

I begin to see myself. I thought I was normal but I'm not. I don't go for what I want. I know diffident people and evidently I'm one of them. I begin to exist in a shadowy way for myself but at least it's myself. It opens me to whatever help there could be.

Most of the time we have no connection with ourselves . . .

QUESTION: Lately I have known more often, especially when I speak with somebody, that I'm false, taking an attitude. I feel myself not being natural on the one hand, and on the other hand I don't know how to be myself—and I am very embarrassed. I have that feeling in me and also I try to get out of it.

LORD PENTLAND: Yes, one must be very careful with experiences like that because they're the result of our work, partly. We don't know how little we think about ourselves or experience ourselves in that sense in which you saw that sometimes you feel you're not yourself. And this is the most precious thing, to be connected with the feeling of myself, even by the experience that I'm not it.

Most of the time we have no memory, no connection with ourselves at all. We are all the time thinking of other people or other things, and we ourselves are just made of wood or stone or something and don't have any significance for ourselves. Now, maybe what you spoke about is just the beginning of something. It's very important. It's the question appearing in you.

Who am I? In a way, you're this person who is speaking; in a way, you don't feel it as yourself. But what is yourself? It's only then that the question appears. You never ask that question at other times. You make plans, you give, you take, but the idea of the egoist, yourself—it never comes into your head. Now it could come into your head. You feel, "This is not myself." What is myself?

You see how easily these sorts of moments, which are important moments, can escape one's attention. One can go through them and, not thinking they are important, go right through them and think that what happens afterwards is important, or what happened before is important. So the answer is really that somehow we have to prolong these experiences. We don't understand how it can be done, but we feel sure, don't we, that we could stay longer in that state of questioning who is myself. But just as you said, we have a feeling and we want to stop it. It's an uncomfortable experience. It's like, perhaps, one asks a question at a meeting and is answered, and the answer doesn't seem to bear directly on one's question, but one knows it is connected and one has a very uncomfortable taste. It's very useful to collect a sort of alphabet of tastes and to know which tastes are good.

The less one invents in this work the better . . .

QUESTION: Some of us are sewing and we are learning quite a few things from the sewing and how important the attention is for what we are doing. I wonder if you could suggest something—perhaps some inner work to try while we are sewing.

LORD PENTLAND: Well, it is a little difficult for me. Although I have once or twice done sewing, it is not something I have experienced enough to speak about. In general, the less one invents in this work, the better. Or rather, in general, I find in trying to see myself there is much too much invention. What is behind this invention? What is behind the idea that something special ought to be going on when I am working with others in the work activities? What is underneath that?

What is behind the idea when I am working with others sewing that there is something I am missing unless I am doing something? What is behind it is my uncomfortable feeling about being engaged in something I don't understand and which I am not prepared for. And what is that uncomfortable feeling? Why is it uncomfortable to be sitting there, sewing?

You understand me? Is it a fair question? You can't just bring questions out of curiosity. It must be based on experience.

QUESTIONER: Yes. It is very strange for me to sit all day and not move around.

LORD PENTLAND: But where was the discomfort? In not being able to move about?

QUESTIONER: Yes. I don't feel free. I can't leave or get up. I think it was the loss of personal freedom.

LORD PENTLAND: Why was there a loss of freedom? In what way weren't you free?

QUESTIONER: I would have to think about that.

LORD PENTLAND: But will thinking about it help? Why can't you just say now?

QUESTIONER: I think it was the inactivity. I am used to being active. Sitting so quietly was . . .

LORD PENTLAND: But can sewing take place without a certain activity?

QUESTIONER: It takes everything I have to sew.

LORD PENTLAND: Well, I think you have a question there. You know, you had time to get this question ready but maybe it is not quite ready. I mustn't take away your work. Maybe you have something. And in any case I think the point is not to agree to add something invented as a work task if there is a possibility you could see what is underneath this wish.

What is this discomfort? You say it is because you are not able to move about. That is interesting because the part that wants to move about is an enemy to the part that can do a job well. Why can't you feel in the movements of sewing that you were there? Why did it have to be that only when you got up and moved about that they were your own movements and these movements of sewing were not your movements? Why can't you regard it as an exercise to push the needle, wishing to get what we want out of meaningful circumstances. Does it have meaning for you that your costumes should be sewn?

QUESTIONER: It takes all my energy—everything—to sew and not make mistakes.

LORD PENTLAND: Yes. But if that is so, how do you have any energy for wishing to get up and walk about?

QUESTIONER: Last time I didn't have any energy . . . .

LORD PENTLAND: Then where is your question?

QUESTIONER: I felt something there, so tremendous . . . .

LORD PENTLAND: But the tremendous thing is in doing it well. And you see it is not true that you can bring all your energy to bear. Certainly there are times when you wish to move about and so forth. It is very far from true that we have intentions able to collect and direct our attention to the task at hand. It is just what we don't have. And the way to have it is not to invent it but to watch. Maybe you have to find a new way to be towards the sewing. To be there. To see that your functions are completely engaged at the job but to let them work freely. Do I work better if I don't stay too close—if you let it be, like when you are walking around? You study yourself.

You never are interested in the sewing to see how you are. You don't know how you are in the sense of an objective understanding—not good or bad or fast or slow—but what, in fact, is your way of sewing.

QUESTIONER: Maybe I get a glimpse of how I am?

LORD PENTLAND: No. You are too occupied with what you call the work and with your task. And between the two, you forget yourself. Do you agree?

The existence of a question depends on a division in yourself . . .

QUESTION: I can't seem to ask questions anymore. I find it difficult to feel that I am with it. I meet them and discard them. I want to ask but it is curiosity; it is not myself. I am left without questions.

LORD PENTLAND: Do you feel you manage to make a division, a separation, in yourself? Because the very existence of questions depends on that. And we place a sort of emphasis on questions because development depends on the division. If one of these separations reaches a division of myself into two contradictory, incompatible parts, the existence of these two parts together is, in a way, a question.

So if I am working, there is always a question—two things I don't understand, together. I am divided, and I work at it from the point of view of a whole. It is a question. But these divisions, or moments of separation, can take place, as it were, on different possible levels of experience. In other words, we have to understand the possibility of relativity, of the idea of the division of ourselves, the idea of separation. I do not see what I am at all.

We have to feel the necessity of a struggle, the existence of two incompatible things, which is felt subjectively as a struggle. This can exist on different levels. If I am feeling in a better state, as we sometimes say, there can be a possible struggle or division that corresponds to that state, but if I am in a very, very low state, there can be a division that corresponds to that. And higher or lower, I am further or nearer from the real experience of myself as a whole. Do you see? But that is a scale of self-remembering or self-realization and, wherever I am on this scale, there is a possibility of feeling a separation, and separation means a question. It means I am a question. For instance, just simply the idea that we are many "I's" and, against that, the idea of a possible wholeness —these are contradictory. I can't hold them both in my mind at the same time. And that represents the possibility of an effort—when I am entirely engaged in my mind to bring the opposite one than the one I am in. Do you see?

Now, take the possibility of trying to hold in my mind a certain aim, and how that makes a separation against the rest of my functions—body and feelings—which always want to go away from that aim. The existence of these two makes a question at every moment, every moment a contradiction, every moment asking who am I. Am I my head which wishes to remember this aim? Or am I feelings and body? But say I have an aim just in the head. What is the use of following what the head says? It leads one to a theoretical understanding of separation or experiences of myself around some thought. There is a division there. Now I feel myself without thought and now I am back again in my thought. And going back in, my thought seems narrow. On the other hand, it gives me direction. When I am out-side thought, I feel freer. Now who am I? Who should I follow? There is a question. Until I finally come to the idea of separation, trying to keep sep-arate the two contradictory parts, trying not to let them mix.

We should wish for this struggle that is the very nature of man, so that I bring my effort in order to prevent this mixing in myself which brings about dreaming and not struggle. So I bring effort to awake, which means to keep separate the part that faces one way from the part that faces the other.

What I am trying to say is that it is a whole scale of possible experienc-ing of myself as a question—do you see? —from the purely mental level up to the possibility of actually feeling the whole of myself and the part, and seeing how the part turns into the whole. Yet it does not mix, it contradicts the whole. But I can't understand that moment, which is the moment of awakening. Yet even if I am very far from feeling, I can under-stand directly the moment of awakening. I can come to a question, to the division of myself that brings me to the level where I am. Do you see?

QUESTIONER: I think I do. There is always a question. And there can always be a question.

LORD PENTLAND: There is always the question "Who am I?" It is, so to speak, a valid question even as a mental question, because even in my mind I can divide between the idea of allowing an absolute escape of energy and the idea of intention. Mentally, "who am I?" It is a question.

Of course we never get very far unless we make the separation from our thoughts, unless we manage to be quiet enough so that we see I am not my thoughts. "She is here. And really all these thoughts that I think of myself have nothing to do with her. But who am I?" There is a question there. And you can't avoid it if you experience it, feeling it as a question—not as a theoretical question, not as one intended as a means to work, but as an actual question.

QUESTIONER: I don't divide enough to ask myself who am I? I back away from questions that I don't feel.

LORD PENTLAND: There is nothing that needs to be done about it. We are all free to make an inner separation. Nature will take care of it. Nature has to produce certain substances. So there have to be a certain number of confrontations even if we do nothing about it. It has to be.

So finally you are entirely free. The separation will be done for us if we don't take care to do it. At that moment, we shall feel for an instant, before we turn against ourselves and pity ourselves—but at that moment—we shall feel very deeply the question, "Who am I?"

I can feel myself as a question . . .

QUESTION: At the end, do you mean death as the separation that will be made for us?

LORD PENTLAND: Yes, but it could also be starting to get out of bed in the morning. The morning is very important. If you allow yourself to dream in the morning, the very first thing in the morning, the possibility of making this struggle is certainly less. You would agree with me, wouldn't you? For a moment you come to yourself. I see this dream or this body. So I say nature takes care of these things. Nature brings shocks. It certainly applies to what you said, too.

If all of you could relax a little—I am not speaking a different language, you know. I don't want to name exactly what events Gurdjieff called these instances. But I think everybody could find it. That wasn't the point. The point is, wherever we are in ourselves, we are able to find ourselves in the sense that we are a struggle. We are divided. Two sides. However near we are to dreaming and however near we are to awakening, we can feel this struggle. And on all these different places on the ladder of being, I can feel myself as a question. When you say I have no question—really this is an inexcusable place to be—it is the one thing one can't excuse. Even nature is bringing us questions in order that we should go on existing as a three-story factory.

I don't really know what will result from choosing . . .

QUESTION: My question, I think, ties in with the idea of contradiction. But it comes to me now that in the moment I was faced with a choice, I was not able to make the choice, and immediately I was no longer present. In a contradiction, should one be able to see the choice?

LORD PENTLAND: I think what we could say, because I understand what you mean, is that at a moment like the one you describe one feels the verification of the way we are trying. You see that later we could have the possibility to choose. As I am, I am not sufficiently there as a whole. And I see that one thing that is never there, or never there enough, curiously enough, is my head, because I never have the feeling that I could choose, a choice that is measured, a choice that is mathematically right. And when I look around I see it is a material world and everything in existence depends on being measured in a way.

So one thing we shall need in any case is knowledge—the knowledge that will enable me to measure, because, while I feel the possibility of choosing, I don't really know what will result from choosing. I can't know the measure. It is one thing that is never there enough. So in that moment one realizes that if one could reach more moments like this, one could be a candidate for receiving the knowledge that would help one to go further. Would you think so?

Searching in the struggle for what is really you . . .

QUESTION: May I ask a question about *All and Everything?*

LORD PENTLAND: Better ask a question about the work you have been trying. For the moment let's just ask about the work you have been trying.

QUESTIONER: In trying to be present when I am with a certain individual, I have found that, during the day, the idea of trying to be present comes to me with two or three other people. I will be with a person and for an instant I will feel that I am definitely present. One I plan to do and this I don't plan to do. Is this mechanical? It seems just to happen. It is not clear.

LORD PENTLAND: I don't entirely understand. But what is right is you try to be present to the whole of yourself in the situation you already decided upon. And what you find is that you lose entirely the little connection you had made, when you worked alone, with what you call a higher or inner part of yourself. You find you cannot keep that, not in the way you reached it when you work alone.

When you work alone, you try to be very, very still. You see that when you start, you make some effort or other. But as you sit and it begins to be clear the effort is quite false and unnecessary, all you are trying to do is be more calm. And sitting there very calmly, trying to see what is going on in you, you become aware that there are, in fact, different organisms together in you and their very presence makes up a struggle—makes up a division of yourself—and that you are occupied with searching in the struggle for what is really you. And the calmer you are, the more the real struggle, the real differences between these three organisms, becomes apparent to you. The quieter you are—you have to be still quieter, more relaxed, in order that the reality of the struggle in yourself should appear.

And after a certain time, as a result of your attempt to see the different parts struggling in you, you will feel the appearance of something that connects you with the higher influences. It appears in you at that moment in a real sense. It has a real force. You know what I mean. It has a real force. It is not just an invented thing. It has a real force. But when later you come in front of this person, you can't find that, not as a real force, can you?

Now tell me, do you feel a sense of relief when you feel this real force? Because if you do, you have never been able to feel it in front of someone else. Do you wish to be asleep to this? Or do you ask who is there; how is this also part of me? If you go down on your knees before it when it appears, you forget everything that went before, turn your back on that. Then, by the same token, when you have to turn back to the world, you turn your back on all this. Man is a question. Man is both. Now how do you understand that when you meet with this wish? Do you see?

QUESTION: How can I have a question about my own personal work when I come here and I am not the "I" that I was when I had the experience?

LORD PENTLAND: Somebody reminds you and although you are not then the same person who experienced your same question, you are related or connected with the same person. You have to be connected, even at a distance. You will never be able to take part in these meetings unless you feel the connection with the question.

Best of all, you feel the question now. But, at least, you have to be connected. You are connected by a certain vibration, a certain kind of vibration which is the vibration of our work and your questions are invoked by the existence of this force. And this vibration can exist at different levels, although at lower levels it is very feeble indeed. But you have to be aware that it is a vibration.

Sometimes you are invoking it in others. Other times others are invoking it in you. And you have something to do with their questions. I don't mean something to do but you are related to this vibration in some way and it comes from them also. So you are related to them in that sense. I don't suppose I understand any more than that.

QUESTION: When I see something to which I am a slave, I would like to cope with it directly. That is, when I experience say a feeling—being overcome by something in me that wants to eat or rest or engage in a particular activity—if I try to resist being pulled by it, I get a certain reward. I go on with this for a while and I say to myself I will not give in. I say various things. I say I will keep on top of this thing or beat it down so that it won't have the power. Other times I see the thing to do is to try to engage in these activities but remain distinct from them. Then I feel it perhaps isn't best to hit these head on. But if I don't hit them . . .

LORD PENTLAND: I understand your question but the point isn't there. The point is to be able to be present to all this—not to say "I" to it all— but to feel all these "I's"as part of oneself. When you say, "I feel," then I exist. That "I" is a part of yourself. When you say "I want to go to sleep," that is a part.

The idea is to try simply to be there, without taking sides at first, and to see the struggle that is going on in me between the greedy part that wants to have a lot of substance and energy and the lazy part that wants to lie down and be big in that way. They are both entirely subjective, both ruled by ego. Until we can see all this going on, we don't have any "I."

So this part that you say gets something from resisting, this could go on in the whole of your life and only at the end one realizes that nothing was going on. Gurdjieff's ideas give us the possibility of trying to be free for a moment to see this going on. And that feels like having a question. We see the incompatible things. One side is lazy. The other side thinks, by resisting, it can get to the crown of glory. But which is "I"? Do you think it is the direction toward resisting everything? You will soon find you are wrong—it is isolating you by a very bad temper or something.

Try to understand that. And you can come to it only in one way that I have ever heard of, and that is by trying to sit very quietly and searching for yourself and trying to be as relaxed as you can and finding that none of these answers that come up is very satisfactory. I am not these thoughts. I am not this satisfaction. Even when something real—a wish—appears, it still reminds me, who am I? And if I feel something within, a strange, formless, something within, who am I? It is just what I feel—who is there? Now as long as I feel "Who is there?", I can't live with any meaning except in these moments when there is a confrontation, a question, because there is no meaning in trying to be stronger. Who is there? Who am I trying to make stronger? Do you see?

(Lord Pentland gave the group a new exercise
to work with and then continued.)

You will see the role you are accepting—wishing to learn, wishing to understand—you will gradually see, if you take it seriously, that this role, wishing for help, is not so simple as you may have thought. We never really wish for help unless we have no feelings at all. When we have feelings we do not wish for help. When we have something which we call existence—feelings—we do not wish for help. When we have no feelings, we wish for feelings. We do not wish for help. When we are dry, we do not ask for help. We say, "How can I get some feelings?" The idea of wishing for help does not belong to the times when you have feelings and it does not belong to the time when you do not have feelings. Most of life is divided between when one has feelings—tolerable—and when one is without feelings—intolerable. This sounds a long way from Gurdjieff's teaching. But I don't think it is so far from living.

The reality is that I am not responsible . . .

QUESTION: It seems to me lately that I make a lot of demands on people around me, especially in my family, but when I try to put some attention on myself and make demands, I can sometimes see that I can't live up to my demands. And yet I expect my children, people living with me, to do it. I can see I can't remember that all the time.

I don't think the goal is to try to stop being that way. I think the first thing to do is to try to see it happening. At the same time, I'm very worried about what is taking place with my children. I'm afraid I won't be able to change fast enough to help them. I feel very helpless about it. There doesn't seem to be time.

LORD PENTLAND: Quite true. I think it's right what you say. I think the work can be a support to us as well as a reminder and sometimes a corrector. I think, if you feel a lack of support, if you feel that there is a reality and yet all the time you feel tempted to accept something less than that in order to be a good mother, or whatever it is you think, you can look for support in the work for your wish to stay with the reality. The reality is that I'm not responsible and that it's a little late for me to discover there are people dependent on me for whom I'm not able to be responsible. But the work can show you that in fact their relation with you is in a way less serious than you think.

You don't know yourself. And you don't know what are good conditions or bad conditions for your children. In a way, if you were able, if you were responsible, I suspect you wouldn't know what to put in their path, whether support or difficulties, for instance. You wouldn't know what was better. The fact that they're growing up without somebody responsible isn't really so awful, if you think about it, because you don't know what would be the responsible thing to do about it.

And so, do you think it would be possible to have the courage to start from the very beginning like you're trying? They would benefit from that. You understand that to be responsible would start from being responsible for myself, and you could begin by trying to be responsible for yourself— that is your concern about yourself, your concern about the work, and so forth—and surely how you manifest toward your children will be better than if you weren't doing that.

One thing is sure, if you try all the time to manifest rightly toward your children, you will not only not necessarily do the right things, but you will also lose this concern for yourself. I think that is put badly. But I think the work can support what you're doing. First of all is the glimpse you have of what is real, and then the work ideas come and support and help to go towards that. But it begins from a glimpse you saw in yourself, not from something you read about.

There's very little doubt that children are not fooled as much as we think and, in a way, a mother who is clearly more aware that she is not responsible is probably a much better mother than one who is trying to give her children the feeling she can be responsible. I think children are very sensitive to the way we can be contradictory sometimes, and also very tactful in not pointing it out. In a way, they're full grown at a certain age. That's what it means, I suppose, that they stop growing in essence at about five years of age. And they know that they need the protection of the mother, and they have to all the time not be pulling down their own concept of the mother. And so I think they see what bad parents we are, but allow themselves to keep a certain picture. I speak from memories, but it is true that one has memories from what was going on in the household when one was very young. So there's another reason—if children aren't fooled, why keep up the pretense that I'm a good mother?

There is the idea of place to remember, too. The place of the mother is a thing that's vacant in the house. The mother has a certain place, the child a certain place, the father a certain place. And instead of being so concerned about adjusting things, try and occupy the place that belongs to the mother, and instead of trying to correct the child, try and have it occupy the place that belongs to the child.

Feeling that things are doing themselves,
a moment of presence to myself . . .

QUESTION: I have tried to observe myself during the day doing housework, taking care of the children, different types of things. I ask myself,

"Who is doing this now?" and sometimes I get to the point that I can see how helpless I am. I will be carrying a pan from the sink to the stove and when I ask "Who is this, doing this?" things start to happen in me. Really, it brings some feeling.

LORD PENTLAND: What does it bring?

QUESTIONER: It is a feeling of—like a big discovery that it really is true that I am not really doing this thing. Things are doing themselves. But then I start daydreaming and forget that right away.

LORD PENTLAND: You should try to understand this feeling. Although it is very fleeting, you should try to understand it more. It comes very quickly and we do not see how quickly it is gone. And strangely, even though it has its side of exposing my weakness, my carelessness, even though it has this side of showing my weakness to myself, there is a great joy in it. It is something very real. It is a moment of presence to myself, a very short moment.

Is there a feeling connected with that which could guide me in between these moments? Is there something more in that experience that I have missed? It is new for you still, but maybe there is something more in it that you will have to understand, which guides you in these other times when you say that you forget.

QUESTIONER: Yes, it just happens. I do not feel I have anything to do with it.

LORD PENTLAND: You feel you are getting something for nothing. This is an awkward position to be in. If you could connect it—how can I pay? There is something more you have to see in that. As far as it goes it is very good, it couldn't be better. But it has to go further and that means you have to see more at the moment.

It always takes you by surprise; how could you not be so taken by surprise? How could you understand what it would mean, this presence, when it suddenly appears, that without it you are incomplete? How could you be ready for that to come? How could you feel that, when you are being so careless, so completely forgetting of the need for this presence? It is as if a child were completely neglectful of its parent, if a child did not recognize its dependence on its parent when the parent comes into the room.

That would be one thing to start from, to see again and again that I entirely forget the need for what you could broadly call help, to see how in fulfilling these ordinary demands I forget that they can never be fulfilled without help—what I mean is, the need of this presence in me when I go out to fulfill these little demands. It never occurs to you that they never can be finished without that; even quite small things get out of hand.

There is no feeling behind your tasks, so the conditions are
not conditions to observe in . . .

QUESTION: I find that the neutral moments, when I'm just busy with duties like ordinary housework, are the moments when it is very hard to observe myself. There are many moments in the day when I remember to try this. They are ordinary moments, doing dishes, driving the car, and I try to concentrate on that, asking myself "Who am I now? Who is this?" But the whole thing is not as interesting as when I try to observe myself doing an exercise, or when I'm negative.

LORD PENTLAND: It is very true, because in those neutral moments I am entirely divorced from this state from which there is a real demand and which, through its presence, could give meaning to my functions. When that experience of being alive is not there, my functions are like children without there being any presence, any grown-up, there. There is no meaning in what they do. And there is no use these children asking themselves grown-up questions. It is absolutely useless asking yourself, "How do I observe myself?" It is just like children playing grown-up.

Now, what you have to understand is that this presence disappears and has disappeared for so long and so often—for generations of our ancestors—that we cannot often find it, even when we look for it. But there is a real demand for this presence, if you could find it. There is a real search to be done. But if you are not interested in its being there, of course you can do nothing. You are acting much worse than someone who never heard of our work at all. It is naive—dreams—based on what? Based on a life that is too comfortable. There are not enough demands. If you were fortunate enough to be in poorer circumstances, you would be worrying about something. You have come into circumstances where there is nothing to do but play with our work. The best advice I can give you is to take up some ordinary interest, so when you are washing dishes . . . .

QUESTIONER: I am very involved with an interest. I am in graduate school now. The other day I went to a graduate meeting and tried to observe myself. In trying this, I felt that the whole meeting was a fight.

LORD PENTLAND: I understand. Do not be worse here than at the graduate school. It was just in those conditions that you were able to find it. In those conditions it is better to try than in the neutral moments. Don't let these meetings be neutral. If you haven't a real feeling about coming, then don't come. It is only when you are more there with your functions that you are in conditions to see your need to search for yourself, for something more stable than your functions, and it has to be a real need. Do you see what I mean?

If you come here and feel free just to play like a child, then these are not good conditions for you. I am not sending you away. Do not be frightened. If you come here and feel free to philosophize about the work, innerly to play, these are not as good conditions as going to your meeting, the graduate meeting you were talking about. Do you understand what I am saying?

It doesn't matter what form your emotions take here, but you have to feel something. If you dislike me very much now, that will do. That situation is also good for work. You mustn't come here neutral. When you are doing your housework, when you wash up, you begin to play in your mind and try to think, "Why can't I do?" Those are not good conditions. It is the same thing when you come here if you are neutral.

QUESTIONER: I have been feeling all the time that because so much of my day is just tasks, that I should try at those times, too, to work. That is why I asked the question, because I find that I haven't very good success.

LORD PENTLAND: But there is no feeling behind your tasks, so the conditions are not conditions to observe in. You do not do the work with any feeling. When you make the bed, you do not think of who is going to sleep in it—that it should be made. When you wash the dishes, you are not aware of what you are doing—whose food. There is no feeling.

QUESTIONER: I see what you mean.

LORD PENTLAND: Any feeling will do. If you cannot find any interest in what you are doing, much better to leave these duties. That is what I said. There is only one demand. Let the bed remain unmade, let the dishes remain unwashed. Then you will see what feeling there is.

five

What could be an education for the whole man? . . .

QUESTION: Would you say something about the conflict or disparity between the trend in contemporary life of seeking more and more self-improvement and character-building and what Gurdjieff said man should seek in the way of experience and opportunity?

LORD PENTLAND: First of all, as difficult as it is to be aware of the contemporary, I think that this problem of character-building is one that always has been with us. Because what we, very few of us, have understood at all deeply, is that a man is not the same thing as his mind. Most of our education goes into the training and filling of a man's mind, and yet we know that a man is more than his mind.

A man's mind is a wonderful instrument because it can reflect the whole of the man and can even reflect the whole of the universe. A man's mind can be a reflection of the truth. But the whole man is something more than his mind. And the trouble, which seems to be growing, is the emphasis that is put on mind-knowledge and our belief in mind-knowledge, because, if you think about it deeply, you will find that the mind always resists the unknown. It always resists what is new, resists the future in the sense that the future is unknown. Therefore this emphasis on the mind is a misunderstood substitute for the whole man and leads to the inability to live with reality, because reality is to be always facing the unknown in myself directly. The question is, What could be an education for the whole man?

Look for the structure of your life as it is . . .

QUESTION: I've understood that there's a new world available to me and that it's possible sometimes to find it within many of the events of life, to find something to interest me more deeply, and that it's possible to find the order that is missing. But I see that the real need is for a part to observe this, as it gets mixed. I don't seem to have a steady place from which to look. I shift.

LORD PENTLAND: What are you really looking for?

QUESTIONER: I'm really looking for myself.

LORD PENTLAND: Then look for the structure of your life as it is. That is what is missing. It's not a structure of some ideal, but my life as it is. Is it true to say I look for that?

QUESTIONER: No, I think not. I look for a structure to which my life might conform.

LORD PENTLAND: The tragedy is that this kind of looking is so unintelligent—looking for a mental structure. So I look upon this part of myself that is caught with a kind of compassion, because this part is always under the illusion that the missing pieces will be found. But if I can turn inward towards myself as I am, there will be this moment of knowing myself. Of course when I say there can be this event, this moment of knowing myself, I don't mean that can be a conclusion. It's an impression and we have to go on. It's just that one can have this moment of awareness. The other approach will not bring me to this, because as long as I lean towards an ideal there will be this mental conclusion.

Slothfulness is exactly the inability to ask a question . . .

QUESTION: It seems to me that slothfulness is a very big part of my life, and I am really trying not to regard it as an obstacle. But I would like to see it. I feel I would like to understand.

LORD PENTLAND: What is slothfulness—what is it for you?

QUESTIONER: I don't know that I could define it. I am familiar with the way it operates. It seems to be perverse, a slowing down in the direction toward which for a moment I thought I was going.

LORD PENTLAND: Yes, but you say you need to find this. First of all, you must know what it is. You say it is an obstacle, but what is an obstacle?

QUESTIONER: In a sense the thing is not an obstacle. Sometimes when I am working with some kind of attention in life—there will be this slowing down process; there will be this drowsiness, this heaviness.

LORD PENTLAND: But what is it before you start? You want to find it before you look at it. Slothfulness is exactly an inability to ask a question. It is exactly in that that this exists. You never can maintain your search, you never can remember that nothing matters insofar as you can understand it, become conscious of it. You see that makes everything a question because even if you know a certain superficial level, you don't know the level underneath. This ability to keep a question is really an ability to think, we are told. So if we are lazy, it is perhaps in our thinking we are lazy, it is in our inability to wish to keep a question.

Everything is changing all the time and everything is a question. The question is changing all the time. For instance, I wish to make a demand on myself. Who wishes? I have to begin from that question first of all. I have to be present. What does it mean to be present? It is in the question I am reminded again. What is consciousness? You see I can always depend on my being able to supply answers, but I can never depend on myself to bring a question. If I keep questioning going, the chain of triad-transformations can be kept going. There will always be an answer as long as I can look at this with a questioning attitude Who am I? What am I?

So the laziness isn't quite what it seems. Nothing is quite what it seems. For instance, this obstacle has a hard feel because nothing is what it seems. Even obstacles aren't what they seem.

How can I wish to work? . . .

QUESTION: How can I wish to work?

LORD PENTLAND: I have to see, I have to realize my situation more and suffer for it in order to find this wish—this help that is always there. You ask how can I wish to work because, although this wish to work is there, you can't make contact with it. You see when you wish to work it is quite ordinary. It is not a real wish to work. First you have to make contact with something extraordinary. You have to see your real situation. You have to see what is your chief feature; you have to see your chief feature is dreaming.

This is what is the center of your whole life. This is what desires. This is what is the source of your feelings, the source of your thoughts, your love, your dislike, your ambitions. It all comes from this feature, your dreaming. The whole of your life is based on this misunderstanding. When you see the truth of that, you suffer for it and it raises another question.

*The effort to be able to experience my imperfections
but to go on . . .*

QUESTION: Something happened to me in the movements. I thought I understood a great deal several months ago. When I would come from the movements I would be very dissatisfied. I would practice; something was wrong but I didn't know what it was. Then later all that seemed to have left me again. And I understood what I had before. I really can't understand what this was.

LORD PENTLAND: I am not sure I quite grasp what your question is. As I understand it, you felt something wrong about yourself during movements. Later it disappeared.

I prefer the first time because it is more likely true. I mean, if you reason about it, the chances are that if the movements could somehow convey to us the perfection that they are, we would see our imperfection in doing them. And the better we did them, the more we would be able to experience our imperfections without being identified with them. The effort to be, to be able to experience my imperfections but to go on doing movements, that is how I would look at it.

QUESTIONER: I couldn't even remember. . . .

LORD PENTLAND: Now, when everything goes, what would connect me together as I am? What would make me a unity?

QUESTIONER: Knowing who I am.

LORD PENTLAND: That would be a long way from feeling that I am meaningless, feeling I am nothing. The feeling that I am doing the movements and it is going well, I think you ought to take with a lot of suspicion. It could mean that you are absolutely blind to these impurities in our movements, and also in our emotions.

As soon as we start to move, we begin to be aware of our emotions. So possibly it is only in the deepest sleep that one could do movements and feel that feeling that it is going well, feeling that it is right. One can't imagine movements being designed except to create the power of attention in the light of which my ability to control my muscles would seem very crude, very much in need of more development. Do you see? It is rather like, to take it to an extreme, even a moderate amount of practice will make one think one can make a good speech or play the piano, makes one feel one knows who one is. So in the same way, sleep has that sort of an effect.

QUESTIONER: I never looked at it like that.

LORD PENTLAND: I don't insist on that, but it could be we need to come to conclusions that are not based on something that has never been seriously searched out in myself. We accept the signals that come to us without enough verification, without testing them enough. For instance, when you are doing movements and feel it is going well—I think we have all experienced that but one doesn't bring enough to question "Is that really right?"—maybe at times like that there is still a little voice wishing to be heard.

QUESTIONER: Yes, I know what you mean.

LORD PENTLAND: A voice that has been neglected and neglected. We have been on these emotional trips so often but the voice is still there. If one could be quiet enough, it would still be there.

I must be able to bear the journey . . .

QUESTION: In the morning exercise I find that now I can pretty well feel that I am being attentive but my mind is not all there. Other thoughts come in. Every morning—I don't miss my times—but I feel I am not getting enough, there is more. Once in a while I feel something real has happened. I see more than one part. One is trying very hard to watch, the other is letting thoughts come in.

LORD PENTLAND: All this that you have said and that anyone else here may be feeling about how difficult this work is—it is exactly what can be useful if we care in the right way. Nothing could show me more clearly that I am nothing than just what you have said. But it depends how you take it. It could increase my concern. It could give me a deeper concern, or it could make me feel, "Well, after all, this is another blind alley and I give up."

It could increase my sense of realism. Do you see, this actually is so? And nothing is better than to be able to say it in front of others because that also affects the purity of my concern. I am able to share my work with others. And then, if the concern is there to be able to come in touch with my essential energy, I shall come in touch. If the right direction is there, I shall reach it.

Only I must be able to bear the journey. I must be able to come back again and again from the distractions to my attention, also holding before me the possibility that I will get lost in some feeling, some thought, or particularly some feeling of interest. My curiosity will take me away. In the long run, we don't wish to turn inward.

QUESTIONER: We think we do, but . . . .

LORD PENTLAND: We don't really wish. There is this concern that has to be renewed. On the way, we come outside again. Perhaps that is why one observes it is no use becoming heavy about doing the exercise—that is not the same as being serious. Sometimes it goes much better if one is leading a full external life. That goes quite well as long as you take the half hour that is needed. It doesn't go when I have no sense of higher and lower in my life. It doesn't go when I have no real sense of higher and lower. It doesn't go when I have no sense of the forces that really make up my life.

I would suppose that, for you, if you would dress yourself up and get all ready to go out and put some perfume on and do everything that attracts you toward the outside, it might go better. It is a question of the forces. If you feel the force of curiosity, if you feel the force of life impressions that attract me to the outside, that reminds me and I find a wish to go inward. When everything is the same, it is just my mind that sees this better; it is difficult for something to happen there. In the long run, nobody can do this work except I myself. What helps very much is participation in the meetings and the movements. That is what I feel.

An emotional whole would be full of contradictions . . .

QUESTION: I have come to a point in observing certain "I's" where I know now that they are destructive, and I have been able to separate from them. It seems that when I come to a meeting, or am less identified, then I feel free. Otherwise, after the morning exercise, the rest of the day is gone. If I forget and I am taken—just a part—I know I will be taken more and more and it becomes quite unbearable. I know now it has nothing to do with true emotion. It is just a mechanical habit. I would like to be able to do something rather than feel sorry for myself.

LORD PENTLAND: You see this habit. You divide it into good and bad. Criticizing myself is very, very deeply ingrained and you can't expect to get rid of it. It even has a certain sense if it could only be in its place, but it must take up the whole room.

In this idea there is something very helpful. We never put enough importance on the idea of wholeness. If you could remember that, it would help you very much to not be taken by the emotion of the moment that says, "Now it is impossible," for instance—impossibility also is part. It is a sense of wholeness and we needn't ever lose that. There can be very many qualities there, but it is our right to have some echo of that ourselves. Why should you give up this echo when you start to work? On the contrary, it is just that that has to be reinforced.

You work to have sensation, but not to have a stronger sensation, only to have a more even sensation. Little by little, you try to come to the whole of yourself. Already you feel a sensation that corresponds to the whole body, and it is because of that it is possible to direct the sensation, for instance into one arm. Unless you had some sensation of the whole body, you couldn't direct the sensation into your right arm. You have the sensation of your whole body so it has some sense—not to pay any attention to the sensation in the legs or left arm but to the right arm—they only have a sense because you have a little sense of the whole. Do you understand?

So what would be the whole of my emotionality, this feeling that now I have failed, now I am shut out? It can't be the whole emotionality. If you think of the idea of an emotional whole, it would be full of contradictions, "possibility" would only be a part.

Now in searching for myself, I am searching for the whole of myself. Some particular emotion comes, like this one. I look at it. It is what I am, very nearly the whole. But I don't get drowned because I have this conception of the whole. A moment later I might feel an appetite of some kind, an overpowering aspiration. It is not the whole. I am looking for the whole which includes all these contradictions. I am prepared for that because, before I was able to be aware of my emotions at all, I had to become aware of sensation. And in working with sensation I become a little—to some extent—I become aware of the sensation of my whole. The more I worked with sensation, the more I saw this conception was needed, because I never am where I wish to be. It is only in relation to the whole that I have the ability to collect attention and place it at that particular place.

The experience of my energy before it is consumed . . .

QUESTION: Lately I have become indifferent to everything, to the people around me. I no longer feel any strong hate but I don't love very strongly either, and it seems there is nothing real. Maybe I have just been superficial all along. There is just a great indifference about everything.

LORD PENTLAND: Everybody has had that question at one time or another. In a way, although I feel this mood or situation is worse, it is no worse than my usual one. If I am being eaten by some inner emotion that I am not aware of, that is making me be unconcerned about everything, it is really no worse than being eaten by outer things. It feels worse though.

QUESTIONER: I am critical of myself.

LORD PENTLAND: The only way to study this is in oneself. From outside, there really is no way of finding what is eating me. I can't have somebody tell me. First of all, avoid believing anybody who thinks they can tell you what it is. There really are some pages in our lives that we can't find in any way but from inside.

We have to look for something that is true, something that is outside altogether the level on which we live. We have to look for that inside us. It is possible to find it and on the way in—or afterwards—we may catch a glimpse of what it is that is eating us.

QUESTIONER: It is very difficult to believe one will find something . . . .

LORD PENTLAND: It has to be a real separation. We have to find something, the bad emotions that eat us. We have to separate something that is spending energy from something that is my energy. Who am I? I am also the pure energy before it is spent, before it is eaten up. In the long run, however, it is eaten up. It always comes to the same thing until I can relate the energy itself to how it is spent. If I could do that, then I could express what I wanted to. Meantime, it is expressed.

My question is, do I care enough to look and search in myself? Because if I can, if I start with the right concern and if I make use of the meetings, I can come to the experience of my energy before it is consumed. Only it has to be what I call a real separation. It has to go beyond what I think is my energy or what I felt was my energy. It has to be a verification. If I could only remember that this energy is there, and look for it. The real trouble is not that we can't reach this separation, but that we dare not admit that we don't wish to.

QUESTIONER: I think I am afraid to . . . .

LORD PENTLAND: That is what I mean. It is a certain part that doesn't wish to, but we are not honest about that. In keeping this wish and pretending we wish, we spoil our real wish. There is a real wish and a false part. In covering up and pretending this wish is there and the false isn't there, we impurify, we spoil the real wish.

So the idea of separation has a sense from the very beginning—it is not to be bothered by what is wrong and look for what is right. Do you follow me in that duality? When I begin, I am in the idea of right and wrong; it is very much present. I must try and separate them. It is not a question of stopping there.

QUESTION: You said there must be a real separation, verification, which seems to me a very difficult goal. When I sit, I begin from some combination of wish and habit, I think. I have enough accumulated experience making me feel I want what I might get. I am not sure why I sit. Then I often don't get very far and recently I have concluded that about the best I can do is this, that I clearly begin to see how many times I get taken by some function or other or some urge or the feeling of how late it is—some automatic function. Then sometimes there is a certain clarity; I do see how badly taken I am most of the time. I am seeing that fact from some position or other which is the closest I can come to defining a separation. I am afraid it is not very well verified. When I can realize though how badly taken I always am, there is a certain clearness that reinforces the wish to sit down next time. This doesn't sound like a very good verification. It seems there is a separation where I get to a vantage point where I see something. Is this a real direction, a beginning of understanding of separation?

LORD PENTLAND: Yes, that is just what it is. It is the beginning of understanding, of separation. But how do you go on? It is absolutely right. There is no complete verification inside. That is what the groups, the activities, are for. Little by little they have to take more part in our work because there is no self-verification at this stage. And the more seriously one takes the work, the more one is bound to depend now on the verification that is so necessary with others.

But the work really begins from what you said. It only begins there. You see that there is something clean about this way of coming to work with the feeling that I have been able to see that I lose myself. It is absolutely right. I absolutely understand these words. The cleanness is the most important thing for our work.

Now where is the work? Because where do I go on from this feeling of, "At last I saw myself"? What is the work? And how can we make work beyond that which doesn't spoil our being clean? This is the whole problem. If I say to myself, "Now where do I lose myself?" in order to see it, it is not clean. Do you see a little bit? How to go beyond just what you said? If I take satisfaction in seeing myself lose, it is no longer clean.

QUESTIONER: I wish I had asked that question.

LORD PENTLAND: You said, "Is that the beginning?" It is only the beginning. The question for you is what is work now, because you have reached your feeling, which is so important, your cleanness. But in the light of that, you see you have done no work. You haven't started to work. Now, what is work?

"Who am I?" is not a mental question . . .

QUESTION: This is my question that I came with tonight. It seems that I come to this finding in myself a satisfaction or a dissatisfaction in my exercise. I see that in order to separate from a part that is in my way, I must not try to run away from it, that if another part of me judges this or approves it, I have to observe that too. I have to hold that in some way that I can't explain. And it seems that I can get to a place where I can follow, in a way, the parts of me, many of my thoughts and a great deal of sensation, and for moments I can resist or find a way of not being taken by voices that approve what I am doing or disapprove of what I am doing. But I don't know where to go from there at certain moments. Other moments, of course, other things start to manipulate. I don't know what work is beyond that. I see my attention is outside of my mind and outside of all this. I can, in a way, hold all of this at bay, but I don't know what to do with this now. I don't know what happens next.

LORD PENTLAND: It means you need to observe more closely. It means you haven't seen what is happening next, because there is something very important that must be missed about then. You feel that in working like that something is displaced in you. You say you feel that you move out of your head into some other part.

QUESTIONER: Sometimes.

LORD PENTLAND: Yes. And always it is something that is difficult, that you can't feel that you do. But when you, so to speak, give up being in these thoughts, you become aware of the sensation of the whole of your body. You seem empty in a way. You feel yourself sitting and empty. Don't you? And suddenly you are aware of that impression, but perhaps what you don't see is that it is yourself that is empty. And who are you? You don't know but in any case this is you. Who it is, you couldn't answer, but in that moment, when you feel empty, when you are displaced, out of your head, just sitting in the chair, you become aware that it is in that chair, in that room, and, of course, it is yourself.

And this feeling of yourself, which is so fragile, is the important thing that you have missed. This feeling makes the question, "Who am I?" quite different. It is not a mental question. It is a question that relates everything together there. Do you see?

And it is conceivable that I could know myself, that I could begin to know myself in the sense that I have a little feeling of myself at that moment. I mean to say that, although I have the experience of a great power of seeing—like we spoke of at the beginning—and also of complete sleep at the moment that you spoke of, I experience myself, which is my measure, to the degree I am related to these. Do you see what I mean?

Sometimes you may have an impression of yourself which is much stronger, in which you feel the "Who am I?" I am much stronger. But it will depend upon your attempt to make a complete separation and, in that moment, there is a little feeling of myself, if you can be quiet enough to catch it.

*There is never any meaning in my life unless
I live between zero and infinity . . .*

QUESTION: I didn't know I was to be here tonight, so I had asked guests for dinner and when I was called we were having a cocktail. I left them. Now I wonder what they are thinking. I just left. Now there was a time when I just couldn't have done that. But I condemn myself. And I am never sure as to whether I did the right thing.

LORD PENTLAND: We never can say enough, you know, it seems to me. That is why we feel between two stools. There is nothing wrong, of course, with leaving one's friends like that, even if, and I don't think it was so, even if you let them down. There is nothing wrong with that really, in a way. But we feel that it is wrong because we don't go far enough.

There had to be a reason for coming here. What you are feeling is that you heard about the meeting tonight, probably at a time when you were having these friends for no reason, so, for no reason, you came here. It is more or less how our lives go, if you see what I mean. The idea can be expressed mathematically. There is never any meaning in my life unless I live between zero and infinity. Of course we see reality upside down. Infinity is below us and zero is above us. When we feel ourselves, we feel nothing. And there is nothing wrong with feeling important and having a dinner party. We ought to do it in many ways, but we only do it in two ways. For our lives to have meaning, we have to live between this nothing, which is infinity, and an infinite number of meaningless parties. Leave your friends more often if you are feeling distressed—but not only for a meeting.

In the olden days they had a thousand shades of color. Infinity below us has become very narrow. We like to have a certain breakfast every morning. Certain people we allow to be intimate with us. We like repetition. There is nothing wrong with going outwards with what we know as the involving force. If we were to go outwards in an infinite number of ways, then turning inwards would have some sense. Then we would see infinity is above me. We have to see this below me.

QUESTIONER: Yes, I see.

LORD PENTLAND: It is a good thing to feel freer to leave your friends.

You have to encourage that. But you will only do so if you find more meaning—this little moment when you connect yourself with the very many meanings I think you have of yourself when you are important, identified.

QUESTION: Some months ago I experienced a separation from my dreams, the dream that things could be different, that I could be different and other people could be different and at first it affected me. I was really lost. I didn't know who I was.

I see more and more it is as if I would see things as a child, with the thought that I could change, that things could be different, with an excitement that things could be different. Now I suddenly find myself looking at things more as an adult. What I see now is almost a stranger. And my question is that in the absence of these dreams I find that I miss them. They excited me to more interest in what I was seeking. I really wonder what takes the place of these dreams.

LORD PENTLAND: This is the point. This is the essence of the thing. All my life until now I was what you call a child. In other words, I thought that evolution was to be free to be exactly the same as I am now, but at a higher level. Some dreamed of higher levels where I could be just as egoistic and greedy as I am now. Now I begin to see it is not like that and something will have to be given up—given up in the sense of relinquished, relaxed, not blocked out but, you know, shed. At the same time, I don't want to give it up. There is the voice that says, "What would take the place of this?" This is interesting. You see, you don't separate there. Separation would be to separate there. Then the struggle exists. You understand what I mean?

You feel you wish to be different, but what would replace the interest which has to be given up? I see that I feel I wish to be different and I see I wish not to be different. Seeing is all the difference. There is a separation in one, in the other they are mixed-up.

As soon as there is a separation, there is a struggle, and it is a struggle for my energy. Not yet, but little by little, we could come to have a little control over this energy. But if it is an experience I could have of the feeling of myself, it will be that amount of energy that I could put onto the balance on one side or the other.

86

First there has to be a struggle. A separation. It is not one process, it is two completely different processes—one real, the other false. One is the wish, the most important thing in my life, the most important thing that exists in me—the wish to be real. The other is the attraction of my various centers, or the chief feature or misunderstanding which keeps me intact, prevents me from suffering. Only they have to be separated. The whole point is in the separation. They have to be differentiated.

This idea that there is an interest which would be replaced has to be seen as an enemy. Until it is seen that this is me deceiving myself, talking about an interest that has to be replaced is wishing to make the confusion in which I live. Do you see a little bit what I mean?

So there was a question of relationships. There was a question of how to make new relationships. But before that comes the question of seeing things as they are—separately.

QUESTION: In trying to be present more often and see my will-lessness in the morning—and I remember very few times—I'm trying to understand how I might find a wish to be present as I connect that with the beginning of a will. I try to relax certain muscles during the day and I recall that there is some connection between that and development of will. But I can't make the connection with being present or what that might mean.

LORD PENTLAND: Bear in mind that we speak of will as "my will." It's not something that can be studied at a distance. Moments of "I am" are what we speak about. Will-lessness also is something to be experienced, but not discussed. It's my will-lessness. Will is my experience of the inner and the outer, for a moment related in the only way they can be related—that is to say it is the result of my realization that the inner and the outer are separate, share separate claims on my attention.

In any case, it has gone beyond the place in this group where we can speak of will-lessness. It is an experience. It concerns me. And will is something I don't have. But I can't tell whether your question is really close to what we have to understand these days or theoretical. The question "Who am I?" doesn't come in enough.

QUESTIONER: I had this experience of will-lessness when I woke up this morning.

LORD PENTLAND: Was it something on a screen, or did it concern you, or was it a matter of your day being spoiled? That is the horror one sees on the screen. It's a different thing. You feel it as your energy is going out. When you come home, you find a burglar has been in your house. That's the kind of concern I mean. All the records you've kept your whole life have been taken. This is the kind of thing I mean—not about somebody else's house, but my house.

The question of will is related to the idea of separation . . .

QUESTION: When I listen to my own words, I am very often struck that they are words that were said to me by my mother and father, that my intonations are from someone other than myself. I hear the words and, in looking in the mirror, there is the expression of a brother or sister on my face. One evening when I was sitting quietly in my boy's room, I had the impression of being a group of impressions from other people. And all of this has made me wonder who I am, because at that time it seemed that just watching, it was part of eternity—because I was just a shell. So the question "Who am I?" is more real to me now.

LORD PENTLAND: When I have had an experience of this stranger, who reminds me of my parents but who still is infinitely strange, the question "Who am I?" is real, not in words, but as a concrete reality. But these are just moments. So I'm more interested in what you said, that the experience means that the question "Who am I?" is more real now and not just words; this is will—if it were as real when I use words.

What I think would help you is to feel how little we understand and yet to see that all our talks have been worthwhile because something has been helped. There is a sort of separation between the stranger and my body— I feel that the stranger has taken possession of my body, but separately. All our talks have been to bring about this experience, and it can't come unless there is this separation.

Now, at these moments when the stranger is there and the question is real, I have a little memory of how my body functions ordinarily. But if I have this experience, I must try to feel the stranger and the functions of my body. And I try to see that these are two. I wish for being. I wish for an impression of these two while the stranger has the power over me, so that when I come into the body the functions will be smaller. I wish to experience them as just a part of me.

In a way I know that the stranger is always there, but I don't come into contact with the question because I allow the functions to have all the play. I have to understand that the question of will is the idea of separation between the two and the attempt I make with all my lack of will—that the two are separate. And when I go back into ordinary life, I try not to let the functions dominate me. I try to keep a touch with the thread, which is usually so difficult to find because I accept to see things upside down— the functions more important, the search less important. And when this has been going on a long while, it takes a big shaking for the stranger to appear. So it couldn't be wrong to pause a little to feel how you are separately like that for a moment—to look at yourself from above for a moment.

six

Observation of yourself in front of other people . . .

QUESTION: It seems like there is one side of myself I can see clearly now and that's a very large weakness in the direction of relating to other people. It seems that my manifestations are based on some very deep inner fear of other people and I relate to them in several ways I have noticed. One is a rather cynical and sarcastic way of poking fun, making jokes about certain weaknesses that they may have, and another is to go into some indifference, which I have always liked to call detachment, which I see is actually just indifference because I am not interested in them. It is just retreating into a place where I can't be reached.

LORD PENTLAND: It's a good beginning, this observation of yourself in front of other people. It's necessary but it has to be a real seeing at the moment. Sometimes I can see my fear as being the background behind my manifestation. Sometimes I can sort of deduce that there was fear. The point is, mostly, I am not present at all in front of others.

How to begin to search, to make room for some feeling—whatever it is—to be observed. Mostly I am entirely externally oriented when I am with others and there is not only no power to see, but no feeling left inside. It's all directed towards you. The only way to have some feeling inside would be to search, as it were, for the source of my life at that moment, quite independently of your being there. And then I would see what I see. If I see myself acting out greed or acting out impatience, it's all the same thing. In any case, I am alive, so what difference does it make which is the more unpleasant? So long as I have understood that I am alive, that my attention has been searching for that, what else do I expect to have?

So I see how I am towards others. Maybe what I have to understand is the whole idea of work toward being and what it involves, and how the relation with others is an exchange of vibrations which goes on in spite of whatever I may be wanting to produce in the form of love or hate. In front of a child, what the child knows is my vibrations. In front of grown-ups maybe some misunderstandings are communicated, but on the whole it's the vibrations. So, one has to come back to the work on being, and then these observations begin to be felt more as facts and less as sins. That's how you were thinking of it?

QUESTIONER: I imagine so, at least as something that should be changed.

LORD PENTLAND: The idea, as I have heard it from Gurdjieff's lectures, is that mostly the forms of functioning are fixed in us. In the way we were brought up or I was brought up, the available forms are very limited—the range of gestures, the range of emotions is very, very limited. It seems hard to believe—when one knows of the existence of acting schools—but if I understand what he said, it's almost impossible to increase this range after a certain age, say the age of twenty. So if we feel that idea could be right, the only sensible thing would be to make the best of it, both by trying to live our lives and by using the relatively small range of manifestations that we have as sensibly as possible, in a more meaningful way. But if one takes that line, one can cast out altogether, for instance, that I will ever be as charming as Clark Gable.

What is missing for me is weight . . .

QUESTION: In my attempts to work with my attention, until just recently, I guess, a large part of the exercise was trying to get the question of what is a sensation straightened out, and I did not concentrate too much on the attention itself. Just in the last week or two I have been trying to work with the attention more, and it is a very curious thing because some part of me knows that the sensations are there and it is primarily a question of keeping the attention moving. It is like getting another layer back and trying to get deeper behind the watching, to just watch the attention rather than to watch the sensations. I guess my question is, does this sound like it might be in the right direction?

LORD PENTLAND: There is such a gulf of difference between "I want attention" and "I need attention." I do not think we could say we know what attention is. It represents what is missing for me. What is missing for me is weight, something weighty so that my little ego is not so volatile, available to every chance interest, person, and so forth. It feels the need of weight and seriousness.

If attention is what is missing, attention would give that. If work is what would bring attention—work in the sense that it is something not ordinarily pleasant in accordance with the whim of the moment—maybe work would give attention. It is claimed that what would bring attention most quickly is to try to make myself follow what is there without preconceptions. We have to prove if that is true each time, because each time we start with preconceptions.

And it is a work because all the time that I need attention I want attention. I want all the parts of me to give attention and all the people to give attention to me. And while I am opening towards attracting attention, it cannot possibly be needed in the other place where it could give me weight, so I feel the appearance of attention in the other place partly as a deprivation of attention from this place.

So when there is a conflict in me, when I do not feel sure that my question is a question, when I am not sure of my intonation, when I catch myself hardly able to bear the silence because there is no applause in it, it may be a sign that I need attention myself rather than following it less. Sometimes one can feel it that way. But only for a moment because as soon as I have made a conception of where to go, it is impossible to really need to go there.

You will see as you work you will follow your conception. You do not actually follow what is going on. The difficulty is to keep on coming back to what is going on. There is no applause in following what is going on. It seems like being against nature. The verification of work like that is that you become more aware of your own presence. You wonder if that is attention. You do not know. Nobody told you. Even from what you hear, it probably is not. You feel nearer to finding attention when you question what attention is; rather than this other way when you demand it, when you know very well what it is.

People look at you. They smile at you. There is no real relationship. You have their attention. You do not have any relationship with them. They will do what you say sometimes, but you have no relation with them.

The whole of me can only be connected towards a reality . . .

QUESTION: I can't help but experience that a question can come from different places in me, and it is a big experience because generally I notice my questions come from a part. I never seem to be able to formulate a more real question.

LORD PENTLAND: Can you feel it even if you can't formulate it?

QUESTIONER: At times, but not often when I am here.

LORD PENTLAND: Is the problem to feel it or to formulate it? Do you wish to speak about feeling it or formulating it?

QUESTIONER: In the area of formulating. Because sometimes I feel the question of our relationship is important. I feel there is something lacking somehow. I come to the meeting and I feel the demand. I also notice that I want something but I am not sure what I want.

LORD PENTLAND: You have to begin from that. If you want to formulate something from the whole, begin from something real that could be wanted by the whole of you. You can only speak insofar as what you want is wanted by the whole of you. You have to begin there and sometimes, if you find that, you can formulate more from the whole of yourself—you feel your foot and nose and eyes are taking part more.

But the first thing is to feel the whole can't take part in forming some question which the whole of you can't be involved in, connected to. That is why we have to begin with being present. Perhaps you all read the teaching enough, to put it intellectually, to see that the only things we can want from the whole of ourselves are food, air, and impressions. Do you see what I mean? The whole of myself can't want a plan for tomorrow except as something I am present to now, because the whole of me can only be connected towards a reality, and for a human being, the only reality in tomorrow is the impression of now. So, try to be present in the moment. What else could I want? I have food, air, and, if I had impressions, I would be balanced, harmonious, satisfied.

Sometimes we can feel that more, even if we can't formulate it. When we are very quiet, we can feel as if we are leading a more complete life—if for a moment we are interested in the impressions—but we can't formulate it. But all the same, formulating does give us something, because the whole idea of being present is a sort of complete exposure of myself to myself, and in formulating, this carries this exposure further. It carries further this movement of the relationship of everything together.

If you have found some problems in your work, please speak about them.

All my life is turned towards expectations . . .

QUESTION: In a meeting such as this, what is it that I am afraid of? Am I afraid of seeing myself here in this situation?

LORD PENTLAND: I suppose so, in a way. Don't you think I am afraid of the unexpected? I live my life in the line of expectations. All my life is turned towards expectations. It is only in the little moments between expectations that I, myself, am more in the field of consciousness.

Most of the time I am hidden because I am occupied with what I expect. When I don't know what to expect it is as if the outer layer is removed. I see what is making me run all the time. I see that it is a part of my mechanicalness which I can call fear. It takes the form of tenseness, too. It is a tense fear.

It is very useful to come to a meeting and to become aware of this more inner layer of myself. If I try to be very still inside, it may be that after a certain time—because it takes its time—the knots of tenseness will be untied. Then other sides of myself, which are the unexpected, will come into the sphere of my consciousness. When these unknown sides of myself appear, they relieve my situation. It is just these unknown sides which I need to be in touch with.

QUESTIONER: It seems to me a great deal is taken up with this fear in an unknown situation and the tension created by it. It seems everything is lost between this fear and tension. If I could have the energy to find myself, as it were, in a quiet place, this would seem more profitable.

LORD PENTLAND: Yes, it could be spoken about like that, but the problem is always how to begin, how to feel I am beginning towards the quiet place. As soon as I feel myself searching for the quiet place, there is some measure of relief. But expecting something, remembering in my mind about the quiet place, is the obstacle to finding it. The quiet place is in an unknown direction.

It could be spoken about as a big stage in myself, the moment when there is no freedom, when I am locked in myself. It is a very great help if I can remember that my work then is to be aware of my situation, my tenseness, my fear. In your ordinary thoughts you don't take that into consideration. You say that in order to be more relaxed it is necessary to get rid of your tenseness. It is not so. It is necessary to be aware of the obstacle to your work.

I refuse the work, but I can be aware of my refusal. Then even though there may not be the possibility of coming to a quiet place, there will be a movement. The movement will go on as long as I don't begin to expect something. I find that in looking I already am freer. It made me freer as long as I didn't get caught in some memory or thought.

QUESTIONER: Yes, the trap is in the thought.

LORD PENTLAND: No. I can be aware of the thought. I am not my thought. I see that I am in my thought. In being aware, the movement begins to exist for me.

I am afraid to say I don't know where the trap is, afraid of the unexpectedness of the answer. You try not to go with this fear that says, "This is the way; that is the way; do this; stop that."

I don't have the right to sympathize with you . . .

QUESTION: You spoke to me about effort, about how you could help me. It is connected with helping myself. It is connected with what you said, about finding a wish when you are empty. I have had the practical problem of getting up early enough in the morning to avoid the household and it is very difficult for me. One Sunday I was very upset about not being able to do this thing. It came to me that I have to get up at 5:30 in order to avoid the children. It seemed impossible. The next morning my little girl woke up at 5:30, which she never does, and went back to sleep again. I would like to know how I can find at least this wish, because the day before I felt I had never been so unhappy and so helpless.

LORD PENTLAND: I don't have the right to sympathize with you. I have to hold myself free from these sorts of subjective feelings. I close myself to the possibility of lifting you in that way from your subjective suffering. I search for something that could be an awakening influence. I absolutely refuse this relationship of trying to sympathize with your feeling. I value my own energy too much to go out to you in this situation. On the contrary, I turn inwards.

I find it is possible to regard these teachings of Gurdjieff as interesting. What is true is that I am prevented from coming into touch with them by lower levels, my egoism, my subjective feelings. These ideas are able to throw light on my life and my behavior.

I am mechanical. Everything acts according to law. My life consists of all these forces and influences which act through me. I don't know what would be good to eat before going to bed, what to read, when to get up, but I am intelligent enough to watch to find an art of how to have a happy life. I begin to find that by getting up early I am in a better way with myself, or by not reading some silly book before going to bed I wake up with more energy. There could be a sort of art of what could make me happiest.

Try to feel the ideas. What is mechanicalness? But you must not go out towards pity. Practice with your children. Practice demanding with them that they also don't pity themselves. Don't sympathize with their self-pity. Don't be all the time defending them when somebody else in the house makes certain things clear to you. You have to practice and practice because we have very little power of preventing ourselves going into this subjectivity. It is possible.

QUESTION: I wish to become concerned with how I am, to be interested. I don't have a genuine interest in myself. I begin to feel if I had something like this it could enable me to begin to work.

LORD PENTLAND: Be very suspicious of this sort of reasoning. Who am I to say what I don't have and what results would follow if I had them? Everything good comes from above. My possibility of having a knowledge of myself comes from above, but I can't say what I am going to know. I have to try to climb up. I do that by not resisting my life but by watching it. If in everything I do there is this reaction, "It ought to be done the other way," I try not to place much importance on it.

Why is there the reaction that I ought to be better? I try to use my reason, which speaks when I am quiet. That way I don't place so much importance on these reactions.

Undoubtedly there is something real in your question, but you ask it in this way, to demand that you should change. The real force comes from above and I am down here. This "above" is always different from what I expected, when I find it. It is never expected. Think of all the trouble people cause who want to make over the world according to their point of view. We are part of the world. We wish to be conscious that we are a part.

The basis of unnecessary suffering is the idea
there is an injustice . . .

QUESTION: I wonder can you say something about unnecessary suffering? Because of my personal situation, I have been seeing in my life how there have been cycles—things have been started, finished, started, unfinished. Relating to this I see that there is a question about attempting to change something. Since I remember in the past it was said we should observe, I see these observations and I feel that this is trying to do something, even though one doesn't try. A wish appears, almost a need, and something is done. I don't know if this is imagination. And the reason I see unnecessary suffering is that something is going on there and I don't understand it.

LORD PENTLAND: In a way it is something very basic and always the same thing—something right and something wrong about it—because at the very basis of this unnecessary suffering, when one thinks about it, is the idea there is an injustice, I have been done an injustice. It is always because there is an injustice that I feel justified in suffering.

Now ordinarily, when we try to explain that or write about it or read about it, we see this suffering as injustice. It is not justifiable because who am I to think all the world should revolve around me? Who am I to think I know the laws of the world? There is a higher justice. God is the Just, so why am I concerning myself and justifying my suffering as if I knew God's laws? And this is where the misunderstanding begins because, as a matter of fact, there is in me a trace of higher energy; there is in me a possible pathway to reality.

So, as I said, there is something right and something wrong. And if I am pointed away—God is out there, he is out there and I am here—my useless suffering is unjustified. I never come to the root. We never go beyond. And this difficult self-pity, unnecessary suffering, useless suffering, plays such a big part in our lives. We feel it is something we shouldn't do—it is just a sign we haven't thought it through, since we feel it is unjustifiable.

Where is God? If God exists for us—a ladder—it is in the inside of the inside of myself. This higher energy, the stepping stone toward reality, permeates the whole universe. There has to be an effort to see what is underneath, behind this useless suffering, not what is over against it. And first of all, I have to try to be free from anything I have read; that has been conditioned and it is wrong.

Then the point where you are at arises from the feeling "I can change," the feeling that supports the thought "I can change," "I can do." As long as the thought follows this general direction toward doing, toward changing, there is bound to be the feeling of unnecessary suffering because I am right in thinking I could know the law, and yet I don't, and things don't go according to the justice I expect in anything. There is a trace of possible connection with reality; it isn't wrong to think about myself as knowing something about the laws.

So you have to see what is underneath, trying to find what would be observing it and what would be the kind of thought which includes, not doing and changing, but observing. I don't know whether you can understand what I mean. It is just the stage where you need, as you put it, to listen to the real demand that is in you to observe, to be present. And you see what resists are the associations, the thought "I must change," "I must do."

The only way I am able to feel this demand to be present, not to be free, is when I become aware of two directions in me. Then I can remember that I am not my thought; there is another reality which can exist in me besides the reality of thought, of change and doing, and this other reality is where there is less unnecessary suffering, because through this other reality I can really know the laws and see better how things are ordered. I can even control my thoughts a little bit.

seven

The valuable part of oneself is the part that is alive . . .

QUESTION: How could I see myself all at once, my faults and everything? How could I formulate an idea about myself? I find it very difficult to accept myself as I see myself. I see a little of myself today, a little tomorrow. I see in fragments. I see myself, say, as a terrible person. I see my shortcomings. It will take so long to see all of myself, to observe all these bits. I would like to take all I see and put it into one thing and say, "You have to accept yourself now." It seems it would be so relaxing if I could accept myself instead of condemning, thinking what an awful person I am. I am so tired of that. There is very little in myself that is worth much.

LORD PENTLAND: The valuable part of oneself is the part that is alive. When you get a glimpse of this part it is very chaotic. It is still the most valuable because it is alive.

The less valuable is the dead part, the forms you give to these observations. When you see this chaotic thing, you are unable to understand that that is a form of your life—you. So you take some past form out of your head and attach that. The part of you that is in movement is valuable because it is alive. It has practically no order. At the very moment I see myself I see my form and I am not able to comprehend that. I say I have to accept that, but this is just the meaningless prose of an ignorant priest.

What possibility is there of accepting it unless I understand it better, unless I know that within that chaos there are possibilities of order, that because there is chaos there are possibilities for order. Because the whole of my life hasn't been anchored completely to some false idea of myself, I am still alive. There is some possibility of order. Life can only accept the living understanding of that. There is no way for life to accept that it has to fit into a label. That is why we need a living knowledge of ourselves.

So perhaps you need to return to the actual effort and to value more the little glimpse you get of yourself. You say you wish to put them all together. Are you sure you wish that? You wished to put together all these snapshots. Do you really wish to see yourself in these ways, two conflicting states together? Is that really what you want?

QUESTIONER: I thought so.

LORD PENTLAND: Then try the next time you hate somebody to bring to that the love. When you are bursting to go out, try to bring the side that doesn't want to get up in the morning. Try.

It would require a wish, also a certain knowledge, an understanding of how to do it, also a great deal of relaxation. Then these two things could be brought together. There are many things in between these two when we are tense. You see?

QUESTIONER: Yes.

LORD PENTLAND: All your life is one. You wish to bring it together. Just think what that would mean. Think what is buried in the subconscious. Think what comes out of people like ourselves who, unlike ourselves, are on a psychiatrist's couch and who, through being relaxed, can be in touch with parts which are usually unconscious. We need to be relaxed. How can we be in touch with the subconscious when we are pressing against ourselves? You follow?

QUESTIONER: Yes. I see what you say. But what does it mean to "know thyself"?

LORD PENTLAND: It begins with the idea that it is impossible for us until we have been brought a certain knowledge, the knowledge that there is a whole side of our nature which we are not conscious of, which isn't figuring in what we reckon we are. Without that knowledge, to know thyself is such a small thing. That whole side is isolated from the world by ourselves. This is the most important part. But we stand between it and the world. You understand?

QUESTIONER: Exactly.

LORD PENTLAND: In order to work we have to be able to turn inward. How to do that in life when we have to be turning outward at the same time? It involves the knowledge that there is something to turn towards inside. It involves something which we don't have, this firmness, this decision, to keep the inner part for ourselves in life.

The whole idea of obstacle is necessary
only at our level of thought . . .

QUESTION: For me the obstacle is that I don't see or don't want to see that I don't know. I fill this vacuum with a pseudo-answer. I try to arrange things, rather than to just see what is here.

LORD PENTLAND: It depends on how one speaks of it, but in naming that as the obstacle one closes the question. You see that there is no such thing as an obstacle. The whole idea of obstacle is necessary only at our level of thought. There is unity and diversity in the world. Everything has its place. The world is as it is, including me with my obstacles. Consciousness means the appearance of unity in all that, connecting the part with the whole. Our mind is not made so that in our ordinary state we can grasp that everything is part of a whole. Maybe at moments, when you are very quiet, you may see the connectedness of everything. You even feel your own reality as being part of that reality which is outside. In our ordinary moments we are not able to have this understanding.

I am trying not to be hypnotized into asking exactly what the obstacle is. I try to move so that, without going off into imagination, I am connected with the obstacle but not identified with it—I am aware of it. I realize there is something else. I look for something else. Isn't it more like that?

What is the real invitation to a higher level in myself?...

QUESTION: The changes which I see lately I find overwhelming. I feel I am going in many directions and have more burdens that I can handle. It is difficult for me to see anything in it except turbulence.

LORD PENTLAND: Of course there are really two difficulties there. One is I am overwhelmed so I don't even think to make any effort; the second is, if I think of making an effort, I make the wrong effort. I try to fight this what I call "lower state" in myself because I feel it is overwhelming. I try to drag it up. I try by calling it names, by shouting at it, to make it disappear. I see that that way nothing gets any better, but I don't really see that—and it has been going on for years.

Am I to blame? Do I shout at you? I see that it produces no effect if I do. I see that, as a saying goes, "You can lead a horse to the water, but you can't make it drink."

Anyhow we have to understand better, and can understand better, what is the real invitation to a higher level in myself. It is there all the time but my so-called "effort" of telling myself I am wrong, then being afraid that I am very wrong and will lose altogether, is something that obscures this invitation to be quiet and come at least to the threshold of my inner world. If I were able to not interfere so much, which I do by making this very tense pressing against myself, there is a part of me that could be heard inviting me. This quieter attitude would be worth something.

We need to question our effort. The first thing we need to do is to look at my day and see what it is I am calling an effort, to question what I am calling an effort. It may be that the effort is something which is interfering with a natural process toward order in myself.

To search means to search for freedom . . .

QUESTION: I feel that in everything I do my mechanical self tries too hard. I try too hard at the work, at home, in the office. I am not really successful in any of them. It seems to be taking away the place for something to come in. I wish I knew how to let go.

LORD PENTLAND: Well, not to beat about the bush, there are two things. One is to know how and the other, if I know how, is to try. The way to know how is by searching, that is to say, by trying to find a way in between the habit of the resistance, and the wish or the ideal.

To search means to search for freedom, in the sense of freedom from habits. If you have a habit of feeling too violently about relatively meaningless things, it's a question not of getting rid of it but of separating from it to be free from the habit—to see the habit, to have it pushing you to run for that bus, but you don't run. To be free means that I am free, but the habit goes on. You see what I mean? So we can say that freedom means freedom from habits, in a way, and as we know our habits we must try to be free of them, not to get rid of them.

A certainty not determined by belief but experienced in myself . . .

QUESTION: At this point I seem to have a negative attitude about the work and I am unable to really make an effort. I try to be quiet and collect myself and find myself daydreaming throughout. I guess what I am asking is what could help me be able to make those kinds of efforts which I know provide the energy for self-observations during the day?

LORD PENTLAND: I think perhaps you could look to see if there is negativeness, not towards the work—because you are not doing it—but towards yourself.

QUESTIONER: You mean watch the negativeness in myself?

LORD PENTLAND: I am trying to understand myself and I find that I am dreaming.

QUESTIONER: But how could I value that?

LORD PENTLAND: It depends on how I value the truth. I find that I am dreaming or find that I am a pig. You are dreaming about food or about your appetite. So you find the fact that you are dreaming or, if you want to materialize it in a kind of lively shape, I find that I am a pig. All right, I find out I am that, but something enters in very quickly that is negative towards what I have found. Just at the moment when I have found out the truth, I am negative towards the truth.

What would it mean if pigs could be conscious? This would be as good as men being conscious. So who said that piggishness was contrary to being conscious? Is it? That has to be found out. There is a long tradition in the search for truth that you have to find out. There is even no use believing in the tradition. Just find out.

QUESTIONER: I think sometimes I feel that but at the same time negativeness enters in.

LORD PENTLAND: Good. And then what you have to practice is a kind of patience, a kind of determination until the negative coloration is drained away.

In a way what we have to get rid of is a tendency to make our work very narrow by assuming that we can't find the truth except when we are in a very good state. And this is really what is in front of everybody—somehow to chip away at that difficulty so that little by little I can find the taste of truth in all of these different states. You see what I mean?

In ordinary religion we are told that knowing the absolute truth is impossible. All you have to do is to accept certain beliefs and so forth and this will more or less keep you on the right side of everything in life and you will go to heaven. In our work we are speaking about the absolute, the taste of an absolute truth, a certainty not determined by belief but experienced in myself. At the beginning we take that in a narrow sense and think we have only one observation every week or something. Now you wish to have more than that. It is a question of a sort of relativity, but still keeping to the taste of this absolute truth.

So I have to assume that it is possible to be aware in an absolute sense of my state, not just when I am in a good state but when I am dreaming, to be able to be aware of my identification when I am identified or my imagination when I am imagining. And you see the work isn't so impossible as it sounds. But there is an enemy which says no, this is not possible. The side of us which doesn't wish to work has got hold of the idea of truth and, from the associations in the mind, tells us that it is no use working at this, you will never get to the absolute truth this way.

How do I open to receive impressions? . . .

QUESTION: I have been noticing that impressions coming to me create a kind of contraction. They come and I feel the impression going into my movements, into my talking. I feel that this process is related to something very deep in me. But I feel the possibility that you spoke of as a real possibility and not just an idea.

LORD PENTLAND: Yes, I understand exactly. But in a way this corresponds to a stage when the impression has been consciously received. So let us first go back before we come to that. How do I open to receive impressions? You see it is absolutely necessary to have a sort of background confidence, to know that it is possible to make this journey into myself, to make this search in myself, to know it is possible to come in touch with another kind of energy. Unless I feel that is possible, however much I try, I won't receive.

But before we speak about what happens, before I do receive conscious impressions, how do I come as far as that? Something has to be opened even before I come in touch with this energy. There is a whole point of view which denies the idea that living is receiving impressions, and we need to become aware of these other contractions. We need to have a feeling of opening; we don't receive the help until this opening is started. But how are we going to open before receiving the help for an opening? Something has to begin.

QUESTIONER: How is this connected with the body? Recently my body seems held back in a closed kind of way. I have tried to find what that is connected with, a kind of negative feeling that seems to block that opening.

LORD PENTLAND: I have to become aware of the tensions. Nothing opens through voluntary effort, yet when I start out, my whole point of view about life is that everything takes place through my own voluntary effort. That is the general effort with which I can start out. I can do. What will take place with an effort of my will? Before anything can happen, I must understand a little that I can't do, that through the appearance of awareness from some other dimension in myself there can come to pass at its proper moment—if not now, then a moment later—a giving up of these contractions in spite of my fear of letting go of this conventional point of view that everything depends on my voluntary effort. Don't you agree? There is a fear of letting that go—I would be annihilated by all these forces around me.

One has to give up something of that point of view in order to become aware of all these unnecessary tensions. I am sitting there and all these tensions are not needed to support my skeleton against the forces of gravity. I am just sitting there and, as it were, armed to the teeth—and now, too. And you can't talk yourself out of it. You can say, "I don't want to be defensive, I want to be open," but a voluntary effort doesn't work. You know how many arguments take place over that. You say, "I am really being sincere, quite open with you." Well, so am I. I find that where there is that tension there can be no consciousness. But if somewhere there is an idea of the possibility, then somewhere the tension will break, and I will come in touch with the sensation of the awareness of my tension, which will make little holes in the armor plate, and I begin to be aware of my body and the flow of energy in it and of impressions. Now what happens when I become aware of the impressions? Why does it seem as if I can't get beyond the barrier? Can you follow if I speak or would it be better if you spoke? It is difficult if I speak all the time.

QUESTIONER: Is that one barrier the tension in my head? If I come to that place and my head takes over, I try to leave and come back down, and I have to keep coming back down to come up against my tensions, to question what is, and my head fights me there. Is this the movement down, is that where it is?

LORD PENTLAND: No, it is not so much just a movement down. It is difficult to speak about lucidly because it is fairly impossible to follow as one is speaking, but you will see what we need to reach is a sense of movement.

We get an impression and at the moment we recognize what we are doing. The head takes part and we connect that with some idea and through that a static situation arises. As we recognize the impression, we find a great idea there—the idea of listening or the idea of sensation, whatever—and we have become habituated to rise to great ideas like fish rise to food at the top of an aquarium. So, as soon as this movement down enables us to come in touch with an idea, to have one impression of the truth, well, it's not so much that we rise, but that we come to a static symbol of the search and it stops the movement that has been taking place, and the movement that has been taking place is the search. It is just that movement we need to have as an impression, not the idea.

We need to get the impression of the movement which has reached a point where something comes to the surface to be recognized by our head—our ordinary consciousness. There is a certain consciousness which is latent, potential, and through recognizing the possibility of this becoming active, a movement has started to take place and it brings a new dimension, a sensation, within reach of our ordinary consciousness. Isn't it like that? And then at a certain moment there is a recognition. It is good to recognize and it is good to have the experience of a great idea, but instead of recognizing the movement, which is what will take us to many other ideas as we continue the search, we say, "I have become conscious of this idea."

Now what we need to become conscious of with our ordinary consciousness is the movement, because if we can feel that there is a movement, then to some extent our hope, our prayer has been answered. We see that this possibility will be realized. You follow what I mean?

eight

*It's only to the extent that I'm not in my life
that I wish to be in it . . .*

QUESTION: Something has crept into my ordinary life. I feel a certain reluctance to even talk about it but sometimes it is as if a certain effort is required, that wasn't required before, in relation to things that have been going on in my whole life just automatically. I've done a lot of reacting to this. I feel very lost. Also I feel a kind of wonder at how things go on. It's being out of touch with whatever is behind what is happening.

I work with children. As a teacher I'm supposed to be concerned with motivation and I see the children moving about and I feel really out of touch with the impulses behind that movement. It's the same in my own life.

LORD PENTLAND: Yes, well the direction to move in is to have more of that, to find that I'm even less in touch with what's going on. It's only to the extent that I'm not in my life that I wish to be in it. We start out thinking that we can control our lives and we see that we don't even live them. That has to be seen with more of me. And there are very many things to see that include the way we've been brought up and even the way in which we receive the ideas here. We can't really believe that we're supposed to cope with all that. And there isn't time to ask.

We see that such energies are involved that we can't believe we can ask

109

about that—it would seem like impertinence. So we don't try or we try a little without conviction. And another part stays behind so that I have something to come back to. This part is waiting for someone to tell me what to do. It's waiting in the wings so that when the time comes it will go to work with the belief it knows what to do. But I have to see all that.

In order to see that, you must try, even with the equipment you have, to try to work at it. One could not do it except as a study. One is so totally unfitted, except when one has the idea that I will learn by trying to study the patterns and movements. Then there is this part that stays behind. But then one begins to see that I'll wait all my life behind. Because the fear gets bigger.

The knowledge that we have is that I can make this attempt to the best of my ability, at the moment when it's done with the idea that I will learn something, I will observe something. Next time I find myself in that situation where I know something is called for in myself but I feel hopelessly ill-equipped, then I see that by manifesting, no matter how awkwardly and absurdly, I will find what I am capable of.

We have to listen in such a way that we distinguish the real from the imaginary. In other words, this part that stays behind—we listen too much to that. We listen to this part that waits, that says, "Later I'll be responsible, not now." I think I'm one of God's little children, "God will see that I get a fair deal in the end." We listen to that and we don't listen to the part that's manifesting. We say this part is lying and it's not really me and later I will tell what I really am and everyone will applaud.

We have to learn to listen and see that that part is the only part that others take into account. Unless I do my very best, what can I expect from others? I'm not earning their love. I'm always complaining that only God loves me. I don't listen to the intonation, the bad temper, the callousness as if it were real. I listen to the other part as if it were real.

It's a question of bringing two lives together . . .

QUESTION: I've found that joy can be talked away. Over and over this summer things have come to pass and very large feelings of wakefulness have come with them. Not that the feelings are all gone, but I've watched—I've watched more and more talking of them to people I knew, and slowly the air of that wakefulness has diminished, but it's still within my reach. It's still extremely clear that I talk too much. And I'm not trying to be funny. It's been a marvelous summer but I see my own self perhaps working against me.

LORD PENTLAND: It's quite right what you say. You'll have to try in a little different way. You'll have to keep in touch with yourself and with the part that sees yourself, or rather to keep in touch with the part that talks too much and with the part that sees that. So in order to save time, I say I'll give up the idea that I'm ever going to talk less and accept that I am both the part that talks too much and the part that disapproves. You keep in touch with the part that thinks everything is wonderful and with the part that carries out these things. The whole of them, together, is me.

Now the question arises, "Who am I?" How could it just be there without any connection to the side or above or below, without having to give an account in some way, without having to produce in another way? We look at it more that way. You see that it's much more interesting to look at it that way because that one who speaks that much is not an abstract thing but a living person and there are all sorts of reasons why she speaks too much, just as the one who sees it is also a part of life. So it's a question of bringing two lives together, not "a" and "b" together.

So it's better to look not so much for the manifestation of the forces, but to try to be aware of the force itself. For instance, be more aware not what you're thinking of but what is this thinking? It's a form of life always moving. It can never be controlled from one instant to the next. Just as with a child, you always have to be there.

Your observation needs to reach a new stage
that is more direct . . .

QUESTION: When I look inside to try to search for what we were calling the Kingdom of God, it seems to me like absolutely nothing, except that there's something else I want. And I feel that if I wanted the Kingdom of God that much, I would already have it. But I can't picture it. I don't know what it is. I think that must be one reason why I don't want it.

LORD PENTLAND: Take it very simply. Something is lacking. Is it that I need a better picture of the Kingdom of Heaven or is it that I need to feel what is the Kingdom of Heaven? It doesn't matter what words we use. The Kingdom of Heaven is a spiritual experience; it's not a psychological experience, as it were. It doesn't matter, the words. It needs new words, of course, because the old words are familiar, but it's just the work we have now to turn the new words into something we can feel.

In other words, I'm not concerned about my spiritual life. My self-observation doesn't penetrate. I feel my work should permeate me. I should be properly penetrated by it. The level of my psychological experience is so shallow that it only increases my frustration, so all I have are one or two experiences. Do I just want another experience of that kind? Or do I see that even those experiences are largely lost in the pleasure in the situation that follows.

So I'm asking for something that would permeate me but in such a way that it wasn't once and for all. I've always wanted it once and for all. There's been a sentimental attitude about it, and as soon as it was over there was so much euphoria that I hardly realized it had taken place. I see that it's something that I need to have again and again, and it could be only again and again if my wish for it was more spiritual, less tinged with self-satisfaction.

So this brings me to what was said, the matter for understanding—it's something absolutely unsentimental—understanding of myself in my situation here and now. I think it's a work that all of us need to know. You probably realize that your observation needs to reach a new stage, something that is more direct, free, new. I see again and again "putting off," for instance. You feel it yourself. For a time one can say, "Well, Gurdjieff was marvelous." But it's not enough now. I need to understand that about "putting off," for example. Or I see that I'm caught in certain thoughts even about the work, a kind of endless circle, and I see these are circling thoughts again. But I need to see how that relates to the wish, the wish for consciousness, the wish for something spiritual.

The action of attention is what we are interested in . . .

QUESTION: It was mentioned that the only thing I have is my attention. Can you say a few words on how to increase attention?

LORD PENTLAND: I think it is indirectly at first; by not avoiding difficulties and not tending to have wishes other than we have. All sorts of conditions which are emotional are the best for seeing the truth, because our mind does not reflect values properly. The action of attention is what we are interested in.

So we can verify to some extent the result of our work with attention. For instance, I know that there are very definite limits to the amount of free attention I have, but there are certain things which are within my power. I discover that it is possible to have enough attention to sit still for one-half an hour. I find, therefore, if I wish to give my attention to sitting still, it is very possible that if I get up after twenty-five minutes I have not even been up to the limit of my attention. I notice that I always have enough attention to lift a heavy weight, do a certain practical job in a certain time, but if at a certain moment I refuse to lift this weight, I am not working to the limits of my attention. I know that it is possible but my attention prefers to lift somewhere else at that time. If it takes twenty minutes to do the dishes, I know if it takes thirty minutes it has been my privilege to spend ten minutes extra because the attention wanted to fiddle with some subject or other.

QUESTIONER: Is it to be understood like a muscle to be developed and that the more you develop it the better it becomes?

LORD PENTLAND: In that sense it is to be understood as a muscle, in the sense that an effort means going beyond the action that is inattention, a mustering of attention to make an effort. In that sense, the more I move almost to the limit of my free attention, I train myself.

Of course what we wish is for understanding. And in a way there is very little you understand yet about what attention is, but we shall understand it in doing these kinds of tasks. It is no use trying to learn about it except in the moments it is being applied. The attention that simply goes by momentum is not the attention we are speaking of. We have to train ourselves, like training our muscles, to eventually reach the conclusion that this is not the attention we are speaking of. When we really reach that conclusion, something new appears.

Life is movement, and as long as we think momentum is movement we are at a certain level of life. When we know this momentum of attention is not movement at all, is simply being carried along; when we, by these tasks, begin to discover that the only movement in our lives is one of dreams—except when a shock appears—and we move with this current, then we begin to look for another kind of movement of the attention which would be life in the sense that life is movement.

As long as we are satisfied with the movement that takes place in the head, as long as I am satisfied with that kind of movement, of course our understanding remains at a certain level. If your husband asks you what you did with your day, as long as you are satisfied with relating the experience just like that, you never really answer the question according to another level, but as soon as what you do today is an inquiry about another kind of movement, then just that day another level of understanding appears. Then there is a beginning, because the understanding of attention is a very big thing.

There are other aspects where we can begin, but for us the first aspect would be to try to understand what would be a real movement of the attention as opposed to the false movement where you follow, where you identify with the banks of the river rolling by.

The idea of resistance . . .

QUESTION: Would you speak about resistance? I seem to find resistance built in and I am powerless in the face of it. I have no control even in attempting to be quiet in order to follow or see where the resistance comes from. I see all the time that I am still caught in it. It is very difficult to work in the face of this.

LORD PENTLAND: Again we come to the point at the end of what you say. It is very difficult to work. Now, in a way this is my starting point. Work is a luxury. I do not mix it with the ordinary difficulties of life. If it is a luxury, if it is a work to be present to a life which is already full of difficulties, then I can expect this work to be especially difficult. I start from that.

What is the difficulty is almost always of my own making. Granted the difficulty of leading an ordinary life, when it is granted, I do not have very much wish for this luxury, for a soul or whatever you call it. The factory only just maintains itself. There is not much energy for work. So I have become accustomed to depend for the idea of work on what I call resistance. You follow what I mean?

Work for me begins where I am, in the problems of ordinary life. I divide this desire in resistance. I do not mean to say I see that exactly; I only experience something as work when there is something to work against. To me there is the verification that there is a work when there is a struggle. This is a misunderstanding, because my work is simply to be present in my life—for that there is no resistance.

The problem is to find something in myself, some energy, some presence that is not needed for the difficulties of life, which can be there at the moment. In a way everything is a resistance. In a way nothing is a resistance to that. In a way everything has to be related to that. If everything is felt as a resistance, I am not able to do that.

It all begins from this problem we have of needing an affirmation for a work effort. I have to try again and again. It used to be said, you remember, that the resistance is also me. I do not know if that helps. One has not much time to think about things like that. There is a sort of satisfaction I take in the experience of working against something, which makes that work very difficult and which creates the other difficulty—that sometimes it appears too much.

The more you think about it in terms of a force, the less you think about it in terms of positive and negative, the better. I see there is a struggle. I know that my possibility of coming to a question from that depends on whether the force can engage directly. The real awareness of living is so close to living that it is like the force appearing directly. It is very subtle.

When there is this sort of substantiation about this resistance and what can go against it, it is not so subtle. This makes for a work that is less useful. It also makes for a work that is very vulnerable to violence. When life comes to me violently because I am not living close enough, I am unable to make use of that. On the contrary, I react violently.

I need very much this naked confrontation with life. So you try. It cannot be done all at once, for we depend for the moment on this experience of resistance in order to feel I am back home again working. But you see we have to get beyond that because this dependency gets in our way. It gives us the feeling that, because of the resistance, we cannot work. We never come to the third force, but it is where I am. You understand better now?

We let go in order to be able to receive help . . .

QUESTION: What is meant by the term "letting go"? And what part of me is or could be helped by that?

LORD PENTLAND: We let go in order to be able to receive help. What does it mean to be able to let go? Have you tried?

QUESTIONER: When it's happened, it's happened. I was wondering how to be active towards that. I see when I try it has never happened.

LORD PENTLAND: It isn't an effort; it is just a realization, a longing. I need to be freer. It is pleasant. Where is the effort? Do you follow what I mean? There is a giving up of my self-importance, the idea that I can do everything alone. Try it. It's something to be practiced, not defined or excused or discussed.

The practice is to let go of each idea or thought as it comes into my mind, to look at it and, because I look at it, I can let it go. As a thought comes into my head, I see it. I see what it means to me and I let it go. When the thought of letting go came into your mind, could you let go of it? Unless you just look at it, you react to it. Everybody must understand that the head needs to be free. I need to practice the effort of letting the thoughts pass out as well as pass in. What use can it be to hang on to the thought? But it is my habit.

I don't know what a free relationship with thought would be. In order to have a relation with someone, one just sits and talks, not worrying about something coming into the thought or that there will be no feeling or the fear of no relationship. It involves a respect for myself that it will work all right without my interfering with it, if I let go.

The point is how to establish a relation
between "I" and my life . . .

QUESTION: I can't seem to come to terms with my life or my place in it. For a long time now I've had many pressures and demands on my time which have always seemed like more than I could cope with. Recently the demands have slackened off but now that I have more time, I can't cope with this either. I brood. Yet having more time is what I always thought I needed in order to find my place in life. So my whole situation has been brought into question.

LORD PENTLAND: You see, we never want to understand the significance of that little word "I." I am using "I" the whole time, but what does it mean, "I this" and "I that"? It is the point from which I relate to myself. But we never question who am I. It means what relation do I have to my life. We don't question that.

In other words, you, like each of us, want change. You want something different, something new. So the pressures were removed and now you see you have less pressure, but it is not the kind of change you want. You helped to mold your life. You wished it in a certain sense, even though there may have been contradictions there, and now you see you really fell from the frying pan into the fire. It is not what you wanted.

The point is not what sort of change you should work for. The point is how to establish a relation between "I" and my life. There is no relation. This change you speak of was not made consciously, was not made knowing the result. I don't know myself. I don't know my life. I don't even think in terms of "I" and my life. You understand what I mean? This is the first thing. But now you come and you have only just discovered that.

At every moment we could for an instant, if we really longed to, really wished to, find this I as something which is entirely separate from all my life, all my mechanicalness. We really have that amount of freedom even in the midst of our greatest pressures. For an instant we could know there is something unchangeable, something eternal, which can face all the blows I take in my life. But there is no relationship. We don't see it is there where something needs to be related.

I need to know myself, but that is only possible through a relation between I and myself, but I never question that. For example, you regard yourself as you, not as a role, but you could take a different role. You come in front of a different thing, a different person, and you immediately take a role—the role of a mother towards someone twice your age, half your age—but it never occurs to you to take the role of a daughter. But this means you don't question. I could question the role. Do you understand what I mean by role? The figure I represent. And, of course, in trying to take a different one, I find I can't. But I learn something about myself.

I like to be a teacher or I like to be a pupil. I could learn something about myself in trying to be a teacher when I am a pupil or vice versa. I would learn I have no power. There is no relation between "I" and myself.

Then it begins to be a question and this question is so interesting, so important, that the changes that take place and have to take place from time to time are practically intolerable—because it raises the whole question of an inner life.

*By giving up ordinary memory, I can
touch universal forces . . .*

QUESTION: I recently became aware that I really wasn't interested in my life or the way I lived. But something in me wished for interest, wished to be connected. I seemed to feel closer to emptiness inside. I was wondering how to look at this emptiness and at the wish for interest at the same time.

LORD PENTLAND: The best way is to try working alone. We are so mixed up it is difficult to have a clear verification whether one is approaching reality. Do you try working alone?

QUESTIONER: Yes. I think that's when I come closest to this emptiness. But it seems to pervade everything.

LORD PENTLAND: Even working alone, we can't expect to find every-thing in a certain order or place. And, if things are mixed, that which we can recognize we can't explain in spoken terms. Words and concepts do not help. What is found inside is not the way of things when I look out-side.

I think one must begin by understanding the idea that there is an adver-sary or anti-force in the effort to live my life. The form it takes feels like a burden. I struggle all the time to live with the burden. Burden is depen-dence on all things, particularly on the idea of responsibility—for exam-ple, that I ought to be able to work better, manage better with relation-ships, carry out things. I have entered into outer life with the idea that to live it I must straighten out all things before starting to work. The fact that it is necessary to deal with the burden creates a sense of guilt.

When we sit down to work we don't begin in a good position. There's often a sense of guilt. A kind of complex of this dependence, and the guilt centers around the fact that I didn't remember this or that, or even that I didn't work yesterday; if I had remembered, I wouldn't be in a mess in this or that relationship. When one starts work, one must give up dependence on that kind of memory.

You know, if you are quiet and not attending to memory which guilt brings to mind—"I must do this or that"—then you come to another memory nearer to yourself. You know there can be real magic which transforms you and you feel such a joy at this freedom from the depen-dent. You are in touch with a level of your own life which is more impor-tant than the other levels of your life. You know it and it gives you what you longed for, gives you a freedom from doubt, a sense of certainty. But just as on the way there when one touches emptiness, which may seem ter-rible to one, one becomes stuck again with something subjective, this magic moment of freedom does not last long. It is as if it is a part of another time.

It is important to try to relate that last vestige of dependence, which is my ego, with the moment of joy. You can find it before you reach the free-dom and immediately afterwards. It represents the reality of my ego. I cannot count on total release; this is only in an exceptional case. I can count on reaching emptiness. There is still a vestige of my ego. You have to try to understand and know that.

Don't forget it begins with a new point of view towards memory. By giving up ordinary memory, I can touch universal forces and respond to necessary aspects of situations. I do not need "knots" of memory. The question of void and the question of memory could be two places you try to enlarge your self-knowledge.

Part Two

1961–1977

nine

*A lot of fears come because we try to make
a morality out of thought . . .*

QUESTION: I have been interested lately in how fear affects me. Tonight as I was standing at the door I could see how the little fears would move me this way and that. Someone came in and I was looking at a fear, just looking at it. The fear stopped me, then I found I moved. Once movement began, the fear stopped. Once I was there, another little fear froze me there. That just goes on.

LORD PENTLAND: Very true. A great deal of the work is in observing our fears and always in situations in which we don't understand there is fear. You can be sure if you come up against a resistance, there is a fear there. So it is very useful, what you started, and you will see that in a way the fear is connected with our attempts to work through thought alone, that all the fear exists through trying to have with our thought a work that can't be done with our thought.

So it is really better to accept that I can't work through some thought-imposed pattern—and in that way to risk not being connected with work at all—than to say, "In order to have a connection with work, I will have to stick to this thought about something," because that almost always leads to fear. "I ought to" leads to fear.

We put a wrong value on thoughts about the work. They are not as valuable as we think they are. That perhaps is too big a generalization. I should say, in order to have thoughts that are closer to work, we have to find their real value. If we keep a big false value on thoughts about work, we will not often have thoughts close to work; we will have feelings. Morality is not a question of thought. A lot of fears come because we try to make a morality out of thought.

QUESTION: What then should we replace the sense "I ought" with?

LORD PENTLAND: What ought we to replace "I ought" with?

QUESTIONER: Maybe that is why I am so fearful.

LORD PENTLAND: One has to observe that this is really me. Even my questions are flavored with this. It is in the moment one recognizes that, that one is whole. So maybe it is not that one recognizes something and frees oneself.

A question is intended to be a relationship between one thing and something other, a paradox, a metaphor. A question is the original relationship between two parts of myself which are there at the same time, because they are not exactly contradictory but are quite separate in their significance. When they come close together there is a question. But when we make a question out of one part, it has no meaning.

How then ought I get rid of "ought"? There is no question of that. One needs to see that, to see how the symbolism has lost its real life, how the pattern in my head has taken over. All that is going on. I believe in all that, even bring it to a serious discussion.

One needs to observe this with a kind of gladness—this is the clue I need, the breaking of the cipher. This is what makes me such a mess. When one receives that without protest because there is such a truth in that, this little thing . . . Can you follow me at all?

QUESTIONER: Yes, if I were to follow that to some sort of conclusion, it seems to me then I wouldn't want to do anything.

LORD PENTLAND: One gets that impression. On the contrary, it raises the whole temperature in me. I see it is quite simple, it is just this little misunderstanding. You have a misunderstanding.

Because I have seen, all the problems of time and distance disappear. In seeing my failure, I supply everything that is missing, everything. That is why it is so important to understand seeing, because every one of us has suffered through a non-supply of many things when we were young. Our whole life has been twisted because certain things essential to a young child haven't been supplied. In the moment that we are able to see it is not supplied, it is all supplied.

Gurdjieff says you can repair the past by this new attempt of being present. Instead of describing and airing one's memories, one should learn to be present. In the present one can supply everything that is missing. One supplies understanding of the present moment and that gives you what is missing.

I am talking about impressions one can have of oneself in one's sleep, asking questions intended to be important that can have no significance. In seeing that, one doesn't feel hopeless at all. If it is seen in a subtle passing way, it relaxes completely the distress of feeling my work is going so slowly. That disappears entirely in that moment.

Being present means I am aware of distractions . . .

LORD PENTLAND: Can you say what helps you about coming here and what hinders you and what you work towards?

QUESTION: It leads me to understand something about work. When I find myself wandering, I am reminded about being here. Being here is an opportunity; from being here I can struggle to be more present more of the time. I find it is an opportunity and gives me a chance to struggle and . . . .

LORD PENTLAND: And that means what? More present in the sense that a soldier is present? What do we mean—be present to the situation here and now? In this situation we see that something wants to work and something doesn't want to work. What does it mean? All the time we see that the very thing we want, that a certain part wants, gets in the way and seems to be our own worst enemy. So what we mean by being present here is that I am aware of the distractions. I am aware of the situation of myself not being here and of the situation of being half here—that would be more present.

If I am here like a soldier, prepared for when the sergeant says "Attention" to hold himself tense, I don't feel the earth, or my feet on the ground. In that sense, you are right. When I am here, I am here to, as it were, bring together all the sides of my life and maybe that is more possible if I am faced with what I don't expect. You see what I mean?

That very part that doesn't want to give attention has to give way. If I am interested enough in the thing that I am doing, hammering nails, or whatever, then there are no distractions. Do you follow? I am aware that distractions disappear through interest in being totally engaged in that attention.

QUESTIONER: The question is how to get to that interest.

LORD PENTLAND: Yes. Well, I don't know what you think, but half is done for you and half you have to do yourself. The conditions here can help you to have that interest, but you can't depend entirely on the conditions. You have to have rather like a conviction, partially you have to remember your own question and be aware of the whole conditions. It's half and half. Do you see what I mean?

QUESTIONER: Yes. It seems very difficult.

LORD PENTLAND: Because we are speaking about the forces of attraction and repulsion. In order to be aware of everything that is going on in the present, we need to be aware of all the pulls and pushes and shocks; it has the effect of moving me to the center where I can be aware of the whole thing. If I keep half of my attention for the whole thing and the other listens and remembers, then there is the best chance that I will be reminded what these conditions are. Any other way, I want to push or relax, and I go to sleep.

It is a help to be aware of the whole thing, including the distractions. If at my job I see a distraction enter, I see only the one part and I begin wanting to do more. Perhaps you haven't been in that situation yet.

QUESTION: It seems as if I come here in order to be surprised. Now I have a lot of ideas about what this meeting would be and I've been thinking about it and making plans to come. Even being here is a kind of surprise and I couldn't suspect what is going to happen just here now. It seems a hindrance for me that this surprise is a kind of shock. There is a shock connected with it and I have ways of reacting to that that close me off to what is going on, ways of thinking and associations. So I am surprised and, right on the heels of that, reaction closes me off to what is happening.

LORD PENTLAND: So how to use the time? How to use one meeting, for me is a question. Suddenly we are together now. I don't think of my life in the old way while we are together. I see my life quite differently in the whole situation. On Monday, if not tomorrow, it will be different; there will be all sorts of old problems. For the moment, in this discussion, I react to the shock and know more about how to live, about how to deal with this or that problem of life. But on Monday, if not tomorrow, will I regret not having settled this problem now?

Now if I am in a more clear state, would it be possible to attend to a problem that is coming up? And maybe I could live this way, in search of a way of trying rather than dealing with things the way I dealt with them most of the time. How to use a meeting—for each of us? Some kind of experience is possible that maybe we could use to seek what would be the best way to deal with these things, and so forth.

Also there are some people around who spent a great deal of time with Gurdjieff. Maybe we could ask how he would have dealt with it, or what he passed on, or, in my case, how he dealt with life problems. When I knew him, he was speaking all the time about little things, little things like, "Don't drink when your mouth is full of food." or "You don't pray in the water closet." Things like that.

So we could use meetings for that but we are not going to and you know why. We believe we have established that almost all of the problems which will come up on Monday arise out of our fear of life. For ourselves, we are relieved for a moment of this fear of life. Do you follow what I mean? All the problems come from that. They are created by our fear of being simple and sincere, and that goes back to our school days. But to get free from that is not so easy. But at least in this instant, we could try to be open, not to be afraid to practice in this moment, here, what is not yet possible in our homes, to be sincere without fear, to be sincere because it is through sincerity we can reach real self-knowledge; because it is through seeing the truth of our sleep that we can find out what is really best for us.

So you see we can make use of the meeting in observing. In a way none of us is very skillful in talking with words, which are very general, but it works because we are all together in that attempt. Try to listen with no idea of remembering what is said, but attempt to relate together what was said and not just in meetings but outside, in work activities.

Work for an acceptance of the body as an important part of my psyche . . .

QUESTION: The study that was suggested last Saturday helped me to be in touch with my body an unusual amount of the time. By the end of the day, I could see that my thoughts get in the way of being more with myself, and there was a definite decrease in thoughts about people—what I thought they should do instead of what they were doing. Just what had to be was there. I learned something about that on Saturday by being there in a different way.

LORD PENTLAND: Suppose one could have a relationship with the sensation, involving a kind of acceptance of my body. We are alienated from our bodies. I don't accept that this is my body. It is rather easy to accept that this is my body when there is a real inner experience and I feel this is just the outer covering. But these moments are rare when I am impartial to my body, can look at it in the mirror and feel this is just the outer covering. Normally I don't quite accept what I see in the mirror as me, so I will never have a relationship with my body, will never be aware of the sensation as long as what I see in the mirror is rejected. So it is a very good thing when you feel frustrated or angry or something, instead of trying to quiet it, to go look at it in the mirror and see that it is not me that is doing all this.

QUESTIONER: One of the things I am now trying to do . . .

LORD PENTLAND: As long as you don't get lost in the doing. So one has to take one's measure in relation to that. It is no use having an idea that more has to be done in this direction. One has to know one's measure. One has to work at it within the measure that is available to me. It is no use picking exercises and giving myself tasks that are too difficult. I have got to do what is just a little too difficult for me.

A lady came to see me in New York, an artist. She had had some kind of experience in Central Park and she had been everywhere trying to understand it. She finally went to a priest. He said, "If you come to my retreat, I will help you to understand it." She was completely a non-church person and said so to him. He said, "You have to learn humility." She said to me, "You see the crazy things they tell you. I was saying I had seen growing things, the spectrum of colors and the man says 'humility.' My friends say that you understand something."

So I said to her, "Start with sensation. You must try till you see me again to keep your face relaxed." So after a month she came back and not perhaps without some help from the beauty parlor, but her face was very relaxed. She said this had been the most extraordinary reminder to her. She talked about that for awhile, and she stayed and went on talking, and I realized I was supposed to give her something else to try. I didn't feel inclined to, because just that work on relaxation of one's face is a marvelous reminder and four weeks isn't long enough. But eventually I said to her, "Well, if you have done that exercise, I can only think of one other one. Make an absolute rule not to shout." She gave me a sort of pitying look and she said, "I was brought up in such and such a way and I never shout." Well, it was too late to go back by then so I said, "Anyway, that is the exercise for you."

She was from a Fifth Avenue family. A few days later I was seeing the friend who had sent her to me and I said, "You know, I understand your friend up to a point, but I am not sure whether she is happy with me." My friend said, "Oh, she is very happy with you. She left the office where you saw her, went out in the street and the first thing she did was yell for a taxi, and she heard it."

This is the work on sensation, if you follow me. It is not sitting still, saying, "I must have contact with sensation." It is a work all the time to have a relationship, that is to say an acceptance of the body as an important part of my psyche and to be aware of the way I make it pay for my idealism. I am all the time taking it out on the body to make it pay for these ideals I run after. So it is a work to make a place for the body, but a work that can't be done fifteen minutes once a day, can it?

Because of your work you are able to see
these forces in conflict . . .

QUESTION: I see that everything runs down. I start something, it goes on for a time, then it begins to run down. I am beginning to catch the flavor of the searching about for rationalizations and excuses that comes when the running down begins, always this repetition. Then I see the need to clean house and have the feeling that I want to make it right. The part that wants to make it right usually either is acting out of the wish to avoid a reprimand or perhaps to get some credit. I would like to be more intelligent about this.

LORD PENTLAND: At least because of your work you are able to see these forces in conflict. This is what we need, this friction between the forces, the different energies. This is what gives the possibility of renewal. You have seen the entropy. But there is now also the possibility of a continuous creation because of being three-centered, all three centers being there, so that I can see the friction and the result of that sensed as a kind of wonder. Do you understand?

QUESTIONER: Is it like not ever letting your house get dirty, of cleaning it before that happens? My house always gets dirty; then I clean it.

LORD PENTLAND: No, it is not like that. I mean that it is possible now to distinguish between different levels of energy—the sensation of moving, emotion, thinking, even higher feeling. What seems to be conflict is actually the appearance of different levels in me. All this is possible because of the work on sensation, to be able to sense, "This is a thought." There is an electromagnetism that appears as a result of this work on sensing the body. This work also brings the possibility of being completely open, exposed to a situation in which forces are being manifested, to simply be in relation to them without resistance or covering.

Seeing the friction between two forces leads to a result, the creation of new energy. As soon as this new energy appears, I see the ways, including thoughts and dreams, in which it begins to be wasted, to be drained off. But perhaps you could just begin with seeing two.

One is never free enough to just try to be aware . . .

QUESTION: I felt very strongly before and after the movements film on Tuesday. Going from my work to see the film and leaving the theater afterwards, there were so many, many contrasts that I ended up by feeling exhausted and I wondered about that. Why? I felt something of what you said, that I missed something, that it was an opportunity.

LORD PENTLAND: One is never free enough to just try to be aware. One is never free enough and the impression of energy going to waste causes a reaction of stinginess in me. One is never free enough to just look at it. There are all these characters or characteristics in me, some of them recently acquired, imitative of people here, some educated, some inherited, some from my childhood. One is faced with the problem of how to be free enough of the moral problem of this or that quality to just look at it. Do you understand?

Now what does it mean to be aware? It means to come in touch with the whole. To see means the existence of some relative degree of wholeness in me. What I see is just a part. So what would it mean as you walked away from the film, or toward the film, and felt this waterfall of energy flowing out—instead of trying to control it, dam it up—what would it mean to see, from your experience of all that, as the result of that, that you were only a part at that moment?

It is very serious. You are walking along to the film or walking away from the film. You are aware of a torrent of energy. You are also aware of your uneasiness about that. And the question begins to form, What to do? How to be? What would it mean at that moment to accept that I am in just a part of myself—nothing else is wrong, everything is right, but I am in only one part of myself. I am lost in this part and therefore I am not aware of the other parts. What would it mean to suddenly recognize that I am in a part, instead of starting to hunt for something to do, or hunt for somebody to ask or whatever?

Of course there is always a catch. I will accept it if it is a means towards coming in touch with wholeness. If it is a way of coming to myself, I will accept it. And it is a way to come to myself. But as long as I think of the result, that it would be wholeness, I am not really accepting it. It is a question of accepting my human condition at that moment—of giving up the whole idea of evolution, of being saved—of really accepting my human condition at that point. And immediately I can do that, the perspective widens. I become aware of my body walking along, on top of the world, on top of the street.

ten

*A struggle begins between a whole other world
and this automatic thing . . .*

QUESTION: You gave me an exercise to do while trying to be present to my wish. For a long time I did it but it came always to the problem I asked you about months ago. And you told me to stop doing it as I was.

LORD PENTLAND: Try to speak in general. Ask your question. Not everyone has the same work. How can you be present to your wish? You say, "I wish." How can you be wishing when you say, "I wish"? All the time in our daily lives we have something going on outside, which we are engaged in to some extent, and inside ourselves something quite different is being thought and felt—so different that it is sometimes continents away from what we are supposed to be doing. So what is the question?

QUESTIONER: I tried different ways to do the exercise.

LORD PENTLAND: What is your question? You don't need to tell anything of that. You don't need to speak about the exercise. What is your question?

QUESTIONER: At a point in the exercise I felt a confusion, not knowing the thing that was expressed at those moments, also not knowing where I was.

LORD PENTLAND: What is your question?

QUESTIONER: What is that confusion that I felt, a feeling of not knowing where I am. It is not really this feeling but rather something I need to understand to go further with the exercise.

LORD PENTLAND: Too lazy. You put your question finally but it could have been said at the beginning without all this about the wish. It makes something ordinary, stupid, which really has a great deal of meaning.

So you see that we have what we might call an automatic life and when we come more near to ourselves the meaning of that automatic life becomes clear. Even though there is everything in that automatic life— effort, work, play, difficulty, struggle—it is all going on automatically, so none of the words have any meaning, any more than the word "wish" when said automatically has any meaning.

When I become quiet I see that this whole business of my life is all automatic. Then a question arises: What do I wish, what is my intention? And for that I won't be really satisfied with anything less than the appearance, even in a very subtle way, of another dimension, something that doesn't belong to that automaticity, something that hasn't been smeared with that kind of automaticness where nothing really means what it says. Now we feel that sometimes another dimension appears suddenly and then a kind of struggle begins, which may not last long because our contact with that other dimension isn't very strong. It is passive. But a kind of struggle begins, not between one thing and another but between a whole other world and this automatic thing. And we feel right about that as long as it lasts, although we are awkward. We feel the need to study how to work with that struggle.

You will probably agree that what you experienced was a kind of sham struggle when you said "this is the intention," when it wasn't really another dimension. And one sets up a kind of mockery of the real work for oneself because one can't find this real struggle. Now how can we be when we can't find the real struggle? That is your question.

This kind of upsetting confusion comes when I sort of put my best into a kind of insincerity. One hardly knows it is not my best, but something knows. One hardly listens to that ever. So what would it mean to listen and at least know I am out of contact with my wish? If one pretends to be in contact, you are doing an imitative work. It is better to say, "I am not in contact." That would be the step for you. "My wish is zero." So I would say, not that I have no wish, but my wish is like zero. It must be there in a way but I can't find it, the energy for it has been spent. Somehow I am still connected with it through the possibility that it will appear again. That way I keep a kind of respect for this possibility, a self-respect, and I think that is perhaps what was a little missing from this moment you speak of. Yes?

What it means to search for the experience of a question . . .

QUESTION: I have a question about where inside me a question can come from. I see the importance of having a question and yet to formulate it takes so much. A blank comes just before I can ask a question. It seems as though I have been observing a conflict. I search for a formulation, then get hung up in something else—a panic that stifles the question, leaves it to the next time, and I hope I will be able to speak of it the very next time. Recently something more has come about, a sort of urgency that I find out what in me can actually ask the question that is with me at the moment.

LORD PENTLAND: Yes, in a way that is our first real question. It is very good you came to it. Our first real question is "What is a question?" because more or less we pick up by a sort of osmosis the idea that we are here to search, but it takes longer before one understands that what we are searching for is a certain period, which we first experience as a question. It is what we are searching for. "Searching for" implies a certain movement. I have to move innerly. I am hardly able to grasp the idea of moving without the image of a result, but I am searching for an awareness of myself in search, and that is what I am in simplest form.

I am a question in the sense that I am two not easily reconcilable sides— without the reconciliation. That is the question. There are two sides to every question. A reconciliation is no longer a question. I am this other dimension, which is limitless—when I touch there—and I am automatic. I am this person, each of whose inner and outer manifestations has a taste of automaticity, of evading the real question, of acting up to my sense of self-respect. So I am this larger dimension and I am this flow of events that absorbs me.

How to be in touch with the larger dimension just enough and with my automatic life just enough so something of the expanse of this larger world comes into my life in a form of sort of inner space, without my falling into dreams? If I were to be in touch enough so something of the expanse of that is felt in my ordinary life, then it would be another stage. It would be a study going on of that process going too far in one direction, going too far in the other direction, getting identified.

But the first thing is, what is a question? The question itself is this situation where I am in touch with one force and the other but no reconciling element. So you have to understand what it means to search, not for an answer but for the experience of a question. And what you call your formulated question will come out of that. It will formulate itself from the experience.

For instance, you see in your relations with one particular person, one particular person not too close to you. You have to see it again and again, so you make sort of an exercise out of it. Try to understand how to have better relations with this person. Try to understand what it would mean to feel him as a human person, that there would be a sense of meaning in what you say, not an automatic relationship, and you see in trying that you can't, that you simply can't. You try again and again and you see that it really does not appear. You make plans, but maybe begin by forgetting altogether what you intend. Even when you plan carefully you cannot be successful in having this something by which you feel the other person as a person. Only when you come to a complete block there, does the question appear, "What is a man, what is a woman?" Only when you feel totally blocked, then a hundred answers appear. That is an example of how a question springs without formulation when you come to a questioning place in yourself. So don't worry too much about the formulating. Take a person, start to work like that.

To come to the wish can only be through a kind of stop . . .

QUESTION: In order to try something like that, it seems to me you would have to have an intention and a real wish to try it. I keep finding in myself that I don't, and I don't know how to come in touch with something real in me.

LORD PENTLAND: That is true, quite true. We do come in touch with something more real and then what do we do with the experience? It does happen that we come in touch with something more real, then what do we do with the energy of the experience? You say you don't know how to come to it, but it is sort of given to us sometimes and we don't really make very much effort to understand at those times. So probably one has to be much clearer that I need to come in touch with that. I need above all to be in touch with that, but when in a tight corner I secure myself before thinking about coming in touch.

It is fear, and fear is one of the big motives for my agreement to this automatic behavior. It is a fear even of not moving. I am lost but keep going. I don't stop because my fear says if I were to stop I would see how lost I am, more lost even than I know. So when one really wishes to come to the wish, it can only be through a kind of stop, through a moment in which this impulse of fear comes to an end and, just for an instant before it comes again, there is my wish, very faint, an echo probably, but it is there all right as soon as the impulse has been allowed to die down.

Inside there is this wish and I hear it only if I am willing to some extent to struggle with my automatic behavior. I may make the stop and do all the technical things that are right but I won't hear the wish unless I put part of my attention to jumping across to that inner level, the only sense of which is that I will then be divided. There will be a struggle.

One of the great merits of my automatic behavior is this feeling that I am one. It prevents me from coming in touch with the wish because when I come in touch with the wish I begin to be divided. So in order to hear this echo, my wish, even if I am trying to listen, there will need to be prepared a kind of attitude that wishes for this sense of something more deeply right in me, when there is a struggle, when with a part of me I am trying even unsuccessfully to see myself.

*Not a tug of war, a search between
the two parts of you . . .*

QUESTION: I was sitting here trying to listen to you and to every word that comes out I have an answer or a question. Now how is it possible just to sit here and listen without this, and is there any chance of that?

LORD PENTLAND: That is what I say, there has to be a willingness to struggle. It is a struggle largely, but there is a kind of posture back in myself where I can bear to listen in spite of distracting voices in me. I can bear to give up my interest in these voices again and again in order to listen. There is an attraction to listen, but I am not far enough back in myself. I am too eager to be in front and with that I pick up all the static, the distracting voices rather than what I intend to do, to listen to something.

It requires a very sensitive work. It is like if you have a few rowdy guests—how to get rid of them? If you ask them to leave, they will not go. How can you gradually sort it out so you are with your friends, the people you want to be with? Not a tug of war, a search between the two parts of you: your wish and the functions as they really are.

So what it comes down to—it is like the previous question—is that there are many factors there which are outside my control. There are big forces at work which are passing even through me, even through a small organism like me. There are enormous forces working, so I can't expect success but a study. A study involves the appearance of a struggle. Struggle depends on whether I am willing to struggle. If I prefer, in spite of knowing a little tiny bit better—because we do have a sort of conscience—if I still go on with this automatic stream of thought, then of course the struggle won't appear. When it appears, then listening becomes more an inner process and not much help comes from what is outside, from reading or hearing somebody speak outside, or from trying to translate these words into the actual fabric of struggle, because the struggle is going on all the time like a kind of dance. Words are slower. One has to do one's best, kind of intuitively.

I would say, generally speaking, the questions we formulate are ahead of our actual experience. We need to share 'round about' the point where we actually are in our work. But the tendency is to ask about something not useful because it's too far from where I actually am. It would be more useful to discuss 'round about' where I am actually and flesh that out with serious ideas and feelings, because the next step isn't an answer—that would be too logical. The next step is that this question is experienced by more and more of me, that the question becomes a sort of more total experience.

Try and think about that. You suddenly at the meeting experience something and feel you are an instrument for a question. It comes through you rather than your inventing it. It is still not your question. It is surrounded with irrelevancies. You feel a question while you are on the bus; you also feel everything that is going on in the bus. How could more of you be in this question? That is the next step.

I am in my life for the understanding . . .

QUESTION: I would like to ask something that relates to everything you have been saying. I received something real during the intensive work week here, particularly at the end, and I was able to see a little bit that when I just automatically expressed everything about it to myself, the whole flavor of it changed.

I find it so difficult to take something for myself. I don't mean just here but also at home in the midst of my life. At first there seemed to be such incredible help to keep something real, but the automatic flow of my life is so connected to other people, how they are and how I should be for them, that after what I have heard here now in this meeting, what seemed to be a simple thing, to take something for yourself, is not the same as I thought it was.

I find the same problem in trying to begin creative work at home. It is very hard to disregard what other people expect and go into the center of what I am making, regardless of all the outer talk around it. It is the experience of when that doesn't stop me and I am really beginning something freshly which helped bring me here to begin with and connects me with the question I hope I am asking here.

LORD PENTLAND: We are very much limited by our fears. We need to see that this whole thing is a misunderstanding, that we in reality have no relationships with other people that are very much, even in the very best cases, and that our illusion about our relationships is a necessary one. If we could really see the poverty of our relationships, we probably couldn't bear it. But one needs to have seen something of that, it seems to me. Only then would one start to study oneself. Only when one really has passed that limit would one give up in a certain sense. One needs to go quite far. We are afraid to go far enough to admit to ourselves the truth of what many people have said: that life is meaningless, that there is no hope. We are afraid to go that far, as far as we have a right to go even on the basis of our limited experience.

All automatic, this book you wrote, this dinner you cooked. One is so attached to it. One says, "Oh, it was very poor," but doesn't feel how poor. It is poor in the sense that it is automatic. We don't follow something that connects with something much larger in me. It is very poor in comparison with that. What Gurdjieff teaches at that point is that by law at the moment of giving up I have to be connected with that larger dimension, but only for a moment, and in order to maintain that relationship with the larger dimension I have to go back to the same automatic life, taking an interest in it this time not as a hypnosis, as attraction to the pleasure, but as a work of understanding.

I am in my life for the understanding. The life may stay the same; my behavior may not change so much. What was wrong was the motive? It was with no motive or an egotistical motive. Through that I thought I had good relations with people. Then for a moment the scales have to fall from my eyes; then I see I have no intentional relations. Everything depends on illusion, on states created by my structure of experience. When that falls down I return to the very same life. Don't you think so?

It involves a work of intention or an intentional contact with my attention—I don't know what my attention is, how it moves according to law, an intentional contact with that, so that something of the larger experience carries over into my outer life, into my home, into my career. And that can't be done by being dreamy; I have to be almost as alert as when I am in my life and my career for egotistical reasons. I have to be right in there speaking, arguing, looking, all right there, but I feel something of the expanse of my wish. Then I go to sleep and I get attached. Well, it works for short periods like that.

Is that what you are trying? You should choose a particular person. You will see how you cannot feel enough the lack of relationship. One's vanity is so great. One is all smiles at practically every passing cat and dog, but you feel practically nothing with this person, nothing real.

A question about my conceptions of ordinary life . . .

QUESTION: How is it possible to take life seriously if we see everyone is asleep?

LORD PENTLAND: Because the whole of my inner purpose is balanced there and I may lose it if I am not serious, and if for a moment I give up taking the simplest outermost detail seriously the whole thing flies away. It is not that life is interesting in itself. The life that we call life is not interesting in itself. It is completely unreal. We can't see it in a way that is real.

QUESTIONER: How to keep the attention?

LORD PENTLAND: We keep attention because we have an inner reality that keeps appearing and for that we have to have a kind of attention that sees ahead, so we take everything as real. But that also depends on whether we are looking to get a shock. It is humbling, this work, a long work.

QUESTIONER: I notice that the intensity I may be able to feel things with changes. At first it was very intense but it has gone downhill almost consistently now. It is very hard to find that, even if an exercise goes well. But at the same time other things become more intense. For instance, I will be able to see that someone I am talking to is not aware of other people in a room or is just chattering. I guess I am worried that I don't feel this physical intensity when I try to work. Is this a normal thing?

LORD PENTLAND: It is hard to say. It sounds somewhat Freudian but probably your question may reflect a tendency of yourself to take this world as only too real. You know, one has someone smart inside one who takes a contrary view, rather is contemptuous of those who take the world as real, but that may mean you share in that difficulty.

QUESTIONER: I realize that.

LORD PENTLAND: If I take this world in front of me as being real, there is no room for it to be sort of brought alive by another dimension which I breathe into it. So what happens is that I come to some meetings and the whole of the work becomes constructed in a place called heaven and doesn't touch my life. In order for the work to exist in my life, I really have to have a question about my conceptions of ordinary life, how much I need the money, food, sex, which are the wellsprings of my ordinary life, and keep me content in this cage. I may have the question in my head. That is life in heaven. The question doesn't enter in when my appetite for this or that is actually working, so you could say that we are completely caught in that. It is an illusion that with our ordinary will we could make a dent in that.

You could say we have to wait until something stops. At that moment we can begin to struggle. And it is a struggle; even with our ordinary, small will, there are things we can give up. I can give up this or that appetite before the form takes shape. When there is no struggle, there is nothing I can do. And to make plans and resolutions that I will be different tomorrow—there is absolutely no result.

When I am in touch with my wish, then this ordinary side that makes plans really is needed. Until then it is ineffective. But we are just the other way around. We think it is effective when there is no struggle, but when there is a struggle we see man cannot do. But the struggle has to be maintained by agreeing to little acts of renunciation. It isn't really a renunciation but that I am so interested to keep in this place in myself that, if I am quick enough, the temptation doesn't take form.

The beginning of a real work in life is the ability
to stay with my confusion . . .

QUESTION: What is the relationship between this renunciation and this feeling I have that when I am touching something real in myself it is a passive experience?

LORD PENTLAND: That is right. The renunciation at the very most is quite temporary. The appetite appears; I can put it aside for a time. It is sometimes necessary to say to it, "Go away just for a time." The wish is passive, has no real activity in transforming me as a being and the appetite will come back, but for a moment I can renounce it.

QUESTIONER: Yes, and I want to ask is this real world we are searching for a world of complete lack of desire?

LORD PENTLAND: I am saying the real world is a world of lack of desire but it happens to be a world which men and women can't enter. So we are more interested in the fact that, through a certain relation, which we can have with the real world, we can work toward being real men and real women. With part of ourselves we can be in touch with the real world. With part of ourselves we are not. Do you understand?

What we consider to be the real world is something we can't enter into. There is a real world but we have to work longer before we can see what that is. What for us seems to be a real world is in fact a world above the earth, the planets, but we have contact with one part of us. We mustn't identify with any one part. One part is in fact real in comparison with the other part. We have these two parts.

But you speak of the world and first of all it is a question of my own life and my own life is confusion. There is not an order of these two worlds, parts of which I am. It is just confusion. In fact if I have fears, if I have doubts, if I am not certain about anything, if I am constantly revising, going back or changing what I have laid down, said, written, it means there is no order in me. It is just confusion.

So it is very useful to take some time out of my life and in a quiet place I can experience what really would be an order. The order I write down on a bit of paper becomes confusion. I have to withdraw from life to experience a relative order and I see what could be translated into my life if I work long enough. The order I write on a bit of paper or is put on a chart or diagram is completely hypocritical as a representation of life. I can't carry it into life; it doesn't represent life. All these diagrams are such a mockery. I can't take a plan I have written down, even a list of things to the supermarket, that I don't change or add to. So a real order in my life will not come from that type of diagram.

In order to live, I absolutely need each day to experience a different kind of meaning for the word "order." Now, in life that breaks down into confusion, so the first beginning of a real work in life is the ability to stay with my confusion, to admit I don't know the answer, don't know where I am going from moment to moment, to study how I am in life, observing myself. It is absolutely necessary to have recognized that my life is confusion. How many try to work in the morning? You don't try?

QUESTIONER: Not every morning.

LORD PENTLAND: Maybe it is good not to try sometimes. We don't want it to become routine, but make the times you don't try the exception. At least one could give that time. There is a certain kind of suffering in not being able to reach what you have hoped, to see that your attention is that flighty, your ability to work is not what you had hoped. One needs that every day.

And you say to your friends, do you, you are in a Gurdjieff group? Have you ever said to a friend you are in a Gurdjieff group?

QUESTIONER: Yes.

LORD PENTLAND: How can you tell your friend you are in a Gurdjieff group and yet you don't do the work that is given? I think one runs away from this intention. I am sure we all have the intention but we run away from it to a thought, into a form, a word. It is a sort of paranoia. It is a fear of not succeeding in experiencing life in the raw and one runs away into something that is pictured, imagined. It is the real paranoia and it is a limiting experience. One runs away into coffee, a cigarette, a plan to go to Boulder, Colorado. One is always running away into a plan. That is what creates all the nerves, the bad health. Do you agree?

Then why run away any more? What is there to do? The earthquake may come. What does it mean? Will you have a question—what is the meaning of this, how to understand? How could one develop such a stability that would have such a question? That is what Gurdjieff says man is on earth for. Yet you say you are in the Gurdjieff work. We have to pay it back to him. If we are in his work, we do his work in a simple way. It could be said simply.

So have a good vacation now. Try not to remember what I said. Bury it in you.

eleven

THEME: *How can self-observation, well understood and practiced in quiet conditions, begin to produce the energy needed to be for the good in our lives?*

QUESTION: This question seems to state a clear purpose—to be for the good and by use of the words "to be," asks us to be. We cannot simply choose the good, but the good demands being, and I think this says also that, for this, a special energy, a new sort of energy, is necessary. Can you say something about this new energy, this new quality of energy?

LORD PENTLAND: It has been said that we're searching for the truth— that means all our work is for knowing more completely the truth, for being more sincere. What this question showed me was that ideas can only take one a certain way in that search, because the search is a search which passes from one level to another. And ideas are quite different on different levels; some ideas that apply on one level, and are useful keys, are not use- ful on another level. For instance, if you take love, human love is a travesty of divine love, say between God and man; but at least in this idea of love is something that works "as above, so below." One could imagine a pure love, as the Sufis have done, which could be a help for understanding the right relationship between the parts of oneself.

But we come to this question—self-observation. How does this connect with the third state of consciousness, which we don't speak of very much but which is what we need—to begin where we are—but which, if we are more sincere with ourselves, one doesn't come in contact with for very long? So there is this question. When I am there in a certain way and I observe myself, what happens to the energy? Because a different idea has to come in.

Let's say I woke up this morning and as I woke up I remembered—I had the impression of my inability to pay attention, to listen properly. Let's say at the moment I was aware of myself pretending to listen and to have attention but instead I knew I wasn't really listening with the whole of myself. Let's say I woke up this morning with that. And let's say you woke up thinking, "It's another day." and immediately the associations started, and you saw it. And so I woke up with an impression of self-observation and you woke up with an impression of not being under control. Which of us would have a better day from the point of view of the work?

There is no question in my mind that, because I woke up with this marvelous observation, I do practically no work the whole day. Whereas you, because you woke up in a hurry, associating, and so forth, because you woke up like that, you work better the whole day. That has been our experience, I think. Most of us would say that is our experience. When I have had a very good start to the day, something that I can give a report on at a meeting and so forth, during the day—the day is not one in which I work. Where I have a very bad start, during the day, on the whole, there is an attempt to observe myself—to be for the good—more than on the day that starts better.

I don't know if you find this but, if so, it is a very sad thing. And that is what we're talking about when we say, "this energy," because if it doesn't go any further than that, inevitably the work itself becomes a pretense. There begins to be a sort of competitiveness of who can put the best question, a kind of affirmation of "I can do self-observation," and all this looking over one's shoulder, as between men and women, or between the people who are responsible and those who are not, or between the group here and the group somewhere else, or between our work in studying Gurdjieff and other people who are trying to find their way with another teaching.

So there is a mystery. We find something subjective after a time from doing what we're supposed to do, what we think we ought to do, observing, being good so to say. We find a subjective taste even when we sit down and be quiet, even when we sit down. Because it has been suggested, there is a sense of imitation, a sense of conforming perhaps, at least on those days. And on the other days, when we really work, I think it is possible because we have no energy.

"Blessed are the poor in spirit." We all have experienced that. We work better when we find ourselves in deep trouble. We are not very connected, so when trouble first appears we don't turn to our work at all then. But when we are humbled, when we understand that we are really in for trouble, we do turn to the work sometimes, when the trouble is deep enough.

So why do we need energy? It seems to me the energy must be needed, as was suggested by one of the questioners, for convincing myself of the truth of what I have observed. I observe chiefly at quiet times. In order "to be for the good," I need to observe at all times. And in order to be able to remember myself for what I am, inattentive, I need to convince myself. The energy is needed for convincing myself that I have that little attention.

And so the question is there—how does this energy which we receive as we are opened, when we are touched by the truth a little bit, how is this energy reinvested to touch the other parts? And the idea of self-observation is simply not adequate for the approach to that. We need the idea of three centers, a new state of consciousness that appears when the three centers are in equilibrium. The idea of a photograph, a stronger photograph, is not adequate for an acceptance of what is. What is needed, what we are talking about, is a kind of glimpse, in a very delicate way. As was said, I go with the associations generally, or rather, mostly I simply assert myself. But when I see I am going with the associations, that is not going with the associations, with whatever is there—in a sense.

We are not speaking about struggle, as if there were something good and something bad. In time we go with the associations and I need to convince myself of that, so that when I come in touch with other people—and we are very fortunate here, we still come in touch with others—then I must remember that I still go with my associations. If there is an intelligence, it is something that arises out of that. If there is an intelligence that sometimes I am aware of, behind, when I am able to bear the burden of being convinced that all the time I am attracted by my associations, if a little intelligence shows through, it is because I have accepted this is not an intelligence I can be prepared for or which can be worked out in advance. But it will appear in the course of an exchange if it is needed enough, if there is enough attention, which there generally isn't, or if there is enough truth—which means enough recognition of the need for attention.

So we are speaking about how to be convinced that we are what we are. We are not speaking about a vague sort of energy. We are speaking about how we can be convinced that the truth which I have glimpsed is really true and not something hidden behind all this energy.

And I think there is no better way than the way Gurdjieff showed. He seems to have said that the search for work is on myself, for myself. But he made no restrictions. In fact he encouraged people who are struggling to come together, and I think the idea was that there is no better way of, as it were, showing energy gone to the wrong place than in our relations with each other. We don't expect them to be better than they are, but being what they are is a help to remembering the truth, if you follow what I mean. We are not criticizing ourselves for having the kind of personal relations we have with each other, but we are here, together, because our relations are reminding us all of the time that we are living in associations, that we live a pretended life and largely a pretended work. But we are not depressed by that. We see that is so. And listening to each other we are reminded that is true, because it gives us the conviction—not in a strong sense, more in an affirmative sense, but in a very decided sense— that we carry with us this burden all the time of being nonentities, of being not only men but modern men and so on, the whole story we read in *Beelzebub's Tales*.

We are not asked to hold our heads low, and it would be awful if we held our heads high from being successful at self-observation. We are just looking to hold our heads. And we can do that from having worked together and seen ourselves, how selfish we are, how vain we are, and so forth, and the way our associations are constantly coming in.

What comes after that? But there is nothing after that. That is the truth. And if more and more of one could be convinced of that, if one would have, not the energy, but the clear consciousness of that being the truth, one could feel the three parts relate when one reaches the third state of consciousness—the sort of touch of one part on another, that particular touch which is absolutely different from our usual use of the sense of touch in our relations with each other. It is that sense of touch, I think, inside and perhaps a little outside, which represents for me one of the signs of being human, and which, when it is missing is a sign of inhumanity, however much I have studied the ideas.

We speak about the idea of self-observation. But the electric touch of one part on another that produces a sort of tingling—maybe that idea of touch and warmth is something that is missing in the idea of self-observation, so that one can't take the idea of self-observation right up to the third level, the moment of the transformation of consciousness.

twelve

QUESTION: I read an expression in a book the day before yesterday. The expression was "the motivating force." That phrase stayed with me. In our group we have talked a few times about why we come to groups. In connection with those talks there is the feeling that when I try to apply any of these very complicated exercises or ideas, it is somehow connected with a situation where I want some immediate result or improvement to make things somehow better. The idea of a motivating force that can follow me through my days seems important, but the only times these ideas appear is through some association or when I feel I have lost my temper or in the morning, because I sit in the mornings. At the moment I can't even feel any reason why I am attracted to these ideas, aside from wanting some improvement. It doesn't thread through my life. It is very infrequent.

LORD PENTLAND: We are weak. I think you are right. We are weak, so we are easily captured by the idea of a motivating force, but we have no force. We have many, many motives, but we have no force because they are all divided from each other. We have many "I's," many motives, but we don't know what altogether we want. We have no central integrated self; therefore we have no central integrated intention.

Now of course you are right, it is always a question why one would come here. But do you feel it except when you are here? You only feel the question why should you come here when you are here. As you leave here you ask yourself why did you come. As you arrive here you ask yourself why, and maybe at those moments you touch something of a result of coming, because of course each of us has to find for ourselves what is this result we can have from coming. But we have difficulty in finding it because the appearance of force in ourselves, of a central motive, is something that is difficult to recognize unless we are helped to recognize who I am as a whole.

What is my duty as a whole? A difficult question, so difficult that even to experience the question is the result that can come from working. What am I now and what may I become? It means, What is the next step of my duty? Do you follow that? What am I now? I have no force. I have no central motive. I sit in the morning but it has no meaning. Now what may I become? I have had some good experiences. Yes? You have had some? So what is in between? What is my duty? That is where we can look for the result. Do you understand? We can't look for the result in the best moments, and obviously it is not what I am in my present condition, so the result is somewhere in between. Do you look for the result there or do you look for perfection?

QUESTIONER: I don't even know what I look for outside a moment and a situation where I feel I have made a fool of myself or I have broken some rules.

LORD PENTLAND: That is what I say, that is what you are. And to not break rules, to not be an idiot is perfection. So the result in between is what you can have. Do you ever look between? At this moment what is the next step? What is my duty this very moment? Some of you have seen a result of that kind I suppose. Yes? I don't like the word duty. I don't mean anything by it—it is sort of narrow—but I don't see what other word to use because the next step is very, very serious. It is even historic. Do you see what I mean? The next step is historic.

My motivating force is a part of the whole motivating force of the whole universe, a very small part, but it has the sense of being an historic step. So the result we get has always that kind of taste of the exchange, the dividing. We have to give up the dream of adding all these little motives and becoming a very forceful person, for the reality of being a tiny part of a very big situation. That is where the motivating force is.

You don't stand as a sentinel at the doors
of your perception . . .

QUESTION: I am having an experience now that I don't understand at all. I was very calm when I walked in but the sound of the music coming from the next room has caused much more emotion inside, and I wonder how I can understand what is being affected. That music is affecting me. I want to know why, but I don't know where to go for an explanation.

LORD PENTLAND: Everything affects me but because I have no attention for myself I never conceive how. It seems as if everything draws me out of myself. At the same time, I am there and I am affected, but I don't know how. So it is as if there were a kind of paranoia, a movement away from myself. Everything is starting to draw me away from myself towards it, not towards me, almost everything. Is there anything you feel magnetized to towards yourself?

QUESTIONER: In a way this music—I feel what you mean by the drawing out but I can feel it much more intensely through me.

LORD PENTLAND: Your body is affected but you are not able to say how because you are there with the music. Your body, your feelings, your organism lets the music in but you don't stand as a sentinel at the doors of your perception, so you can't tell what is going on. So how to be, not just towards music but towards everything and everybody?

You have a tension; it affects your breathing. How to be towards that? You want it to go away. Now how are you going to be able to relate yourself to that? You have a headache. You know it is not just a question of wanting it to go away. You begin to feel it is just a question of letting it go, that you mustn't fight it, that if you would just drop it, it would go.

How to let it go? You can't drop it but you begin to see that really the truth is it could be let go. Now I have to let it go. How to work with that? Do you follow what I mean?

QUESTIONER: Yes.

LORD PENTLAND: What I know is that at a certain moment I sort of pass back into myself. The music is there. I am listening to it, but in a sense I have let it go, and now I am listening to it so that I can not only watch its effect on me but with much less fear. I even feel a sort of confidence that, within limits, I can control its effect on me.

The first stage of digestion is a kind of transformation . . .

QUESTION: I need a work for more depressed emotional states because it reminds me of what Gurdjieff said about being under more laws when you are sick. It is almost the same feeling, except coming from another place.

LORD PENTLAND: Let us look at it in a new way. You are in an inner situation. We can follow it best if we can see a little bit our inner situation now. And it doesn't satisfy me when there is so much that blocks the sense of freedom within my body, that it is as if I were sick, and I want to understand what is work at that moment. It occurs to me that I am under more laws at this moment than at another time when I don't feel this resistance as such a block. But of course that doesn't help—just to make that connection between the idea, which is a good connection, but it didn't help you. You asked if that were so but it didn't work.

What would it mean to be conscious that there is a block, without changing anything? How would I be able to describe, to associate about, my experience if I became conscious of myself, as I am, in this state of being blocked? This is the problem. So let us look at it from the point of view of impressions.

I am receiving impressions all the time but only one at a time—impressions in my head I mean—and I am following this stream of impressions, little images, including about myself being blocked. And every now and then with some shock or other it goes way off into some other area which has been touched because my body or feelings have been touched. So I am coming back to impressions of this inner state so far as I can see it and I am asking what the work is then. And I remember that we need to digest these impressions. Perhaps we never understand the scale of what that means.

You see that these impressions—even when you associate them with the laws, the food diagram—are all of a certain level. It is as if I were looking at something on a screen outside me. But the first stage of digestion is a kind of transformation. Suddenly I have an impression of myself.

It is an ordinary moment, the stream of thought impressions is going on, but I am aware of myself in my fear. I am not looking for answers in the stream of impressions. I am still limited, but I am limited by the area to which my attention will extend. If my attention is round about my body and if I am very careful, and provided no shocks come which upset it, I can keep a certain amount of this impression of myself for a minute or two.

Another step from there we need to speak about. It might seem that another step might be to extend it, but there is another step taken between for the digestion of these impressions. So it is not that we are just trying to extend the area, the circumference, of the circle, but that each of these steps, if you remember in the food diagram, represents new dimensions of the experience.

You see, once you come to this impression of yourself, whether sick or not, it relieves a certain way in which you are hunting for answers among the flow of these other little impressions. Do you follow? It lifts you right back from these impressions which are like thrown on the front of the forehead where you are following them—and this lifts you right back—and you understand that this could be a useful moment for your being. This could be a work that is worthwhile. It lifts you right out of the attraction to the information media in a totally new direction, towards the attraction of what I am. Maybe that could help you. Do you follow what I mean?

And you see now that you are listening. Somebody will speak and you are listening in a different way. You have the impression of all your functions being changed a little and you are sort of listening before, instead of listening or following after, with your inner eye. And here you are sort of listening before, so that you hear something quite different; the same thing looks quite different. If you listen after, you want to know what follows, but if you listen before, you want to know the quality of the sound, you want to take in something of the sound itself.

Very badly described, but you see what a big difference it means. And it is just marked by two little lines, one line, on the food diagram. It is said the first impression of that level we can have is an impression of myself. And we lose our time in looking for that kind of order in outer impressions, in impressions of the world outside, although in rare cases it is received by coincidence by the perceptive apparatus of a man. The first impression at that level, the first digested impression that we can intentionally have, is an impression of myself. You have heard that before.

Every conscious impression you
receive will help you . . .

QUESTION: For a long time now I had been thinking that my thoughts were myself and that I was my thought. But I feel that a part of me, or perhaps what I would now call more honestly, myself, is tired of the thoughts, perhaps a little suspicious of them, or perhaps just not interested, and I have a wish for some sort of quiet. And I wonder, I seem to be in some vague way trying to do something in that direction. I am not sure what it is I am trying to do and I am not sure if I should be doing it. I seem to be somehow saying to what I used to call myself all the time, "Oh, go away," because I would like to hear something else more real. And I am puzzled by the idea that it is not possible to do anything in that respect.

LORD PENTLAND: Yes, it is quite a good piece of reasoning, that, but we misunderstand. We wish to be conscious. It doesn't mean to be different. It means to be able to be what we are, perhaps not with intention, but at least with a certain acceptance. So we find that we are always chattering and making noise. Do you follow?

QUESTIONER: Yes.

LORD PENTLAND: And the difficulty is not to get caught in a kind of reaction to that but to realize that to be conscious is to be able to be consciously making noise. That is what it means.

Now it so happens that in becoming conscious a whole area which I am not aware of normally comes into view. So consciously making noise is not as bad as I think it would be, because consciously making noise is the little peripheral noises that go on when I am in touch with a much bigger part of myself. So we don't need to be as afraid as we are of being what we are, because in being what we are we get a big compensation for getting rid of the fantasies. We come in contact with a whole area of ourselves which makes the talking, the noises, quite bearable for the moment.

Then you have to work like that, realizing that every conscious impression you receive will help you. You understand? Every impression of yourself will help you, will be like a building block, an atom of a kind of possible crystallization within you which doesn't exist now. But at the same time, every impression of yourself—this is the other end of the stick—will inevitably be occupied, taken over, by ordinary thoughts too. You follow what I mean?

QUESTIONER: Yes.

LORD PENTLAND: There will be the fact that this creates something new in you. This transformation of myself is a transformation on a minute scale of the energies in myself, which creates something new, which unfortunately is quickly dispersed because we haven't experience enough to realize that when an impression is taken by my ordinary thought it adds to my information and, therefore, I still remain attracted to receive instructions from this type of information that is always going on in my thought, that is always kept up to date on my latest discoveries by stealing them. Then there is nothing for it but to take the risk, to not fight that, so to speak, to consciously allow that most of the time, to consciously follow these instructions, consciously be a slave most of the time, and at certain times to gather together my knowledge and try to come directly, without preparation, to the impression of myself that I spoke about earlier. Do you follow what I mean?

It is better not to be thinking about the work most of the time, better to consciously accept to be what you are, to be conscious of what you are, instead of reacting to the noise by thinking of quietness or something, to consciously be the noisy thought-ridden people we are. If we try that, we become interested in the work of these functions, and what it leads to, how to connect. So you try to consciously be that except at certain times and then, without ado, without preparation, you make this passage we spoke about earlier to another dimension. Do you understand?

QUESTIONER: That is a great help.

LORD PENTLAND: It is better to try that way. It is still not easy but, trying with that kind of struggle, one can find one's way. And the most important thing for each of us is that we reach that stage, which we all reach, in which we don't feel dependent on books or outside people to help. It is up to us. We still need verification in the group, exercises, but we are making our own program, if you see what I mean.

Some of these prayers or symbolic sayings have
a life of their own . . .

QUESTION: I wonder if it is possible for me in the state I am in, in my situation, to take something from *In Search of the Miraculous* like, "I wish to remember myself." I wonder if it is possible for me to use something like that at a definite time in the day to question myself a little more, for example when I drive to work. I have been trying this but wanted to ask about it.

LORD PENTLAND: I think that some of these prayers or symbolic sayings have a life of their own and we can receive them directly, but we can't follow them as instructions. They are sometimes, like the Lord's Prayer, arranged in a way that corresponds to the way in which we are arranged. So if the proper instructor is there, he can use these prayers as a kind of exercise similar to the exercises we are given that correspond to a structure.

QUESTIONER: By an "instructor" do you mean an outside guide?

LORD PENTLAND: For me, it seems the recognition that I am experiencing something like what is described in a prayer comes after I have experienced it. It is a very great help in that way. There is something very extraordinary I feel in experiencing something which corresponds exactly to something I have been told, by which I remember I feel I belong to a kind of circle of people. It is always very mysterious, that. I don't know if you have had that kind of experience but one may sometimes hear something read on Sunday in one of these readings of Gurdjieff and later, or before, one may see he is speaking about exactly the same thing. And one wonders that a sort of confused person like myself would be able to receive in that direct way the knowledge which he gives, but it apparently is so. So one feels very much strangeness that one belongs to a kind of circle which Gurdjieff was part of, for that moment. And I think it is more in that way one might come to understand the prayer that you give.

Of course at a certain level it is useful to discuss it, perhaps, but I don't think that leads anywhere. And I think if I had to answer what use can be made of it in advance of such an experience, I would say—which amounts to the same thing—if one was in a very, very quiet state, in a conscious state maybe, one has a certain freedom then to bring before one certain associations rather than just watching the ones that are there. You might bring this before you then, and see if you understand it differently.

QUESTIONER: Before, I tried to do another prayer and asked a question about it a year ago, and I think at that time I had the idea I could sort of churn this into where I was, in order to force myself to receive some sort of benefit. I don't know if that is a true statement, but it was somewhere along those lines. Now I feel for the first time in a long time, in the period before I am going to work, that I have become a little more quiet and feel I have this time between Sausalito and the park which I drive every day.

LORD PENTLAND: In any case, you see from the way we have been speaking that our effort is more to try to intend what we are doing, to be with what we are doing, in order to be conscious of it then, rather than after doing something to try to change it by seeing it is not right. It is all right to be mixed-up in order to see what mixed-up-ness is, or to be sick, or whatever.

So one tries to come down, to be what is going on. Then maybe the other parts will appear. But the other way, if one is fighting oneself, they cannot appear. They also can't appear if one is fighting oneself most of the time and making too definite a plan about certain times. If it is too definite, one is really creating two parallel people in oneself.

CHAPTER TWELVE

Fear has to do with a relationship with what
you are interested in . . .

QUESTION: I feel that fear in connection with what you have just been speaking about, and my usual way of covering up that fear is doing a kind of violence to myself. And I think that partly that fear is based on a misunderstanding of what a relationship is, both with myself and with other people. I don't know whether all of the fear is because of the misunderstanding, but partly I feel it that way, but don't know, in my case, what that misunderstanding is.

LORD PENTLAND: In any case, the fear has to do with the relationship. So exactly what part it plays, what the fear is of, I don't know, but the fear has to do with a relationship with what you are interested in. It doesn't have to do with the thing itself. So if you accept the fear, if you can go with the fear without being swallowed up by it, you may be able to understand better the relationship. But if you fight the fear, you fight the very thing you are aware of that has to do with this unknown relationship in myself.

The relationship is what I need and all there is is fear. But until I accept the fear I will never discover the relationship. Maybe I am grateful to the fear; maybe it has to be there always. In myself it is the relationship between two parts of very unequal value. Why wouldn't there be fear as they approach? Sometimes I don't know which has more value than the other but they are of unequal value. I don't know what the fear is of, but it is a signal that I must go with it.

About fear between people, I think there are so many different kinds of fear that, though it could be analyzed, one can't immediately place that fear between people. In a sense it is the same, because mostly there is nothing between people, just nothing. One sees that so much, just nothing between people. People even bump into you on the sidewalk as if there is nothing.

A real freedom where the thought and
feeling are more together . . .

QUESTION: This afternoon I was sitting at a meeting at the school where I work and we were discussing one of the children who goes there.

159

At one point I made an observation about the child and after I was part way into the sentence I realized that I wasn't speaking only about that child. It occurred to me that all of what I had said to that point was an account of what had happened the previous evening with my own child. As soon as I became aware of it, I tried to cover and back off by saying something more relevant, then discovered that I was going further along in the same direction. There was a moment when I really had a sense I was trapped in some sort of cage and that there was little I could do about it.

LORD PENTLAND: All the time the difficulty of being free. You see you cannot be conscious if you believe or have judgments about what you observe, if you feel wrong or something. Maybe it was there and you lost it. We are all the time losing our attention like that and in a way it makes a relationship with a child very difficult, but not impossible, if we could be freer. You understand what I mean by freer?

QUESTIONER: Yes, the way I think of that is to have moments when I wasn't so identified with all my workings and thoughts and reactions to things. It is not quite free but perhaps it is partially free.

LORD PENTLAND: In order to be more free you need to be in touch with your feeling, which is much faster than your thoughts. And you kind of receive signals with your feelings but see you don't respond because you are so tied to your thoughts—I mean with a child. It shows the feeling is there but it doesn't work. You understand? It is only by accepting that, by really being this person who has no feeling—which means by not running away from encounters with the child—it is only in that way you can grow. As soon as you see you have no feeling you start to avoid the situation where feeling is needed. Do you understand?

QUESTIONER: No, I don't think so.

LORD PENTLAND: You need to have a taste of a freedom that comes through feeling, a real freedom where the thought and feeling are more together, and for that you have to not avoid the encounters which show you you have no feeling. But once you have the taste, then it is something else. If you have the taste with a child, then the work is to have the taste innerly. I don't think you understand.

QUESTIONER: No, I don't.

LORD PENTLAND: Could you put the question differently and say what if anything interests you in what I answered?

QUESTIONER: You spoke of encountering the child and avoiding having no feeling, but I don't follow what you mean by no feeling.

LORD PENTLAND: It means the child is laughing and you are feeling very serious. How do you understand that? You have no feeling for the child. There is no perception of the child's mood, otherwise you wouldn't be so serious. You would have caught up with the child, but you are getting in the middle of talking to it, and the child has already thought of something else. Until that becomes a fact with you, it is better not to avoid the encounters with the child. You won't increase your feeling that way but you will increase the need for feeling. The real relationship with feeling is in yourself and you don't get that with children, but you can get the taste of a need for it with children. I make a distinction between the two, perhaps you don't see why.

QUESTIONER: Why you make a distinction?

LORD PENTLAND: Yes.

QUESTIONER: Well, being aware of the need is not the same as experiencing that.

LORD PENTLAND: Exactly, you understand what I mean. And also one gets to be dependent on a certain situation. We wish to have a relation not just with children but with all sorts of levels of nature.

*Recognize this part that works from
a false picture . . .*

QUESTION: Some time ago in trying the exercise in the morning I felt a kind of change came about in my attitude about it. Whereas before I had been moved by some desire for peace or a quiet state, I began to feel less involved in the part that just wanted peace and quiet because I found that it had become a static thing. Now I feel much more that something is missing. This morning I felt much more distracted than I had earlier but more awareness of being distracted. I felt movements in myself, changes in myself, very strongly in a way, but without any purpose. I don't know if I could have a sense of purpose about what is needed. It seems sometimes the morning exercise has life for me in the sense of being in touch with this movement, being taken away, coming back. Some understanding appears but I feel something is missing.

LORD PENTLAND: It seems to me one has to see the whole work inversely to how one does, as if we are naturally aware without trying and all that we try gets in the way. If one would look at it that way, one would misunderstand less, if you see what I mean. And we have to try. It sounds funny to say that, but we are so unconscious of ourselves that we don't really recognize the existence of this "try-er" except in others. So one really has first of all to recognize this part that works from a false picture, that is greedy not only for energy, experience, but also for information. And we have to recognize that to enter a work like this can't be done without taking that part with us. Don't you agree?

So, more or less, the scheme of things is that through something that is touched by the knowledge we receive and exchange, we have conscious experiences, but in a way the highlights are always put on our efforts, which get in the way, sort of. It is not so stupid as it sounds, that. It has to do with the difficulty of accepting to be what I am. Mostly I am reacting, going away from myself, getting in the way of the light that is there the whole time.

So if one could get over the first shock at this idea, allow it to be assimilated, it could be a help, because one of our greatest difficulties is to go along with what we see and not be so shocked that we go back to explaining it. I am always subjective and have this opinion of myself which can be lightened but can't be altogether cast out. So in this way all my efforts, to a greater degree at least than we recognize, are blocking-efforts rather than helping-efforts.

One begins in that way to be interested in the part in oneself which is the resistance, is blocking, and to see it, to bring it up out of the unconscious, to see it reveal itself and to see the sort of camouflaged creature that it is. We don't see it. It is right in the middle, but we don't see it.

To remember that I am, and I am my enemy . . .

QUESTION: Is there a right attitude one can have toward the idea of resistance? I mean, could there be the possibility of a new way of working? I see, well, resistance has become rather clear to me, and how to confront it? What to do when it's there? It seems there's emerging in me something that wants to struggle with resistance and it lacks intelligence to the point where often when I see that something is resisting, without really stopping myself or anything, there's an urge to just struggle with it without realizing what the outcome might be. Is that right? I also see the possibility of a more intelligent way of becoming aware of the habitual parts that kind of take my attention without my knowing it or take my energy without my knowing it. And upon becoming aware of this, there can be a struggle it seems. Along that line is there a way I can understand resistance and what to do?

LORD PENTLAND: You see you touched on many things as you spoke. But not on really as many things as we experienced as you spoke. You touched on too many things for us to comment on. Yet you weren't able to keep pace with all the things that came up as you spoke. So one sees that my concept of myself has to be enlarged. Until you spoke, we had no idea how many things were myself. You spoke about many, but as you spoke we saw many more. And we can be conscious of all these things. We can expect our consciousness to be aware of all these things up to a point and then we find resistance. Now, is resistance the other things? You can't say that because we weren't aware of any of these things till you spoke. So what is resistance?

QUESTIONER: There is an I that wants to say.

LORD PENTLAND: Resistance is when you move into the other things. It's not the other things. It's the fact you move into them—and you may only move into one thing. Can anybody follow? Maybe you were dividing yourself up to you and the resistance. But in fact I understand it doesn't exist until somebody speaks and touches me and as you spoke, you spoke of somebody else and, listening to you, I thought and others thought of other things. Now the resistance is what stops that expansion. And what spoils that expansion is not other parts of you but that you moved into a part that doesn't want to expand. So you see—you're two. You are your enemy. I am not your enemy. You are your enemy.

QUESTIONER: This part, where I want to expand . . .

LORD PENTLAND: It doesn't matter what part it is. The sensation of you was expanded until you moved. And you see there's a natural law that you have to move. It isn't a question of your voluntarily moving because you are your own enemy in this sense of the expansion of consciousness. So in the work I am, and I am my enemy. So that brings us to the beginning of your question. What is the attitude I can have to remember that—to remember that I am and I am my enemy? And as long as I fight myself, I won't fight you. So if the idea is to lead a better life, to do the least harm, the first beginning is to experience myself as my own enemy. And what I am trying to say is don't let's be distracted as we usually are by what is the resistance and where is it. Essentially, the resistance represents the movement of myself into, what shall I say, my ego—something that doesn't want to change. And the possibility of self-development depends on recognizing, first by logic and then by experience, that if I can move from myself to my ego, there must be a movement back from my ego into my wish. So the possibility of work now depends on the degree to which I have faith that because I moved into my ego, there is a way I can search for making this movement back. Then I shall be distracted if I think, "Where is back? Which part is back?" because essentially the structure of it all is the movement of my interest, what I take myself as at the moment, my attention if you like.

We are speaking about the appreciation of quiet . . .

QUESTION: If I understand correctly, certain things are possible if I can become more quiet. But I approach it with some kind of violence—as if I could make myself quiet by violence—and, as a result, I never seem to move from the mental process, and I wonder if these moments of quiet I do have are the result of something that I am not able to affect directly or whether they come from something along the line of acceptance of myself. At moments like that I experience fear of relaxation and I wonder what an idea of quiet might be.

LORD PENTLAND: Yes. It's difficult to speak about these things because we are speaking about the appreciation of quiet. It's nearer to emotion than an idea and it is hard to speak about. But it's very important. We must try because it's a recognizable event for all of us, which we have to understand.

Now to begin with, there's this misunderstanding where I try to become quiet and it doesn't work. At the root of that misunderstanding is a wrong idea of self-observation. You see, we wish to work and if we can't sincerely get the taste of work, we try anyhow and we convince ourselves we are working. And so we start to observe ourselves with the mind and then looking at myself with the mind gradually allows me to try to do something to myself from my head.

At the very beginning, when we were just finished reading the books, we wouldn't have tried that. But now, from self-observation from the head, it gradually becomes changing myself from the head, making myself quiet from the head, from my ordinary will. What is my ordinary will? It's just a desire, in this case you could say greed, ambition to make progress in the work.

So the first step will be to come to a right self-observation, that means seeing from my sincerity. I always have some. So then I begin to see my greed at the same time as I see myself imposing the attempt to be quiet on myself. And I see I have to come back to that again and again. What does it mean to come back to that? Can you bear with me a little longer?

It's an interesting question. We are speaking about what is right self-observation and we are speaking about what will is and how, from a deep sincerity, one could see from a whole more this part that wants to be quiet before I am quiet and that doesn't have much action on myself. I have to come back and back to that again and again. What does it mean to come back? Then again, one could go along and have a little idea of coming back to that. In the right way one could have a sort of longing wish for a taste of that kind of sincerity.

Eventually something takes place and this quiet appears in a lawful way, naturally, spontaneously. It's like we were listening to somebody and— you can't be above the whole thing, you know—you're not free enough to listen and be in contact with yourself and all that. And suddenly, quite spontaneously, you're able to take in the whole conversation: yourself and the person and the conversation. That comes about suddenly, doesn't it? It may be connected with a kind of determination to go on trying. What, one can't say, but sometimes it's a kind of determination not to be in such a narrow frame and longing and longing for that. Suddenly one is able to listen to the conversation and at the same time to see all sorts of distractions, and see how little one is able to remember, to be aware of how impossible it is to follow. I don't have the attention. Now, the quiet appears like that, spontaneously. It's almost the same thing.

thirteen

*To know myself is a precarious balance between those two greatly
enlarged meanings of "know" and "myself" . . .*

QUESTION: Several weeks ago there was a meeting that I have thought
about a few times. I am always amazed at the "I's" that come here, and the
experience of being different with people in the work made me wonder
about what seems to be my "work personality." My work personality is
very shy and frightened so that I don't speak often. I was then able to
observe myself in different circumstances. In this non-work situation, I
was very different, very active, bold in offering my ideas. I thought about
these two different aspects and realized that the bold "I's" are not necessarily me and it made me question the possibility that the shy, passive "I's"
aren't necessarily any more true, and that perhaps the more bold, active
set of "I's" are more useful. Is there a way of struggling against this set of
"I's" that might have developed and am I struggling against them now?
Or is there any value in this group of "I's" that come here?

LORD PENTLAND: We identify with everything, you see. And you
identify with what you think would be an image that would come here to
meetings, so you come like that. It may not be very successful. You may
not be giving the impression you think. I do not find your question partic-

ularly shy, for instance. But to understand your identification, you should be like that. It's just an image that you somehow framed in your head.

When you come to meetings, what "I's" are there isn't the point. You are giving your energy to that; therefore you can't be here at the meeting. You see? If you want to get anything here, you have to be here.

Now about the other one, you speak as if you have seen yourself as a bold person and don't like it. It means you don't see it. When you really see yourself, there's no doubt that's you, and when you see it there's a sort of jar. I really know that's me. You see what I mean? So bold or not, if you don't like it or not, it's you.

QUESTIONER: I tend to not like the shy one.

LORD PENTLAND: You don't, I know. But you identify with it. If you tried to come here not shy, you couldn't do it. There are many things one can't do because one identifies with a picture of oneself. You don't have a picture of yourself like that, so of course you don't like that; so you want to be different. But the point is, the other one—it's also of no value.

We need to know ourselves and we make the mistake of thinking this is quite simple. But if I ponder what it means to know myself, you will see then I become very, very quiet and I see that to "know" is a word. It has to be enlarged. It means to know in every part, in the whole of myself, of my body. To know I would carry it into action. To know it means to understand it and myself. There are so many sides of myself. I never stop enough to allow these various sides to come together—and to know myself is a very precarious balance between those two greatly enlarged meanings of "know" and "myself." But it does take place as a sort of gift and then we come on it partly through our own wish. So you don't need to ask "Is it so?" It is so. And we don't need to try to accept it. We do accept it.

So the preparation is in recognizing that things are not what they seem, that the observation, for instance, "Know thyself," is a cipher that needs to be decoded. There's no deceit in it but all the same the words don't convey it. Any word, like "mother," any word as long as that word is there, you don't have a millionth part of it. So you see, gradually you free yourself from images that make you what you are. But I free myself from the inside out. If you free yourself from the outside, it makes considering. You play that shy girl to an inner audience the whole time, but the real change comes from inside.

You begin to understand how the forms give only the tiniest part of reality and the more you understand that, the more joy begins to activate you. So little by little it can come to a better balance. The balance is love. But there again you don't know what love is. We don't know the word "love." God is love. Love is the balance. We take a word like love and apply it to things that don't have to do with a particular balance, which is knowing what it means. Even then it requires something to be given.

The movement of consciousness is magic . . .

QUESTION: When there is no movement of consciousness, what initiates it and once it is in movement what retards it, if I see this as a flow between people, relationship? What suddenly gives it life and what causes it to die, if you are talking about life as the movement of consciousness?

LORD PENTLAND: The movement of consciousness is magic. Life is magic, would you agree? What is magic? It is life. You can't understand life, it is the miraculous. Now there is magic going on in me and around me. The audience says, "What starts it, what stops it, how does he do it?" But that doesn't apply to what is going on. Do you understand? That is the best answer I can give. It is an irrelevant question.

The point is, this magic is going on now and in order to experience it I have to have a very open muscle structure, an attention that contains all my energy, so I have to have a open inside of my psychic muscles. There has to be an attention that contains this like the cup contains the liquid, and I find that, in trying to come to that, these questions that you ask don't last and the wish to come to that endures more. Do you follow what I mean? So gradually I get to be what I am, the player not the audience.

All the books you have read, all the movies you have seen, all the television you have watched, this has created a tremendous habit of experiencing passively, you know? Now I am not saying that that is wrong. I am saying that there is a movement starting from there towards a more active attitude towards my life, and this movement starts by itself as soon as I recognize the passivity of this type of participation in living. At the moment I see the passivity of it, it can't be avoided that I get up and leave the football ground or turn the television off. It takes place as a law. Everybody has felt that; it just stops. It isn't that I do anything, but this seed of consciousness that is in me begins to act, maybe not very often but that is the way that works. So you could say in a way that it begins when I see what I am in this passive state.

Now there is a whole traditional way of living that has been given by the various traditions, which agree to a great extent as to what type of program one should adopt during the day: the need for certain periods of meditation, what type of food to eat, how to make use of the sex energy, or in what kind of exact postures one should sit in and work in and sleep in and so on. There is a whole vocabulary about that, which can't be ignored, but the more we learn that, the more that is learned, since you and I are unique questions or cases or problems, there is not going to be learning absolutely right. So the more of that that is learned, in the long run, the longer it will take.

I am not saying there are not these types of questions to be dealt with but first I have to be sure what I am talking about, to look at things from inside. Then through this vision my intelligence, if I am very fortunate, may begin to give me discriminating answers on some of these questions within the framework of common sense. But I can't build it from this kind of knowledge. It won't appear that way. It appears from seeing the passive way in which I live, I think, and you think so too, everybody thinks so. In a sense there is something I find out, which is that everything is in me, everything is included. Wouldn't you say at moments you feel everything is included? Except what?

QUESTIONER: My desire to stay there, probably.

LORD PENTLAND: Except these kinds of questions. They disappear. Everything is included except dreams. When I have this sense of being centered, everything comes inside and I feel it is almost possible that an achieved man might indeed be a universe. But some of these dreams do literally stop in order for me to come inside. I don't stop them, but they stop.

QUESTIONER: I have experienced that in the morning exercise.

LORD PENTLAND: So there are some animals that don't get into the ark, some questions that can't be answered because they don't come inside. Do you follow what I mean?

QUESTIONER: Yes.

LORD PENTLAND: For instance, you look for sentimentality in *Beelzebub's Tales*, do you find sentimentality there? You see what I mean?

fourteen

We have to listen for a knowledge of how to listen . . .

QUESTION: Today I was on my way here for work on crafts. I got in the car and couldn't find the key and while searching for it I confronted quite a feeling of "Gee, I don't have to come, there is a way out, I have a good excuse, can't find the key." On the other hand, I wanted to find the key because I wanted to come. This is the way it is most of the time. What is it when I am not here that can be a reminding factor that will work?

LORD PENTLAND: Ideas.

QUESTIONER: They seldom penetrate farther than my head.

LORD PENTLAND: That is quite true, but what would penetrate? The idea that we are asleep, the wrong connection between centers?

You see that you lose your keys and begin to wonder if one of your friends hasn't purposely hidden them or if God didn't arrange it that way because you need rest. Your thought comes into action and you begin to listen to your thought. You lose your keys, let us say, and you are living with a friend who doesn't want you to come here and you immediately blame her, think she probably hid the keys because she didn't want you to come. She wanted you to stay home. Does that happen? You imagine she hid your keys to prevent your coming. You listen to that, then later find your keys in your own pocket and you come to the meeting, but when you come back you have destroyed your relationship with her. You know the sort of thing I mean.

It means it is no good listening in that way to everything that comes along like that. So the only rational thought—one doesn't have many rational thoughts, but that is unseen—is that she wishes for you to come here to get you out of the house at last to some decent place, and yet you suppose the other. And when you meet her again there is this wall between you, and then between us.

So the only way will be to listen for the knowledge of how to listen. Because we all listen in that way to everything that comes along. If we want a cup of coffee we listen to that—we have a cup of coffee. If we feel we don't want to come here, we listen to that and it presents an obstacle. As long as we listen, we have to listen for a knowledge of how to listen. I become very quiet. Is there such a knowledge? And the ideas can help, all the ideas that you remember. As soon as you start to listen with the knowledge of how—instead of using what you hear as a knowledge of how—it acts directly. It has an action on you. It affects your nervous system, prevents your having this kind of narrow vision. Then you find your keys.

See the full organic harmony of our sleep . . .

QUESTION: I was driving my mother somewhere the other day and showed her an article about the chemistry of abnormal children which I had cut out of the paper. She read one or two lines and said, "This is about such and such." I said, "Read the rest." So she read the whole thing and said it was interesting. I was aggravated that she wouldn't get it, and suddenly I saw something tremendously interesting about my own superficial way of listening to my outer life. I found I would wait for a word I could react to automatically.

I find now this premature commentary of my head is never enough to give me what is real. I see I always interrupt people, never wait quietly long enough to find out what a situation really is. I am happy or afraid, so some part of me always comments as soon as it grabs onto something familiar. It is just in my head. I don't listen from deeper parts of myself.

I am getting more deeply dissatisfied with the way I am always at odds with life because I don't listen long enough. I am interested in how to be more quiet, listen long enough, how not to give in to that first artificial familiarity that comes about in life.

LORD PENTLAND: You see that we are afraid of other people.

QUESTIONER: Yes, I do.

LORD PENTLAND: You see that.

QUESTIONER: More of a gut feeling, not just intellectually agreeing to that idea.

LORD PENTLAND: Not emotionally, not intellectually, you recognize that we are not comfortable with other people, that as single organisms we are not free of that. Therefore the very shadow of an appointment with somebody else is enough for me to start looking for ways to please him in order to hide from myself my fear of other people.

Of course, there are times when my fear is hidden, when I feel a success, but normally, when not on the wave of success, I fear other people, and so any prearranged meeting with somebody starts up a mechanism in me to find a way to cover up that fear by bringing them sometimes very inappropriate things. For instance, you see it is inappropriate to bring your mother something about how to bring up children, something organically inappropriate. Perhaps you have never really recognized that she is your mother, you are her child. And by some miracle I can speak, walk, do all these things which somehow went on in the interaction between her and me at an early stage. One hasn't recognized that, so one actually tells one's mother about how to bring up children. Nothing could be more insane. If you saw a young chicken teaching a hen how to lay eggs you would say it was insane.

So you have to recognize the breadth of our sleep. When you say you don't want to just intellectually understand the ideas, you have to see the full organic harmony of our sleep, all the chords involved, and the result is that one accepts that the only way to relate to other people more successfully will be to accept this sleep. By seeing all the time my insanity, I will be able perhaps to cure others of their insanity. By being honest about the way in which I listen to the most illogical demands and put my energy into the most illogical changing fears, putting all that together will be a better way of living with people than by trying to please them. So one has to make it little by little by little.

You don't have the knowledge of how to manifest in accordance with your wish . . .

QUESTION: I felt very much what you said about fear of others, and it has seemed to me lately that the hardest thing is to wish to work for myself. It is a real obstacle, what others think about me. This sounds very shallow, but it seems so hard to wish in that way. I lost it as soon as I started to speak, but sometimes I really wish that.

LORD PENTLAND: So it is more complicated—the how. Then you speak. So you wish and it doesn't come. How do you reason about that?

QUESTIONER: I don't think much, I react a lot. I just want it to stop, just want it to change, but I don't know how to think about it.

LORD PENTLAND: That is the emotional side. You have a wish but you have no mother. When you were just an infant you wished for something and someone brought it. What do you expect to happen now when you wish?

QUESTIONER: Maybe that.

LORD PENTLAND: Yes. So one has to listen to the grown-ups around one because one is not grown up. One is neither in the position that every want will be satisfied at once by a loving mother nor in the position of having the knowledge of how to have one's wishes act on one so one can manifest rightly. You find your wish but the manifestation doesn't correspond with the wish. You don't have the knowledge of how to manifest in accordance with your wish. You can't go back to the crib where your mother will bring you a bottle. All you can do is try to understand from more grown-up people who have written books how they managed in your particular circumstances, instead of stamping and saying, "I am wishing, I am wishing, and nothing is coming." Do you follow or not?

QUESTIONER: I understand. Something says I don't really do that.

LORD PENTLAND: You don't stamp? You sulk? Which?

QUESTIONER: Sulk.

LORD PENTLAND: Instead of sulking you have to turn the energy that is released by this emergency—that your cry for help is not being attended to—towards understanding through the various texts of the grown-up people how they managed in that condition. You have a lot of energy at the moment that you are crying for help, and instead of that being gradually wasted in the self-pity, one has to find some way to use it to observe.

Very small people have very big emotions. The difficulty is to reduce the apparent size of one's emotions to the particular detail which is being emoted about. You know I am just a detail, you are just a detail, but one's emotions are as big as the universe. You have to be able to reduce them to your own size. You are looking all over the place, but some of the knowledge you want is in you. You are just a tiny person. One doesn't look there, one looks everywhere else.

Like Gurdjieff said, a raw potato is less intelligent than a cooked potato. When one is emotional one has a power one lets loose on the world instead of cooking one's own potato. One doesn't think of oneself as an unintelligent raw potato, one thinks of oneself as a chrysalis that is overdue being a butterfly, but we are not yet a chrysalis but just a little grub. We have to turn this energy onto ourselves, this is the healing of ourselves.

As we are we just try to make ourselves logical . . .

QUESTION: During the past months, from time to time I have made an attempt to recognize where I was in relation to what I recall of myself when I am here. A handful of impressions have come out of that, sometimes a sense of affinity with myself here and sometimes a sense of distance. One thing that is very different in my usual state out in life from my state here is that there is much more tension in life. It is grounded in fear and anxiety and that prevents more moments of a certain clarity which seem to occur more here—more lucidity and less tension. That tension somehow also seems related to a difficulty I have in opening to other people. There is a fear of other people which seems like a big obstacle.

LORD PENTLAND: Obstacle to what?

QUESTIONER: To returning more frequently to a more centered clear place.

LORD PENTLAND: You see our work here is very much the same as our work in life. The only thing that exists here, sometimes, is the whole idea of the place as a sort of lightning conductor to help us receive influences from above, rather than ordinary life, which is trying to adjust without help from above to make its peace. But actually we can't say it is much different between ourselves here and in life. The difference is that we have a teaching that shows how to receive one's inspiration by living from above. That means the idea of consciousness, of awareness.

So all this that goes on in our heads about ourselves when we have learned the lesson that we are here for ourselves—all this takes us in a wrong direction. We categorize our impressions of ourselves and they point us towards a kind of precision, but the direction is different, it is toward being aware of myself, present to myself, aware that I am crazy.

The link to that higher is through the awareness. It isn't a question of wishing for change in one; it is a question of being able to recognize the changes that are going on in you. When you are quiet and watch, that produces changes in the attention. You see you can't conform for long; you want some other change. The idea here is to be more active, more dynamic, in order to follow all the changes that are going on. The idea in coming here is to try to restrain one's subjective desires. Yet when one walks in, one wants to be on a different team. If possible we arrange all that, but then one wants to change oneself, which wouldn't be bad if we had an intelligence, but as we are we just try to make ourselves logical.

But the possibility of wholeness depends on all these parts, and the wish for change represents a sort of surgical operation on one's psyche, leaves us without the necessary elements for love.

The changes that are going on are more beautiful
than the changes we can initiate . . .

QUESTION: I have found it very difficult to distinguish between when I am a coward and when I feel it is necessary to change. In the teaching we are told we cannot do.

LORD PENTLAND: Do you come to some of our classes here? For instance, we had classes of people who tried to make designs without pre-meditation. Although it is very difficult to be quiet enough, one sees that one is able to make more beautiful designs without thinking about it. It means that the changes that are going on, if we can follow them, are more beautiful than the changes we can initiate. One has to allow that extraor-dinary fact to explode inside one. So we need to work at that, because we have been educated differently, and here also, because we are always talk-ing to ourselves in ordinary terms.

So what does it mean to be actively passive, passively active? How just to listen? If listening is the thing you are engaged in, how simply to listen, to be able to listen better, instead of listening to the meaning that is being said. I won't go on, because I know as I am speaking that nobody will try it. We need to be more ambitious to realize the possibility that is actually in us and less ambitious to realize the very stupid suggestions that we are taking in—less ambitious to imitate, more ambitious to realize what is really there.

QUESTIONER: It is the same as the cooked potato.

LORD PENTLAND: The ambition comes when the potato constates it is only a potato and not a fairy princess. Imagine if you woke up tomorrow and found yourself only a cauliflower—you would get busy.

We must oblige ourselves in some way . . .

QUESTION: What can be the basis for a real exchange? I see the ques-tions I bring, even if I don't ask them, are questions about my manifesta-tions. And yet I have sensed recently, and especially tonight, that there is the basis for something very different than that small manifestation I am always wanting to change, and that is why I am here. Maybe I am asking how I can listen for that in myself, because I know sometimes it is there.

LORD PENTLAND: Yes, we need to be more concerned for myself, for I. What happens, how do we lose that in listening or looking at other people in an exchange? We must observe. It is unequal in each person, this appearance of I. There is something corresponding in this exchange and something that is sick, has all sorts of pictures of what the exchange should be and loses itself in these pictures.

Now the trouble is, as soon as we have understood this, we begin to have pictures of what a real world would be. So it means coming back again and again to the appearance, to the presence, of myself here. Because each time we arrive here, we tend to take away with us a picture. In my opinion, we can't speak about it except in terms of pictures. So we have to have an exchange sometimes without words, but when we speak a picture is given.

A picture that might give a right suggestion is that at a certain stage we might change the picture of the work from a school to a war. This effort to be present corresponds to the beating of drums. The work is much more active. At first, it is a work of listening, like a school, but in order to go further it has to be active, to come back all the time to the experience of being present, which is never so easy. It depends on so many things, includes so many things. Finally, it is done as a service, not done in order to get anywhere. It is done because that is what has to be done, because at this stage the source of the work comes from above and no longer from a sort of taking in part-pictures of ideas of what comes from above.

The source comes directly from above. So this effort to come back again and again is absolutely unmotivated from the point of view of ordinary progress, has nothing to do with climbing mountains, crossing oceans, things like that. And there is another thing which it is perhaps not too early to mention, that to have even glimpses of this kind of effort, of course is impossible without some understanding of what real will is, real attention, and how that can lead toward real will, real transformation of oneself. We don't have that, but we have to begin to oblige ourselves in some details.

If you listen attentively to the teaching that is given in various books of

Gurdjieff, you will see that though self-observation of the centers is the main idea, he doesn't make that a narrow idea, and includes the idea that we must oblige ourselves in some way. We can take some tiny detail, some diminutive thing, and say, "Never for the rest of my life will I do that without attention." We can take a kind of example in that sense, in reminding ourselves that we are serious about this and that it is not being done out of fear or guilt, but to reach a stage where the motive comes from above, from higher influences. And this opens up the whole possibility of a school and the right kind of friendships for mutual correction or whatever you call it.

My whole view of the world depends
on how I am now . . .

QUESTION: I have begun to have a question about associations and inner talking, based on having read some data acquired by men who probably are not familiar with higher ideas but who tried some experiment. I have begun to wonder about the constant inner talking, where it comes from and whether or not it is simply a complicated habit perhaps, the way my hands move nervously. What I want to know is whether thinking—associations— is some sort of substitute for dealing with impressions which come to me from my life. I feel if I knew a bit more about that in a simple way I wouldn't be so taken by associations. I might see them in a simpler way.

LORD PENTLAND: I don't understand how this data done by somebody else comes in.

QUESTIONER: I see the data only as thought-provoking in terms of what we are here to discover for ourselves.

LORD PENTLAND: But outerly the question is provoked by somebody else's data.

QUESTIONER: Not altogether.

LORD PENTLAND: Provoked.

QUESTIONER: Yes.

LORD PENTLAND: What is interesting to me is the communication, the relationship between you and these strangers. Somebody is researching and you feel "I am doing that too." And how important is that? Where does that lead? There is an idea that attracted your attention. Out of thousands and thousands of things that are there, that particular research attracted your attention, made you feel, "I am interested in that too." And whether there is an answer to it or not, I don't know. I suppose it depends on you, on him, on me, but how does something like that get into circulation? How does my conception of what living is get affected when I suddenly see what a big part can be played by that kind of communication?

In other words, if one were asked to make a statement about what human life consisted of, one might speak on the literal level that it was eating, sleeping, career, family, getting up, dressing. But what an enormous part is played by ideas, and why is one sensitive to ideas in that way, even from a stranger? It can really be seen that human nature has this psychic side, and one doesn't really accept that in giving account to oneself about one's failure or success in various tasks. One says negative emotions got in the way, as if that were abnormal. For many people the question of living doesn't really include the idea that the psychic side is so important and can be set alight in that kind of way you spoke of.

QUESTIONER: Yes, that is what is missing—no acknowledgement of a higher nature.

LORD PENTLAND: And without that the question of turning thoughts is rather stupid. Without that there is only part of me that questions. If one thinks of crime, that is so much promoted now through the television screen, obviously the people who arrange those programs don't put the psychic side in its real place. Otherwise they wouldn't present all that, or Watergate, for example, as exciting and unusual.

If people understood attention, it wouldn't be so dramatic—the lying that goes on. And yet, as you say, ideas about the whole nature of man, and the way turning thoughts can get in the way of understanding the psyche and the body together, ideas like that communicate very well. But perhaps in the very work of studying them, they become abstracted from the question of myself, as if nothing in my view of the world becomes real except what I experience in myself at the time. It is just because people don't experience the psychic side with the other side that there is this understanding generally, that my whole view of the world depends on how I am now. It is obvious in a way, but it doesn't suggest itself from what you say. It is both obvious and always forgotten.

QUESTION: So why are we so interested in things that really are not interesting—Watergate, crime, and so on?

LORD PENTLAND: It must be because that is my present state. I have read about other states, have experienced other states, but at the moment I am in the state in which if somebody asked me, "What is your life made up of?" I would speak on quite a formatory level. I would bury the fact away from people that I was very negative today or had some special moments of presence. I would speak in a literal way, would say, "I forgot this; I meant to do an errand for my wife, but forgot and she got very angry." This is the sort of way one describes one's day, as if the world were round and made of earth, as if there were no psychic side at all. All we have read about the forces that brought the world into existence, it is not present in me now, so I look at the world in the same old way.

A change in attitude, not to the negative emotion, but to the
sense of identity it creates . . .

QUESTION: There have been times when I have seen that the negative side in me has brought forth a question. Is it possible that it is a less worth-while question?

LORD PENTLAND: I have often said it, but it seems very true today, that in a way there is only one thing that we find difficult about the negative side in relation to our work to be present and that is that we resent our own negativity and so we are sorry for ourselves when we are negative. We cannot of course be present if we regret the state we are in. So I don't think really enough attention is brought to the point. The point is not that negativity is in itself a complete identification, but resenting it is.

QUESTIONER: What is the step past that?

LORD PENTLAND: Isn't that for you to say?

QUESTIONER: I don't know, but it seems that my reaction to negativity most of the time is to resent it.

LORD PENTLAND: So what is the next step? I am taking the position that I don't resent it, so it is for you to say. If everything is mechanical, if there are certain influences and everything that is manifested by us is drawn out of us by these influences, then what is there to be guilty about? If I wish to be present, it means to be present to the forces that are acting on me, and the fact that I was just negative has nothing to do with it.

I am no longer negative; I wish to be present, and you do too. So why not let go of this reservation you have, which is fundamentally a fear you made a fool of yourself, by being negative, in the eyes of God and man. Why not let it go? You wish to understand yourself. Why assume you cannot let go the shame of being negative? One feels caught in that because the reasoning is not good.

There is no connection between one moment and the next. One can contradict oneself quite easily. You know, one feels like this today, tomorrow different—even between two moments. So why does it bother me so much that I was just negative? That moment is past. This moment is the one in which I wish to be present to understand the forces. What is so attractive about going back to that other moment when you were negative? Can you say?

QUESTIONER: I don't feel I have an answer.

LORD PENTLAND: But you must have thought a lot about this before you speak in a group. What makes our attention be attracted back to this impression of being angry, or to the television screen where there is crime?

QUESTIONER: Maybe it is louder than anything else. That touches on the question of identification. In identifying there is a pleasurable feeling; for some reason the association gives pleasure. At the stage where one realizes that one doesn't want to let go of that pleasure, it is unclear whether I am bound to the attitude or what.

LORD PENTLAND: In other words, the question is whether I can feel the shame, the attitude, or whether I feel it as a pleasure. Something has to change in my attitude, not to the negative emotion but to the sense of identity it creates. One listens carefully. I am ashamed of that voice, that way of coming together, but there is a pleasure in it because it is a particular kind of togetherness. In that state there is a feeling of knowing the answers, a pleasure in that.

So the question works out a little bit differently than how we looked at it. The question is, is it a pleasure to me that I carry this idiot with a sense of identity around with me and at any moment he manifests, or is it a shame? It is not so much a question of getting rid of him as my attitude toward him, and this is what can change. As long as Gurdjieff is right, that at twelve for girls and sixteen for boys the mechanism is settled and only an intense work can change it, what could change is the attitude I have toward carrying this idiot with me. Repeated observations would show one that regarding this part as the whole and forgetting the rest is not only a shame, it is not intelligent, not reasonable. I make myself very small if I say I am the idiot. So I need to know it as a part of the whole. Then why is it so attractive to go back to impressions of negativity? That is not attractive.

We reinstate negative emotions into a part of the process of being able to experience myself in the present moment . . .

QUESTION: I find that the body is a help in sorting things out in the way you were speaking. Sometimes I have been able to put my body in a posture in which it becomes obvious immediately that it is a part that is active. I have a question about that now because of what you said. I feel the shame you were speaking of, but also a feeling of freedom. Am I just avoiding something?

LORD PENTLAND: No, I don't think so. What do you mean by the body, exactly? Is it your whole lower self or the sensation? I think you mean your lower self.

QUESTIONER: I am not very clear about that, but I have been in a negative state and the idea has come to me that if I found a certain position it would become clear that this negative thing was a part.

LORD PENTLAND: But the problem is now how would you manage when it is not convenient to put your body in that posture? In the meantime you have a marvelous entree to this secret, but every time we put ourselves in this posture we have to improve our understanding of what takes place, because we may want to use this secret in a particular situation where we are simply not able to be in that posture.

The secret has something to do with coming into the present moment, out of a sort of resentment of how I was in the past. I cannot feel the past except in the present moment, and some postures somehow break this attraction to go over the past. It has something to do with that. If it is just a technique, a superstition that this takes place in such and such a posture, it is no use. The whole point is, is there some connection between me and the change. It is there one has to follow it. It has something to do with coming into the present moment and the present place. In this posture you will see you gradually come into the present place. Without that it hasn't much sense, because the point is that in coming into my present state, my present place and time, I come into it with a very much richer experience of the present—through the fact that I have broken this strong attraction—than I would if I were just living my day passively. The greater the negativity, and attraction to go back to it, by so much the more can I feel the present moment. This is why we work. It has nothing to do with negative emotions except the more electricity the better. And probably something very wise in you is understanding this, and this is why you found this posture. It is not so important to get rid of the one as to come to the other.

So there is a double reason to work, because it would be so rich in impressions if I were present, and if I were present I would be facing the unknown situation. But no instant repeats. And in facing it like that everything that took place would be for observation. So if I am doing something for observation, whatever comes can't be resented.

So the two things come together: the gradual freeing of myself from negative emotions goes with the richer impressions of myself and my environment. If I go into a situation without a preconception of whether so and so will be on time, then I don't resent it if she is late. But if you go in with a preconception that as soon as she arrives we will go somewhere, you become very impatient. Then you become negative. So it is one of those things—it is either double or nothing.

And one begins to see that the subjectivity and tendency towards identification is part of the same ball game, part of the same work as the moment of presence, that they are not in opposition at all except as they are opposite poles. And insofar as we have no individual power but are always being acted upon, these two poles represent the line of our inner movement, and one can't come off that line altogether. On the contrary, we tend, not in any regular way, to move a little bit in one way, a little in the other, and this represents a tremendous understanding when one experiences it.

When one gets into negative states one sees that only through them shall I be reminded to come back, because we have no higher thought that is able to pinpoint our situation, or very little. Most of one's thought is associative, is not directed in a way that would illuminate what my own state is. So it is really only through a movement toward my subjective way of being, it is only in the sense of my coming in touch with those things that obscure my vision that I am enabled to recognize what the opposite direction is, so to speak. It is only through realizing that I am an idiot— that the idiot is the crystallization of the parts around some thoughts, such as thoughts of injustice—it is only through that I am reminded that I am me and that the first step is to separate those parts.

So in a sense we reinstate the idea of negative emotion, which has become profane, into a part of the process of being able to experience myself in the present moment, and then one doesn't so cheaply say to one's friend, "I am negative, don't speak to me." Without that we don't know the way to be present. And in our present state, which is full of leaks, the more force we have the more we are likely to come into the field of our negative emotions—fortunately, because through that we shall come back. Only we shan't come back unless we live carefully, don't get too tired, live moderately. The more force builds up, the least mistake will send one downhill.

To be sincere is also to be quicker . . .

QUESTION: This morning I was sitting for ten minutes trying to be quiet. My cat jumped into my lap. I just continued trying to be quiet. I started to notice there were times when I didn't feel the cat sitting on my lap. She had no weight, no existence because my thoughts were occupied. When my thoughts stopped, I could feel the weight of the animal. I think I already knew this, but it reinforced the idea that my thoughts determine what I see and feel and don't see and feel. For a time that animal didn't even exist for me, and I realized that much of my life is that way. I don't see things, and opportunities and experiences don't exist for me. I feel right now, to some extent, a kind of need for a fresh start. I have a lot of information I can use, but would you suggest the stopping of thoughts as kind of an approach to help me to see what is real for me?

LORD PENTLAND: To be sincere is also to be quicker. You see you need, as you know, to feel your own weight, not the cat's weight. And you would have to say that immediately the cat jumped on you, you knew intuitively you had to put it away, but you weren't quick enough to do that, and I have to recognize that it is no use blaming myself.

It is not a question of my being intentionally slow or lazy but I do tolerate myself living at a speed that gets me cats in my hair, and there is really not much trouble if one acts at once in simply putting things where they belong. This is a particular form of passivity which all of us suffer from and there is no cure for it until one comes into this movement between the two poles of negative subjectivity and the present. When you get into that for a time you are speeded up.

But the way we live—it is said we have to learn sincerity. We not only don't put the cat out at the right moment, but we are so constructed that this error starts a mechanism that will insist on inventing reasons for leaving the cat where it ought not to be.

QUESTIONER: Using the cat as an idea of comfort.

LORD PENTLAND: Worse. You constructed a whole book about the weight of the cat. But the whole point is what is said here: the change we want is a change in I. So in the long run, measurements of cats, though they may have a certain metaphorical use, they don't help. So I feel we caught that one in time. Do you agree, or not?

QUESTIONER: I hope so.

LORD PENTLAND: We are very complicated animals and we have plenty to do understanding ourselves without getting into cats and dogs. What is that? It is the question again: What is that identification, that one sees something should be done at once but one is stuck to a certain plan, almost as if one had foresight, and one finds oneself going from one trouble into the next? One sees very well I should stop. You are ill, you have a fever, you should stay home—but you go out, waste your energy, and you can't stop it. We have to understand what that is. If you can get the taste of that, you can be free. Through knowing the taste you are directed towards something other. It isn't that you don't know, but it is the opposite of being free. You begin to look at that much more freely when you realize it is part of the whole situation. You don't have the sense of being tongue-tied, manacled, going from one idiotic thing to the next.

Everything is impressions . . .

QUESTION: I don't see how it is possible in my everyday life to have this attitude we are speaking about.

LORD PENTLAND: It is very important to understand that, to understand that everything is impressions. How to have this in my everyday life is how to have impressions of my wish in my everyday life. There is no point in saying "I wish." I am stuck in this kind of identification. The question is, can my attention, if there is any free attention, notice something in the direction of my wish? Can there be perceptions of my sensations which will draw my attention toward the sensation of the body rather than toward these events which I am identified with?

And in working in this way, one begins to understand that it is simply a question of the attention being stuck, and it can't be unstuck; you only give yourself another toy, the sensation. If baby wants to play, it will play, but if you are quick you can take the teddy bear away and put something else there. So isn't that what we can do?

Through our work with the sensation we begin to know the kind of tensions which are recognizable, for instance the feeling that one's hand is full of something. Suddenly if one has the impression that one's hand is full of something when it is quite empty, or it can be open but feel it is clasping something, that can bring attention to the body. I only mention it as one of the examples.

But everything will change as soon as the attention is drawn toward an impression of your sensation. After that it will come back again. Instead of being totally identified, you will see that your thoughts are turning. You will see a little more objectively, a little less subjectively, because there is no permanent inertia for attracting my attention to my sensation. So it will mean that you will be looking out again.

Already you feel your shoulders relaxing. And then you begin to come in touch with the instinctive functions. This is a help, because they are much less conditioned. Some of the instinctive functions are less affected by the identification. When you begin to notice your breathing, you begin to think, "This will give me a heart attack," so you begin to calm down. Or you listen and see that you are really quite deaf. Then again it pulls your attention. I don't do anything, but the attention notices the body breathing or listening—the impressions that come from that.

Then it goes back again to the subjective side, this attention that is moving, until I have a sensation of the whole of myself—then there is a new situation. I know which is my head and I know the distance from head to hand. It makes a different situation. But when we are very subjective it is different—we don't know where anything is. So we have this work. Like the first photographic plate being developed, we have it a little bit, then we lose it. It never becomes very precise. At first my presence is a cloud; it can't be clear.

QUESTIONER: It seems this is where you have to be very light and quick.

LORD PENTLAND: One has time to get quicker because you become more inward, because you see the identification less subjectively. And feeling it as a shame—this concerns the feelings and the feelings are faster—speeds it up. You know the speeds—48, 24, 12. For example, a sense of injustice is a mental thing.

I can control myself only through observing, understanding . . .

QUESTION: Recently, the times that put me most into question are the times when there is a conflict between my need to be here and accommodating my life. I see that partly as a question connected with the need to obey what is given here, a call, and yet it is difficult to be here at times. I see that part of that is self-indulgence and part is that in the moment it is more comfortable to say I will do something else. The central question I can't find has to do with the sense of disparity between my sense of the call and the pulls in my life. I sense being in between. It opens up the view of myself out of control, that is, I saw very clearly at one moment on Friday I wished to come here and thought, I will. In the next moment I agreed to do something else—in the same moment! And I am not sure whether the central thing I need to learn is related to what in me could obey the call to be here, the call to work on myself, or coming to the decision to struggle more with the side of myself that wishes to be comfortable.

LORD PENTLAND: You know I need to understand myself. I need to be sympathetic and understand myself. I can control myself only through observing, understanding. It begins there. There is a kind of call to unity. I don't hear it. If I heard it, there would be this voluntary obedience that interests you. But even here, even now, I don't hear it. On the contrary, I am being swept away by all you are saying and all she is saying. I am listening and imagining. I am away, imagining what it is like when she speeded up on Saturday—all of that. This is being swept away from the possible call to unity which is what I am here for. What I am wishing, in a way, is that I would have this voluntary obedience in myself so that I would be all the time listening to myself, not carried away by myself, able to control myself, to stop myself and so forth. I may have some information about how this movement towards unity appears. A certain rhythm is necessary, a certain tempo, a certain time of day, a certain posture; even perhaps, in certain conditions, in certain groups of people, it comes about that I experience it more. Even with certain groups of people, in spite of all they do to distract me with their questions, their voices, their faces, even there I may feel myself being called together in myself. But then I see that this information, this attempt to find something, becomes too intellectual. I become taken by the memories of such and such a movement or such and such a rhythm that was felt all over the body, but even so it has migrated up to the head. In any case, I know that this obedience can't be something which just appears out of the blue, that the call to which it will be an obedience is something which I have to come into contact with by a work—a work to come out of my dreams, a work against my willfulness, against the taste of subjectivity which wants to dream.

What is very important is that I justify this dreaming. When I do have an observation of it and of being carried away, that moment is associated in my mind with this meeting place or the movements or the group or my family. The dreaming becomes justified by all of that. The observation produces a certain reaction which connects me with the particular circumstances related to that and which, in fact, represent the resistance to my wish for unity. But in the moment of observation there is a freedom and then all of this resistance comes up. The people are the resistance. The movements, in the sense that I want to dance them, are the resistance, etc. And all of that comes up. This is what it means that we see things upside down, and I start to base my work on all of that which, in fact, is the resistance to my wish. I don't know whether anybody agrees with me. I doubt it. All of that is below the surface. The resistance lives below the surface. I take the resistance to be the ego or something, but I don't see it. The resistance only comes up at a moment of freedom when I have this observation, and then I react to that. You understand?

fifteen

Whereas we need confidence to work, confidence seems to
be given with the results of work . . .

QUESTION: I have been working in the movements hall this past week. It has been late and hard work, with a lot of disappointments and interruptions, and towards the end of the week I was really tired. I was able to study energies because of that, the highs and lows. Towards the end of the week, a lot of things were going wrong and I reached a state where I was just too tired to be tired. I seemed to move more into my moving center. If I could just get my body to move across the room towards something that had to be done, it would just go, and this seemed very right in a way. I don't know what the question is, but I keep leaning towards application. I got there. What can I use it for, and to get to that place do I have to go through a week of what I did?

LORD PENTLAND: It was a very exciting effort that some people were making for the past week. If the experience that we are looking for is given, given from above, something that we reach when, you might say, we drink from the waters of remembering, it seems to descend on one. And the main thing about it is that it gives me a certain confidence, a sense of certainty, a sense of less doubt, less negativity.

It is a curious situation because this sense of certainty is very desirable and even seems necessary in order to work towards the experience, but in the sense that this is part of the experience itself, the situation sometimes seems hopeless. Can you follow me so far? What we need more than anything in our work is a kind of confidence, but one difficulty is that my ordinary state is one of self-doubt and no confidence. So whereas we need confidence to work, confidence seems to be given with the results of work. So it is a sort of circular thing. We find the approach to work very difficult.

Now all of that is something that one forgets when one is in a better state, but the difficulty is not so much to put oneself through the various motions and carry out the actual efforts you have to do there. The difficulty is the approach to work. And then suddenly you find that you have this overview. You have this sense of being more conscious, an overview of yourself. What we must try and try and try is to remember then to have the impression, to have the taste of it. Otherwise we remember it by associating it with all the literal efforts we made. What we need is to associate it with the taste. Can you understand? Otherwise we associate it with all the motions we went through, many of which are unnecessary. For instance, I suppose many stories are told about the search. It is put in the form of folktales, myths and legends as if it were like a journey up a mountain. And this is like all the work you did there. Suddenly you get to the top and there is an overview of the whole thing, or you get to the top and there is a view of the valley on the other side of the mountain. Unfortunately, we tend to think of the work as climbing mountains. We don't think of it enough in terms of the taste, which is relatively absolute, of an overview. You follow? Try to remember that. Once you have had that taste, it should be enough to be able to give up doing projects that keep you up all night.

So the legend I like is about the two birds who are talking. One of them is saying, "I want to know how to have this beautiful view of the top," and the other says, "You just fly up on this mountain and then you see everything." And then another bird comes along and says, "There is a much quicker way—you fly through the mountain." To my mind, the real legend is not about the journey to the top of the mountain; it is about the journey through the mountain. Certainly it takes more than one turn of the spiral before one can fix this taste, but it is all the time a question of whether you associate this with a certain sensation of yourself, and a certain feeling of its sacredness, or whether you associate it with the people you worked with, the long hours, the lack of sleep. And one day you will see which is the way you will tell this experience to others—whether the emphasis is on inflicting all these things on them or on bringing them this taste.

*First of all I have to be quiet. I have to allow
something to take place . . .*

QUESTION: Lately I have been feeling what I call an ambiguity in myself—this tug-of-war—between that part of me that wants very much to be in the work and have the work in me, as it is said, and the part that forgets the work. Often I forget all about applying the work ideas and principles in a particular situation and it is only afterwards I remember about them and feel a sort of remorse because I forgot. The other day I was speaking with an older woman who has been in the work for many years and I could see that the work was really within her. I can't say that about myself, and I saw for the first time how desperately I want that, but sometimes I feel so helpless.

LORD PENTLAND: Yes, that's very interesting what you say. Of course, it would be useful to have the work in my pocket, but is that possible? And what is my relationship to the work?

I was looking at the book of the lectures we had last year. I think it is beautifully done, and as I was looking at the first page and the acknowledgments, it really said that I would like to acknowledge my gratitude to God for providing all this for study. Then I looked again and it wasn't there. Sometimes one recognizes that there is an impudence in us that we don't recognize as impudence—"I would like to acknowledge my thanks to God for making this possible and to my editor for editing"—which means that a certain process of dissolution of this personal, egoistic way of looking at things has to take place. Therefore, for me "to be in the work," or "the work to be in me" would be something I wouldn't say quite like that. In a way everything is in me. It depends what sort of knowledge you have of that word "me." It all can be me, but first of all I have to be very quiet. I have to allow something to take place which, as you put it, is a tug-of-war. Do you experience this strongly now, or were you just talking?

QUESTIONER: I experience it right now, but it's never as strong as when I am here.

LORD PENTLAND: What is important for all of us is the way of taking what happens. Do I constate what happens or am I trying to make something happen? There is a big difference. When you sit in the morning, perhaps nothing happens. Are you content? Are you able to sit there if watching is all you can do? There is a big difference between being quiet and this egoistic point of view that thinks it can remember, that thinks it can work.

What is our starting attitude when we sit down? What has to happen so that I am content to constate what happens and what brings it together? If I am very quiet, there is an awareness of my sensation, and the same evening I will say, "I have been working on sensation." It was simply that having been quiet for fifteen minutes, my sensation became something I noticed. There is a big difference between saying, "I have got the work on sensation," and an attitude that, "a certain sensation began to appear in me"—completely different. We need to work so that the thinking center is most present in the moment I am quiet. I have sensations. I am sitting very still. Now it notices that I am breathing; evidently there is a connection there. This is not the same as the average person who says, "I want to work on sensation." It is a completely different game. You are called to work, you are called to play.

Now, you want to work again. Are you going to start by saying, "I will remember what was just said and then I will get to work," or are you going to start by saying, "All that is useless, let me just notice what is going on"? I see there is a tension in my throat, in my eyes, there are the remains of some waste emotion that make me feel inferior. What I am noticing is all related. As soon as I make my head notice, a step towards more unity takes place.

Most important perhaps is the relationship between the head and the body, but this only appears after quite a long practice of work, both in years of experience and in time elapsed after I start to work. The head prefers not to put its attention on the body, which to it seems limited and not always beautiful. Work contradicts some of the head's pet ideas. The body also doesn't cooperate; it wishes to indulge itself. All of that dulls the mind to the sensitivity needed to connect it with the body. So this connection involves a certain reduction in the animal requirements of the body. If the body and the head want to team together, there are various conditions that have to exist in each.

Only a very lean body is going to support a mind that is sensitive, subtle enough to be in touch with the body. We in general don't take a lot of exercise because of what Gurdjieff said about sports. Even jogging is inclined towards the mechanicalness of the ego. At the same time, any sort of grossness of body is going to affect the speed and clarity of the mind needed to make the connection. Just because sport feeds the ego, we can't ignore that the body needs some rest and some training. It's the same with the head. The ego grows if we allow the head to be demanding, and most of us live in the head most of the time. Nevertheless, we need to give the head its proper value and realize a thought is needed to connect the various things that are going on in the moment—to take a step towards the unity we want.

QUESTION: I feel this need to be trying things. Every day I have to be trying something and sometimes it seems helpful and at the same time it seems like I am trying to pry something open.

LORD PENTLAND: It seems to me the freedom which I need is not so much to be used up in trying things as in finding some sort of encouraging relationship with somebody else or something deeper in myself which will enable me, while trying these things, to remember why I am trying them. I am constantly trying things, but I forget what the grounds are for trying them, so if I come up with a result, it is not measured against anything. This trying comes from a kind of wish that wants life to be more stimulating, not a wish just to observe life as it goes by.

There are times when I want to make my life richer. Then I need a companion, a friend in myself who will help me remember how to contemplate this or how to try that. Without this companion I try this or that, but I get obstinate and I am going to try in the same way again. What I need is the ability to hear what comes to me alongside myself, as it were, rather than what comes to me either from above or below. It is not so much that I need to follow or be obedient or even to be pushed. I don't have a strong enough will to carry out the instructions I do receive within myself; I know that I need to call somebody or get up early, but I don't always do it. It seems I need a companion.

I am not so unsubtle as I make out. I do receive psychic messages. It's because I have a very weak will that I regard myself as inferior. I don't think the problem is quite so obvious as most of the textbooks make out.

So what kind of help do I need? I know that if I am on the highway and stalled it is very cozy if someone comes along and offers to push my car, but it is still better if they give me some gas and get me going on my own. It is not much use having a lot of people to work for you or agreeing to be helpful; we need something in the middle. There is something about our relationship in the group that needs to be both separate and enjoined. What we need is this ability to give my attention rather than to be actually joined. I have to come right in the middle. I need encouragement and I need a feeling that it is really true that if I don't live today, I will miss a whole day.

sixteen

What is progress? . . .

QUESTION: I was reading, because it had been given as an exercise, and I had the impression that I wasn't actually reading but dreaming. The reading was a sort of background music for my associations. When I saw that, I tried to be present, to be able to say, "I am reading." I saw that it was something quite beyond my capacity to do. And I had a sense of what "man cannot do" means, in that impression.

I was doing it, as far as I know, because it had been suggested and because I had managed to see interesting things from it in the past. But what the content of the observation was, something about the difficulty of obedience, even in such a simple idea as to read—I saw I really wasn't reading.

It seems, somehow, that that's where I am now—the question of obedience and the balance between what is to be obeyed and what obeys. For example, if one doesn't have enough wisdom in what one attempts, then in failing to be able to do it, one becomes discouraged and thinks that it's useless to try any more. On the other hand, if one has too much emotion about what one attempts, then perhaps one succeeds but the wisdom itself is weaker, and instead of attempting out of a more pure place, one attempts for a specific result one has had in the past. So, from those two sides, if there's an imbalance in either direction, something is wasted.

LORD PENTLAND: Are you trying to find a theory that will show a way towards progress, so to speak?

QUESTIONER: Yes.

LORDPENTLAND: Yes, I thought so. What is progress? Why progress? Because what we regard as progress is to be in touch with a theory which explains and shows what I am, not a theory that shows how I could be better. There's quite a big difference. You see what I mean? You have an interest in finding, with your mind, a theory that will communicate with yourself and so make you better. Is that right?

QUESTIONER: Yes.

LORD PENTLAND: Well, we're not looking for that. We're looking for a theory that will communicate with myself and so show me what I am—with all the warts. Yes?

QUESTIONER: Yes.

LORD PENTLAND: So you have to work, first of all, of course, to get a wider acquaintanceship with myself and then, at some point, to accept my acquaintanceship for what it is and discover in that some kind of structure, some kind of axiom. Yes? So we're speaking about a widening of the view and an acceptance and you're speaking about a widening of the view and nonacceptance. Yes?

There's quite a big difference. You see what I mean? I will not accept this that I am. I, potentially, let's say, have wings and until those wings are grown, I will not be a man. We're saying, I seem all the time to want to have wings, but since observation shows I don't have them, I have to make more and wider observations in order to show that I don't have them and convince myself that I don't have them. Yes?

QUESTIONER: Something keeps saying . . .

LORD PENTLAND: Quite a difference.

QUESTIONER: Is it possible—there might be things I don't have that I have the possibility of having.

LORD PENTLAND: That's why I say one has to make wider observations to make quite sure. Yes? Make quite sure. It's always possible that somebody will come with a little piece of something in colored paper on your next birthday and say, "Here are your wings." But, you follow, one has to be quite sure before one accepts the situation.

But time is going on. We're told that this kind of thing is settled by the age of, you know, three, four, five—in any case, in adolescence. And we still haven't accepted that there aren't new developments around the corner. So this is delaying the possibility of an overview of myself which can be reduced to words, reduced to, as we put it, consciousness—whatever that means. It needs to be able to be put in words.

A kind of quiet that we receive rather than create or make . . .

QUESTION: When I could, I tried the reading exercise that was given and I found that if I read, if I tried to read a work book, that something in me thought, "This is a work book so I should try and pay attention." But if I picked up a science fiction book, then I thought, "Well, I'm going to read and relax now." And I felt in myself that there was a resistance to wanting to pay attention. The question of what you said about success touched me last time and I don't know if it's related to the reading exercise but I felt after that I'm always trying to do something.

LORD PENTLAND: I think you'll understand more if perhaps we wait, before answering you, for somebody else to speak who tried the exercise. Yes? Please.

QUESTION: I tried the reading exercise and mostly I tried it with things I read supposedly for pleasure. I read a lot of detective stories. I mean I've read hundreds probably—this week was the first one I ever knew "who did it," because I found that I skipped maybe twenty percent out of habit. I went to the museum yesterday and I found I do the same thing with what I choose to look at and not look at. I had a completely different experience.

I've had quite a different experience of my life in general just from noticing that same sort of skipping constantly, without realizing that I do it.

LORD PENTLAND: Yes.

QUESTIONER: One other thing I noticed is that there were places where I felt that I would go back. Even when I went back, I couldn't understand. And sometimes it was not only my attention at the moment but it was like I had missed something way, way back where there was some knowledge of certain things that I didn't have.

LORD PENTLAND: The question that arises as you're speaking, what interests me, is what is that particular attitude which you found in which this observation of your attention while reading became possible? There is a particular quiet, a kind of quiet that we receive rather than create or make, which makes that kind of observation of myself possible. And you may have some other way of describing it but it's a universal experience and, without knowing it, I think we are all looking for that, both in our inner and our outer relationships. We pick up sometimes the outer covering of that as if that was what we were looking for, but in fact what we are looking for is a particular kind of quiet, a sort of injection of some kind of bliss, in a small way, that we get when something is going on like you're speaking of.

And as you speak of it, it makes me ask myself, what about now? Why am I speaking about being quiet without beginning to wonder, to search for what is that particular grace—if you like, quiet—which makes this observation of the inward movements in me so simple? Do you see what I mean? Or not?

QUESTIONER: I think so.

LORD PENTLAND: Yes. Because if we skip that step, we can get results such as were just reported on by the first speaker. Not that these results are confined to him; they could have been mine or yours, except that you happened to be able to find this, what I call, state of quiet. Yes?

And you see that in choosing, or imagining we choose the events of our lives, that it, in a way, begins from wishing for that quiet, but we end up by choosing from all sorts of other reasons. So that on the whole our lives are very parched. And this quiet, it comes from above; it's like rain, sort of. It's what we're all wanting and it makes it possible to improve the work of the attention.

Did anybody else try?

QUESTION: I tried the exercise once on the evening that you spoke and I found myself trying to read a historical novel. I was only going to read a part of it, and I was completely swallowed by it and finished it at two o'clock that morning. I couldn't put it down. And then I wasn't reminded to try again until before I came to the meeting tonight. I couldn't say I really discovered anything. I just picked up anything—it happened to be Winnie the Pooh—and I found myself trying to look for these secret meanings in everything that I read, like I couldn't just read it, just the words.

LORD PENTLAND: Yes, what I just said is important for you. You have to fail until you can create some space, create this quiet in which to do the reading exercise. And there is no doubt whatever in my mind that unless you hurry up to make this space, to create for yourself this quiet, then when it does arise in your life, if you haven't learned enough about it to create it for yourself, you will grasp at it in whatever framework it arises. If it's an object, or a man, or a book—not understanding how this quiet arises, you will want to possess the book or the man or the object. Does everybody understand what I am saying? Yes. Do you follow me? In order to possess this quiet.

QUESTION: I found that the less interest I had in the material, the more moments there were of seeing the lapses in my attention. The quiet you speak of, how does this relate to the interest in the material? Where there is less interest there are more moments of seeing the lapses of attention, and is this sort of quiet a moment in which you can see those lapses?

LORD PENTLAND: It depends on where I am in myself as to where I have to go to find this quiet. I have to begin from where I am. But the attention works, it seems to me, according to the degree of my actual commitment, like this prisoner or whatever who threw the note through the hole in the wall. The attention does work better for the states and people in which I'm more invested in this work. It works when I have my back to the wall better than when the situation gives room for any kind of curiosity to be part of the inquiry. You find that too?

QUESTIONER: Yes, I understand.

LORD PENTLAND: What exactly that implies is, of course, left for us each to work out. But what this means, that I give body, soul and mind, or whatever it is, to living that moment, what in fact that means I have to give up, what dreams I have to give up and so forth, that's all another conversation.

This misunderstanding that one needs a fixed point
from which to observe oneself . . .

QUESTION: I was reading *Views From the Real World* and I came to a sentence that hit me in a new way. I didn't want to read anymore. I just wanted to understand the question and look at my life on the basis of the question—wanting to know what is said, what it really means. Maybe there is something from within that is present to the words, that seeks clarification. I don't know. But it is not the mind. Outwardly there's a stop in the reading—but something has happened, something has come up, evoked by the words.

LORD PENTLAND: Yes, what interests me about what you've said is in this misunderstanding, that obviously is deeply implanted in you, that one needs a sort of fixed point from which to observe oneself. So that you stopped on a certain concept in order to provide a fixed platform, so to speak, from which to look at yourself.

Now the whole, or one of the points, of this exercise was to show us that that way, wherever I am in myself at the moment I stop, I can only get further from myself during the period of stoppage. You follow what I'm saying? And the observation of the way that works, how in going further from myself and going into my head I solve the problem intellectually, is something which each of us needs to pass through again and again, in order to understand how we have come to certain progress which we value in our lives, based on stoppages which caused us to look at ourselves from outside, so to speak, from the intellect, and come to certain conclusions which were rational conclusions and which were not the observed truth. You understand what I mean?

Now we've been in the work a long time and, even during this period in the work, we have added to the confusion in our lives by these kinds of conclusions very much mixed up with work concepts. Wouldn't you say that? Can anybody follow me? Yes—and which need to be dissolved out. Just to come together and hear somebody saying that this is wrong, this is right; this is not useful. We need to dissolve out these conclusions, so to speak, and the patterns which have appeared in our lives as a result of them.

QUESTIONER: The question now is . . .

LORD PENTLAND: The question is now, is how to put the accent more on the way in which it goes on after being stopped and to see that in a way—whatever you call it, the truth or this quiet—it depends upon my not grasping it, trying to possess it. And the stopping comes from trying to grasp it, trying to possess it.

This quiet is the basic idea of self-observation. In other words, I let things happen to me. We're told everything happens; we're not given the corollary which is, all right, let things happen. Do you follow what I mean? We can't let things happen. We choose between the things that we allow to happen and the things that we prevent happening. Of course they go on happening all the same. Everything happens. What we're faced with there, this idea that through things happening we shall understand the laws behind them. The possible control will come from allowing things to happen—not from stopping and looking at things through a telescope from the head. Isn't that right? Can you see that? Yes?

QUESTIONER: Only the thing is, it wasn't the head that was present; it was other parts as well.

LORD PENTLAND: You could say that there needs to be more present. It's true. In order that you see it was just the head. Do you follow what I mean?

QUESTIONER: Yes.

LORD PENTLAND: Yes. You need to have a map in order to see where it is. And therefore it's true, the whole of me has to be present to some extent in order to see that what interests me is really a way of evading the universal law. And therefore I stop to use some formulation in the book or something, to see if with this passport I can evade the forces, the laws that are sweeping over me or sweeping under me or beside me or around me.

The question is to allow these forces to happen in order to observe them. Now that means not to be afraid they're happening. That means to be more relaxed and that means, of course, that I become more emotional. And that means in order not to get stuck, as you so rightly spoke—for all of us it's the same problem, not just you—in order not to get stuck, even though I'm emotional, there needs to be some of this feeling of what I call the quiet, which can keep things from getting out of control when I'm emotional. Because I value that little stream of quiet so much, as long as I'm in touch with it I can let the emotions rise like a wave. As soon as I lose touch with it, I start to struggle with emotionalism—it makes it worse. It gives it more of a hold over me.

The quiet depends more on tempo than on time itself . . .

QUESTION: I feel a kind of violence in myself to want to grasp this quiet moment because I guess I'm not in touch with it.

LORD PENTLAND: That way you lose it. So, as I said already, in order to keep in touch with it, I need to learn more about what is up to me in coming in touch with this. Maybe it's a gift but it requires something of me. It's like the wind, but I have to put up my sails for it. Sometimes that's a lot of work.

If it's got to do with time, it requires firmness to have enough time. One can't be altogether sorry for somebody who is always saying, "I don't have enough time," because after all it requires a little firmness and then one will have enough time. Yes? But I think the quiet depends more on tempo than on time itself—on rhythm and tempo. I don't think it depends on linear time. I think it has a great deal to do with some kind of spiral of time, if you follow what I mean.

seventeen

*Are we going to go for consciousness or are we
going for emotionality?. . .*

QUESTION: What would help me develop real feeling? I found myself
reading an article about people in prison and I noticed that I was removed
from what I was reading but it was interesting—what is experienced in
that situation. I observed that there was very little in me that could appreciate what was occurring and, yet, there was enough interest that I wanted
to have real feeling, appreciation of what that situation really meant. But I
saw that I was removed from it. The question that rose in me was where
could a real feeling come from in me and what would be a direction that
would help me develop my feelings—not a feeling that would be just
identified or a feeling that would be "feeling sorry," but a real feeling of
appreciation?

LORD PENTLAND: It's a good question, everybody's question. At the
same time, it's a rather stupid question. You see that even now you're concerned about developing feeling. Yes? Even now. It was not only at that
time when you observed it, but even now. Yes?

QUESTIONER: Yes.

206

LORD PENTLAND: I might say, are you looking to the awareness with which you saw that or to the concern with which you feel that, as the main avenue, the main approach to real feeling?

QUESTIONER: I think there are both aspects involved in it.

LORD PENTLAND: Yes, that's why I mentioned them both. Which are you looking to? You're saying, "I'm not aware." You're saying, "There are both these things—don't ask me to come down one side of the fence or the other." In other words, let me dream, leave me in peace. And it's that, it's exactly that, which has to be given up: this idea that without differentiating illusion from reality I can come to reality.

All of life has the mixture of dream and awakening and has this mixture of consciousness and concern or passion. Now are we going to go for consciousness or are we going to go for emotionality? You say, very rightly, you want both. You want to be able to be respected and useful, even successful, in the world and you want to have an inner life that is virtuous. For the last you need consciousness and for the first you need to be a warm person, an emotional person, an outgoing person, and so forth. All of this we can have. If, when I'm with you I can be outgoing and when I'm alone I can be virtuous, this is all right. What we can't have is a confusion between these two things, but we don't differentiate illusion from reality.

QUESTIONER: I wouldn't disagree with anything you've said.

LORD PENTLAND: Well then, to the extent that now you're emotional about this, are you looking carefully at this emotion and seeing that really what you are saying is, "I want to be successful at achieving real feeling?" If you're trying to get success in that way, you'll never get it. If you want to have real feeling, you have to try consciousness. You understand? But, as a matter of fact, that does not in any way rule out that I could be a warm person, an emotional person, when required. What it rules out is that at the time I'm being warm, I think I'm being conscious or vice versa. And that's what we do all the time. We sit there for five minutes every morning, or perhaps longer, dreaming. Then we say, "Now I've done my morning exercise."

What has to be given up is the insincerity, something that I already

think I've given up, the little jumble-up of ideas that I make privately—
"He said it was good to be conscious, he said it was good to be a warm person, therefore being warm is a way towards consciousness." That's what I take away from remarks like those that have just been made. But the law is inexorable. Nobody will get enough satisfaction out of life to work on themselves unless they are reasonably emotional with their friends. And nobody will come to inner development unless they recognize that this emotionality is absolutely worthless in the work of attention.

In order to be able to include success in our lives, we have to understand the whole process of failure and success . . .

QUESTION: This morning in pottery, someone showed me a movement and I couldn't—I just could not—get the movement, so I left it and went away and sat for a little while. When I came back and began to throw again from the beginning, I came to the place where that movement was necessary. And this has happened to me before, something just connects. I'm really interested to know—what connects? And why aren't I there to see what connects? I'm really connected with my hands doing the right movement, but it's as though I just arrive there. And I really wish to see the thread that connects—how did I get there?

LORD PENTLAND: Are you saying that you were more present at the moment of satisfaction? It's almost unbelievable.

QUESTIONER: Well, I sensed—I sensed the moment of frustration as strongly as I sensed the connection.

LORD PENTLAND: Are you saying that when the frustration gave way to a feeling of satisfaction, that this was accompanied by a strong feeling of yourself, there, satisfied? Is that what you're saying? Or not? I'm not sure what happened—whether perhaps your birthright was sort of given up for a pot. Yes? It's the process, you understand, that in order to be able to include success in our lives, we have to understand the whole process of failure and success. Without that, the moment of success is the moment, really, of putting all the accent on my most material side. Do you follow what I mean? So it's like going to the very bottom of the ray of creation at that point. This is something everybody has to go through, which is quite unavoidable, but which, in families and even in businesses, everything is done to avoid people going through, because it's felt that there's no return from that.

There is a return from that. So we can allow this success to take us but we mustn't imagine that that is the object of our work here. Our object is to find the whole process and, in order to understand the process, we see it consists of two processes. And one of them comes to a stop at the point that you reached. One of them comes to an ultimate stop. I'm completely satisfied. I've no wish to understand myself because I'm satisfied. So we have to understand that as part of the process, and it can be a great help. Without success we shan't be able to work, do the inner work. But to start with, I think it's a misunderstanding to imagine that that moment is one in which I'm more present.

I think it's quite a question whether, if I do have an instant of presence there, it's not immediately taken up in the euphoria of having for the first time understood some process. Yes? I'd be very interested to know the anthropology of that and what the aboriginal tribes do when for the first time somebody learns to center a pot—whether they throw them in the river or what they do—because probably it's a dangerous moment. The gods have to be propitiated at that point, or something.

Because self-observation, if I am a process, means that I can
follow to some extent what is happening . . .

QUESTION: I was having a very spirited argument with someone and, at one point in the argument, I unleashed something from within myself which was exceedingly sharp and bitter, rather ruthless and clever, but, as if it were a friend, something I knew and recognized. I saw it and there it was. I just let it go. It had always beaten the other one down and won. I was standing there and there it was. But whatever it was, it was recognizable and I found that I was not angry about it, or ashamed about it, but there it was. It was as if I had a space in me where it had been and remained until I needed it. This went on for quite some time and the person I was arguing with didn't even recognize me, but I recognized me in that form.

So it opened a question about the space I have inside of me for things which were useful to me long ago and are still useful to me if what I think I am—perhaps the ego or whatever it is—gets into trouble and wants to be saved. It was like, you know, the knight with the lion; only I was no knight but that was a lion. That's what happened and it's gone now. It's as though I had just put it back in its cage and said "Good boy and that's that for now." It wasn't a shock but almost as if I was visited by a friend. But the whole business was being watched and seen for what it was. And I saw how I keep within me this menagerie, at least this particular one.

LORD PENTLAND: We speak of a wider observation. We're at a point when we understand I need to observe myself more. At the same time there's a part of me that feels ready to go beyond self-observation.

What does it mean that I am a process, for instance? It's no longer possible to excuse that a certain animal pops out on the grounds that it can be put back in place, because self-observation, if I am a process, if my reality is a process, means that I can follow to some extent what is happening and where this springs from. This wider self-observation really means that I am in touch only by fits and starts with a kind of potential self-observation that is permanent. I can't be so easily satisfied with a moment of shattering truth followed by a moment of relative relief. There's something going on all the time and it's the same in those around me.

Now what am I protecting—that also comes in—in unleashing remarks like this? What in myself is being protected against the other one? And why? There's a whole situation begins to open up. What am I defending? What has got out of balance? Is there some idea that I'm defending? Is this what caused the energy to be unleashed in that way? You follow what I mean?

I don't think the idea of the ego is very important. One's dealing with ideas like essence, or the three kinds of energy, or five kinds of energy, or seven centers, however you like, and one's dealing with manifestations and one's dealing with sleep. Where the ego comes in, it's not important. Sometimes in these very fragmentary periods of clear consciousness there may be a small ego or a big ego around, but that doesn't effect what comes through.

There's a kind of new hope appearing, of greatly widening my relationships with others and with nature through understanding myself as a process which exists also in others and in nature. So self-observation becomes something far beyond the psychological sort of stories that can be related to nature by the head, as in the idea of a menagerie or something. All of that is old hat, so to speak, compared to what's at stake.

I'm talking about a kind of microcosm of the whole of nature. And pinpointing the different forms as different animals is child's play compared to what's being spoken about in terms of ocean currents and weather and electronic storms and so forth. You follow what I mean?

My form is the form of a man, not a dragon or a rat. Now we're talking about how this man works. And the dragon works the same way; the rat works the same way; the world works the same way. And we can't expect to more than touch the very tiniest fringes of it. But if we want to go beyond self-observation, we're going to have to see that the self only exists as a composite of energies which is taking a different form, a different "I," at every moment. And to reduce that to terms about an animal that's put in a cage, let out of a cage, is a reduction of an absurd kind. Yes?

There is a danger of technique becoming important in its own right . . .

QUESTION: I have read that there is a way of getting centered, I believe it is in one of the Shiva Sutras in which you sway your body from side to side shifting from one buttock to the other and suddenly you find a position in which you get centered and illuminated.

LORD PENTLAND: Yes.

QUESTIONER: This of course immediately suggested that the exact posture of the body is most important. Would that apply also to our body posture while listening to your answers or while doing any exercise? Should one sort of study what effect happens in which particular posture while doing an exercise or whether the shift of posture changes it? Or, perhaps I should put it, what is the right posture one should adopt when being in the group asking questions and listening to answers?

LORD PENTLAND: Yes. I must say straight off that if we were to rename ourselves the Spiritual College of Science and Technology, I would put that under the heading of technology. All the same I find it important.

I, some years ago, introduced a kind of standing as an exercise in my other groups and in the groups here. I think it's very important to learn to stand; one spends so much time standing. And I was beginning then to try to understand what it means that we are always in movement. And so I introduced this exercise of feeling the weight moving, you know, from one leg to the other. But, of course, one can also do it forwards and backwards. And a very good way is to treat the body as a kind of straight line and make an inverted curve with the head onto the ceiling, do you follow, from a point below. And, of course, you reverse it the other way.

And if you work then repeatedly with that, it seems to me that I come eventually to several conclusions. One is that a very, very tiny movement is necessary in order to satisfy this need to move and satisfy a need for non-restlessness, but that also, gradually, as I come inside myself and try this circular movement, for instance, it does I suppose work this way—it refines the attention. And finally it creates a kind of central place which I want to occupy—which, as soon as I occupy it, becomes static; so one has to start again. But still, it does give one a sort of feeling of being centered, there, you know.

Now, since then I discovered a lot of other tricks and I've tried to pass them on, too. But what interests me now is that it seems that ninety-five percent of the job is done if one can come to a sort of wish for this quiet, if you know what I mean, if one can really be in an attitude that will receive that. And then, probably, not always, one needs to use these techniques. But often, if one's quick enough, they seem to offer themselves out of some higher part or something; they just appear. You know what I mean? The necessary technique comes at once.

So, I don't think it's at all to be sneered at, this kind of work with centering like you spoke about, not at all. But there is a danger of it becoming important in its own right and becoming therefore a kind of technology. And it's a constant danger. Constant danger. It's why we need to be together, because mostly we are very uncompassionate towards others getting lost in their technology. You know what I mean?

CHAPTER SEVENTEEN

It takes some discrimination as to what serves
my aim, and what doesn't . . .

QUESTION: I had a very deep impression of the extent of complete passivity and automatism in trying movements today. I don't know how far I
would have gotten on my own without a demand of that sort, because I
lost contact with the sensation of my body, a rather complete, good feeling, which I had when sitting quietly. Although I lost contact with my
body completely except to know it was jerking around, it still was a very
valuable impression of the difficulty of having it move to an activity. These
functions are lazy, are very lazy. I had a great impression of myself as a
machine, really, with habitual limitations. But how do you relate the effort
of movement to the effort of being centered? There seems to be a tremendous requirement for activity there and I can't relate that to what I know
about a certain kind of good passivity. I really have a hard time relating
those.

LORD PENTLAND: Yes. It takes some discrimination as to what serves
my aim and what doesn't in order to know what's necessary, and through
knowing what's necessary, not to be so taken by the unnecessary, such as
my self-importance. So, in a way we're all the time lacking this ability of
movement, of discrimination, which could serve me towards what is necessary. New impressions are necessary all the time, impressions of myself.
And, as has been said, there's a tendency to want to succeed rather than
get these new impressions, or to have impressions related to some big principle that's being spoken about like the center, rather than to get the
impressions where they can be had.

I see that my laziness is very much connected with not having seen
enough the need for togetherness and for unity, even not having rational-
ized about that enough. So, I'm inclined to value what is novel, or what is
creative and so on, in a scale that doesn't give enough value to the value of
integration and unity. To come to a center, like a central place between A
and B, doesn't necessarily put me in touch with C and D. I may have to
find a pencil and paper or something to remember about E and F—they
just escape me altogether. I forget, because a way of putting everything
together—which is what we're lazy about—is something we've never

been educated in and yet it is, to coin a phrase, the central idea of our work.

So one has to find the way of putting things together as a necessary ploy, rather than take techniques, any particular technique, as a necessary technique. There are no rules. The field is open, as long as I'm really bending towards this task of getting myself together. This is the point of being here and we continually get lost in this or that means—I can ask other people what I've lost, or I can get my notebook, I can jump up and down, or do a craft.

Somewhere we're all learning that in order to come together we need to find a means that touches my body—that actually touches me physically—not always painfully but not necessarily pleasurably. Well, it's getting back to something like that—that nothing is necessary that doesn't involve my body some way. Of course that's an overstatement. I was thinking about letters—are letters necessary? Well, remember what Gurdjieff says in the Third Series about letters. He never answered his letters unless they had a check with three zeros or something. So maybe it's not so far out. Nothing is really necessary that doesn't involve my body because the presence comes from the body, not from the words, not from the head.

eighteen

QUESTION: I have a question about attunement. If I understand you rightly, it's something that I call "informing my parts." And in the work that I've tried, I've caught myself several times acting as though I were conscious and I don't even know what that means exactly. It's a big word. But then when I ask myself what am I conscious of, then it feels rather ingrown or something just having to do with me, a little empty in a way. And so, I ask myself what could I be conscious of. And of course I don't know, but there is a movement then, inside, which tends to become serious and it ends up that I'm quite afraid because what is there to be conscious of? But to turn that into active and useful work is a question.

LORD PENTLAND: I think you have to begin at the beginning. You have to try and trap one impression, reopen the whole question of work— why we work. Then you can move on to attunement. The idea is that the higher entities, the sun, the planets, and so forth, are broadcasting their emanations the whole time, like a television station. And I have to tune in—like to turn the knobs of the television set—in order to get the picture.

You say the pictures you get are all crap; well, but life consists of tuning

215

in to get the picture. That's what attunement means—adjusting myself, so that these perceptive instruments begin to produce a picture—focusing myself. And then these pictures begin to act on me.

You see that, for instance, this morning maybe some vibrations were reaching you telling you that you ought to be working faster, or slower, or more quietly, or in another place. But these reached you in such a way that they didn't represent a call to make any change, they were just in the background. You see what I mean? As if these rays were out of focus. I'm sorry my ideas are so outlandish. Could you understand at all? Then you need to tune in to it and as soon as it's in focus, it produces an action by itself. I can't inform anything. The relationship needs to be established between the various condensers and valves and all these things so that things begin to happen.

Emotional states which present a possible avenue towards unity and those emotional states which don't . . .

QUESTION: Yesterday in pottery we were going to have a small reading at eleven a.m. concerning the subject of art. The moment before it began, someone said, "Wouldn't it be wonderful if there was a possibility of seeing a perfect image in the air which I could then copy?" And this addressed itself actually to what was going to be read. It was an excerpt from Coomeraswamy concerning a possibility of what he calls a divine image within, or a more perfect image, which addresses itself to real art and which is the only way objective art might be moved toward. In any case, as I began to read, I saw that I was reading from the wrong place in myself. Somehow my wish was swallowed by an attitude that didn't permit the reading to be coming from the right place. I would clear my throat in a kind of absurd embarrassment. And this went on. I saw it and I tried to be quiet. But even from the beginning the material had weight. What was being done had nothing.

I felt ashamed that this was occurring and I couldn't stop it. But within my difficulty, or the difficulty that I had created, there was a great question of how what I considered a possibility was lost. And my functions wouldn't follow a kind of demand that I had, and that I had once wished, but were overcome by that kind of personality manifestation.

LORD PENTLAND: We come to a sort of new possibility through the work on sensation, as if it were possible to classify our emotions into those emotional states which—although relatively far—present a possible avenue towards unity and those emotional states which don't. Maybe far back in time, at some meeting or other that's never been recorded, this is what Gurdjieff originally meant when he said negative emotions. I don't know.

It doesn't matter what he said, in a way. The point is that I don't know myself; it means almost I don't know my emotions, because I am so often lost in my emotions. And there seem to be now some unknowns which are possible, or relatively possible, as starting-off points for a gradual work to come to sensation and to unity. Yes? And there are some emotions which I also don't know but which are impossible. Do you follow what I mean? So in that way I get to first base. Because if it's impossible, it means already something in me sees a possibility—but not in the ordinary way; it's not just a question of wishing. There's something deeply divided there.

The difficulty is just to accept this, this totality of my experience . . .

QUESTION: I've been trying to keep myself in view in a light way. Numerous times when I was going to meet a certain person, the thought would cross my mind that very likely my attention would be distracted by this person in some way that I wasn't prepared for. And this usually did happen but I would only realize some time later that I had lost my attention. And I began to get an impression that there were more subtle things going on between people, more subtle transactions between me and other people, than I am in the habit of paying attention to.

For example, in the things that you say, there are ideas that serve as a kind of mine of impressions throughout a week. Now why do they do that? And why is it that they last for a certain amount of time and then a given idea for working becomes less possible in some way? I'm thinking about what you said last week to someone else in this meeting, "How do you see yourself?" That struck me very strongly and in a way was the center of my work for a great deal of the time in the week. I feel now that the energy of that idea is running down; I have some taste that it's not as fresh as it was at the beginning of the week.

I'm trying not to ask the question of how to maintain that so much as to understand the process by which this goes down. For example, with some of the people that I met this week, I had the feeling that they took energy away from me, that I went out too far toward them. Other people, on the other hand, by reacting and by making me react, gave me an opportunity to try to work, or at least to see myself not working in that situation, and those increased my energy. But the net result seems inevitably to be downhill because there are factors, there are people, that I couldn't take into account. I didn't take into account in advance how strong that reaction would be, and therefore I lost something.

LORD PENTLAND: You're mixing up, aren't you, two different possible thought structures, two different thought structures about a possible work. At the end you spoke as if one could prepare in advance for energy situations that are to come. But here we've been speaking as if that's not possible, as if there is not just one process—that in which everything runs down—but two processes in us, one by which everything runs down and one, which is hidden from view usually, in which everything runs up, so to speak. Yes?

QUESTIONER: Yes.

LORD PENTLAND: Well, you see you have to make up your mind which process, which thought structure, to use as a basis for conversation here. If we're trying to work towards this idea of two currents, then the idea that you have to have something ready with which to withstand the downhill current doesn't make any sense. Do you understand what I'm saying? Anybody?

You can't speak like that without bringing evidence to the group of people here that your point of view can cover the actual experiences that we all have. What experience do you have of having been able to, as it were, visualize or materialize in advance a kind of arrangement of energy that will automatically transform whatever influences and forces appear? Do you have any experience of that? If not, then why don't you try to understand this other idea that there is a process by which everything goes downhill? Yes?

But we can make the experience also of being in touch with the other process by which everything goes uphill. And inasmuch as we experience the one, we experience both, because that's what we consist of. And then the difficulty is just to accept this, this totality of my experience. Yes?

So the difficulty is not so much how to stand outside it to prepare for it and so forth, which is what you've been doing, but how to get involved into it. Because what is there to lose? You see? Can you understand any better? No?

I don't want to know the way to the source,
I just want to be there . . .

QUESTION: I have a question about your use of the words "the source of a reaction, the origin of a reaction." I see a reaction, for example, in my job situation, a question of an anxious feeling about how they feel about me, about how well I do my work. And I see this as being connected to an attitude about myself as being very outstanding and spectacular, which of course isn't true.

A proper attitude seems to be that they are not concerned with me as much as concerned with themselves. So that this opinion which I value, their opinion, is an imaginary thing.

When we speak of the source of a reaction, are we speaking of the reactions within myself which are called up by a certain set of external stimuli, or is that combined with what I see to be a source, a deeper source, which is my sense of myself?

My sense of myself inside is a very tenuous, feeling self which knows—something inside knows—that there is not much to stand on. What I can meet that situation with is a sense of myself which is separate from that, which is separate from my body and which is more open and free.

Now, what I see as being that source of the reaction is the fact that I am not in that place which is separate. That is what I see as being the real source. Now, am I on a totally different wavelength from what you've been talking about or . . .

LORD PENTLAND: In a way, in a way you are. Now, it's as if there's a map spread out and we're here in San Francisco and we're saying, well, what's the source of the River Indus or something. And we look at the map and you're saying, the source is there. We're here and I'm there, or we're here and the source is there. Do you follow what I mean? And you are describing, in terms which could be said to be two-dimensional, that the source is there.

I'm saying, what would it be to discover the source? "Oh, I'm at the source of the River Indus; this is what it's like." That's not the same as being on the map and explaining where the source is. I'm saying, what would it be to discover the source of reactions? In other words, as if the discovery of the source of reaction would give me a kind of freedom from traveling. Do you understand what I mean at all? We're not speaking about traveling. I'm speaking about experiencing something. Does anybody understand what I mean?

QUESTIONER: Well, I thought I was, too.

LORD PENTLAND: I'm tired of all this traveling and getting up early in the morning and, you know, getting the pack horse ready and all that kind of thing. I only want to be at the source. I don't want to know the way to the source. I just want to be there, because once I've been there, that's in a way, I feel, what I'm here for. It's one of the things I'm here for—to have come to the source of that stream of life which I call reaction.

And I think that's an indirect way of putting the work—to say you can study and come to understand what is the source of reaction. And so, by the same token, I can't explain what I mean. But I can tell you that there's not a single thing you said which may not be true. But it may be false, too. What you said was an explanation of reactions, as it were, a theory of reactions, so to speak, based on moments of truth, but worked out now in your mind. Do you follow me at all?

QUESTIONER: It's worked out now in my mind but . . .

LORD PENTLAND: Yes.

QUESTIONER: But it came from, as you say, it came from my experience.

LORD PENTLAND: It came from your experience.

QUESTIONER: And at that time I was studying anxiety.

LORD PENTLAND: Right. This is what Gurdjieff means when he says all the travel books are written by people who never traveled. He's speaking about what we speak about, and I speak like you do, I try to explain reactions. But in order to be there, you have to experience at the time and it's quite different. You don't say, "I can explain to you the origin of reactions." But when you're there, you say nothing, you just say, "Oh, ah." You don't need to explain.

So in a way what you're saying is only, as it were, half of the story. Now, we need to continue this work; it won't be done all at once, if it's true that we can only really be through being both these currents. Yes? Do you follow what I mean by this?

QUESTIONER: Yes, I do.

LORD PENTLAND: Then it means that anything which only belongs to one current is questionable, is doubtful it's true. It's only true when we stand in both. Do you follow what I mean? So I'm saying that your explanation may be more or less true but it'll only be true when you stand in the other current as well. And then there's this question of moving the accent from one to the other until you come to such a place that you can say, here is the origin of reactions. Yes?

We're speaking of a higher power whose wishes are on the whole beneficent for me—on the whole . . .

QUESTION: I have a question about distraction. Sometimes it seems that I'm on the verge of understanding something and something comes in—maybe somebody will ask me something, or I'll realize that I'm hungry. I see that I don't know how to be in relation to those distractions. It doesn't seem anymore as if it's a question of simply sticking to what I was doing.

When you speak of the influences coming from the sun and the planets, I wonder about being on this earth with all of these other forms, and I just don't know what my responsibility is. There's something about accepting whatever comes my way that seems right sometimes as an idea, yet I guess

I don't know how to. I find myself just reaching in a way that's not very helpful.

LORD PENTLAND: So it makes me ask myself, is it really part of my experience, quite apart from the beautiful idea of it, that there is a higher energy which may come from the sun or the planets, which is higher, which has effects, which I would wish to collaborate with in me? Is there a higher power that has a wish which is accomplished in the heavens and whose wish I would wish to see accomplished in me? Because that wish cannot not be accomplished, in a way, whether it's what I regard as acceptable or not. You understand, the whole thing goes back to the word God which is the same as the word for good. But we're speaking of a higher power whose wishes are on the whole beneficent for me—on the whole. But we're not equating them with my opinion as to what is good.

So I'm asking myself, do I find it possible to experience, whether on a one-shot basis like a trapper catching a prey or on a more continuous basis to which I, myself, have found the approach, do I find it possible to experience a current of higher energy which perfects me? And am I cooperating with what would be its effects on me, so that its wish should be accomplished in me as it is in the celestial regions? Excuse me, I just want to fill in one thing, the possibility of a fear of misunderstanding about that.

Is it possible that this higher energy—if it's experienced at all, is obviously a dangerous energy; in the sense that it's higher it's more powerful than I am; in the sense that it has a different quality nothing that I've accumulated in quantity can be set against it; it's greater than I am—is it possible for me to relate directly to that energy, as it were on a one-to-one basis, without intermediary, without fear, in order that its wishes should be accomplished in me as well as up above? This is what we're talking about as I understand it.

The adjustment came out of the listening . . .

QUESTION: I have a question about cooperation. This idea is very difficult, very complicated to grasp, in terms of just working every day, coming here to work, you know. Here it's easy from a mental point of view but when one just tries to work with it, something inside shuts up, just closes right up. It's very alarming. Almost nothing can be done. I found myself, today particularly, skimming the surface of this and finding no way to be able to enter myself—on the outside all morning, just nothing seemed to open up—just being carried off with this idea, or that idea, this association or that association, just ordinary things that most of us experience.

And I didn't quite know—I just didn't know—I felt kind of upset at myself, upset with the fact that there didn't even appear to be a need in me to attune, not even a wish to attune, because I was being taken off with all the other things.

In other words, I allow myself, the energy, to be taken up with the task, with the people, the team, and trying to find out what is a way to be in that. I find myself completely taken away from myself inside so I'm not able to balance the two in some sensible way. So this idea of attunement that you spoke about this morning, does it have to do with a level of coop-eration that I'm not aware of? What could that be?

LORD PENTLAND: I've tried with some people the actual work of try-ing to tune our voices—and most of our voices certainly need that work—and what we found helped was to go on trying to tune them while one was singing. You understand what I mean? While trying to make a vowel sound, for instance, to go on adjusting it—to go on adjusting it while one is making the sound.

We started by trying once and then again and then again to try and hit the exact tune of the sound. Then we found that by going on and on try-ing to make the breath for it, gradually the voice got tuned. You see what I mean? Do you hear what I say?

QUESTIONER: I follow what you're saying.

LORD PENTLAND: Yes. Well, I don't see why there would be different laws on the physical level, the psychic level and so forth. So I think that is of interest—that I can report as an experiment that was tried over a period of years—that if you just try and hit the right note, you sometimes go on. If you've got a teaching like we have back of you, you go on trying and trying and repeating and repeating. What we tried was different. We tried to keep a note going and as it was being sung, to adjust it, to listen to it, and the adjustment came out of the listening to it. And again, and again, there was a sort of refinement process going on. That's what I call attunement. You understand what I mean?

QUESTIONER: I think I got the point.

LORD PENTLAND: Yes. We're talking about something that's been the subject of relatively little research, and that chiefly among saints. So we can't expect to sort of move along at a great pace, but we can bring our results like that. And if you could try that way this afternoon—maybe not today but maybe one day—you'll have your own contribution to make.

What I'm drawing attention to is that, whereas we tried again and again—starting again and again—the idea was suggested, which sounds so simple, just to keep going and adjust it as you go along. But where we'd be if I hadn't brought that idea—where we'd be today—I don't know. That was the key to what was being tried. And this is the kind of knowledge that I'm interested in sharing.

nineteen

We must look at things from the point of view of possible unity . . .

QUESTION: I'm in a place right now where I'm feeling rather confused about my relation to the activities here. In one regard the work has not ever seemed so immediate and meaningful to me, and in another way it seems that often I come out of a kind of considering. I don't want people to be angry with me, or I don't want them to think badly of me, or I want "to be good," or I feel greedy and I don't want to miss anything that I might miss, or occasionally out of the sense of wanting to pay for something. And I don't really know how to work with what I'm experiencing in terms of my way of coming into what's happening here.

LORD PENTLAND: Perhaps we could say that things are always changing and new rearrangements take place, so that the question arises now for you in a new way about how to be about coming here. And you really feel lost about it. In fact, of course, we could assume that again we must look at things from the point of view of possible unity. Growth would mean growth towards a possible unity. So, we can't understand ourselves very much. But, you see, at least it's a good sign that you find yourself actually asking about the main question of why you're here when you're here. This is like a kind of unity—that you're not asking about something else.

225

You're asking about now, here, and you're asking it now, here. So this makes me feel that perhaps you're on a good base in your questioning.

You see that the work is about that relationship between you and the work. And you're asking about that. And that's what the work's about. The work is not so much about whether you're afraid and if you run for cover. Growth is about the gradual turning towards these direct relationships—for instance, between me and the work. That is the possible way towards unity—when you are here that you are wondering how your attitude is towards here. Whether your attitude is what it should be depends upon some little bird in your head that has been told what it ought to be. You follow? But the fact that you are questioning what it should be doesn't depend upon that. It depends on the directness of your relationship. And my ability to respond to you depends upon the directness of my relationship to the work. You understand?

If I run for cover, if I try to shoot at the side and so forth, that also means, now we're facing each other, the unity will depend upon not so much our formation and the way in detail we react to each other, as on our returning again and again to this possible relationship. Yes? Because out of this confrontation, we are told, a third, neutralizing principle can sometimes come to make for unity. So if growth is a process, we can say it depends on this wish for unity and that manifests itself through a more and more direct—is that intelligible, direct?—a more and more sincere confrontation in the various activities.

We don't understand how easily different forces can act through the same vehicles. For instance, we can be facing each other. It's not often that a force relates us in such a way that there's a real exchange. You understand what I mean? And it doesn't need to be always. We have to recognize that it can't be always. But it's absolutely necessary for our growth. So far as growth is in our lives, this direct relationship is the only way because it's only towards unity that real growth takes place.

Growth is not a matter of giving up smoking or something like that. It's a matter of the relationship between me and the cigarette. You can say that cigarettes are harmful. You can say, "Ask a woman for advice and then do the opposite." All these things are true. But as far as growth is concerned, "Ask a woman for advice and do the opposite" is no good. It won't produce growth. It may produce good advice. Do you understand what I mean? Giving up cigarettes may be good for your health, but it won't produce growth—necessarily. Do you follow what I mean? These forces are working. It's so obvious though. Yes?

QUESTIONER: Yes, I know it's so obvious and yet I . . .

LORD PENTLAND: You see now. It's quite obvious, yes?

QUESTIONER: It's only obvious when you say it.

LORD PENTLAND: Yes, but as long as you hear it. As long as you see it. No need to harp on it.

*That which I am identified with is
the unconscious . . .*

QUESTION: On my last visit here five years ago I asked you a question about fear. I did not fully understand your answer. You ended it by telling me that it's obviously something I will have to see myself, first. But I have since tried to observe whether there is any fear in me and, apart from obvious situations of physical danger, I can't say that I have found any. But it does seem to be spoken about in our groups in Australia. It was spoken about yesterday. You have spoken about it today. So obviously it's something that ought to exist, so to speak. Am I abnormal in this way? If it is an abnormality, is there anything I can do about it?

LORD PENTLAND: Are you afraid you are abnormal?

QUESTIONER: Well, I don't know whether or not I've experienced fear other than the ordinary physical fear. So I would like to know whether it's something to be sorry about or proud of or just indifferent. I don't know.

LORD PENTLAND: It could be related to what seems to have been a kind of theme tonight, and that is process. You know I mean by that the emotional process also. Yes? And do you experience the release of tension when you sit quietly, when you come in touch, when you try to come in touch with the wish, there is a kind of tension that gets in the way and it is released? I don't release it but to some extent, up to the point it goes— it is released. I can't say I do that.

Now, what would be necessary for you would be—and it all comes back very quickly—to try to observe how it comes back. Yes? Because I was just saying we have to begin at the beginning every time and that's because these tensions that have been dissolved, that enabled me to open to a wish that can connect all the parts and come in touch with an energy of a higher level in me—as soon as a certain action ceases, the tensions begin to come back, not absolutely instantaneously but very quickly. It could be interesting for you to try again and again after sitting quietly to see sometimes what it is that brings them back. For instance, in a cold climate—you'll be going back to a cold climate—you'll perhaps sit in the morning someday and the point comes when you've finished, you have to go out. Is it like that? Sometimes. You put a coat on?

QUESTIONER: Not usually.

LORD PENTLAND: Not usually. Is it ever cold enough for that? Yes. And you put it on. Would you say from memory—it's not good to speak from memory, of course you understand that, but speaking now from memory—would you say that in putting the coat on, in opening the door where there's a big, blustering, cold wind, have you ever felt tension in your body and sort of fear the cold?

QUESTIONER: Well, I didn't call it fear but perhaps what you are describing could be called fear for me.

LORD PENTLAND: Connected with a tension. And I don't think it matters what I call things. But is it not fear? Is it not your body defending, being defensive, putting up defenses? Yes?

QUESTIONER: Yes, I can see what you . . . Yes.

LORD PENTLAND: Yes. Maybe you could look at it as an example, but there'll be other examples. Yes? Then also we should approach the question from the other side which is that in order to understand myself, I need to know myself as a process, a very complex process. And certainly it's unlikely that I'm quite abnormal; therefore probably there's fear there, as something that arises and goes away, not as something of a sort of offensive label which you've put on somebody—that he's a coward—but simply as part of the process. It's a very, very important question that you've touched on there and I think what's important is that to some extent you were open enough to want to know the answer. To some extent you would still ask out of curiosity, so to speak—why am I told about fear?—but to some extent you begin to suspect that there is fear. Is that true?

QUESTIONER: Yes, I'd say that's true. And what sometimes annoys me, if I can use that word, it makes me angry if I can't see it. Other people speak about a similar situation which I've experienced but I don't somehow call it fear, what I see in myself in a similar situation. This annoys me to be—how shall I put it?—to be perhaps unable to observe. It seems to me I ought to observe the same as anybody else.

LORD PENTLAND: Right, you can't. You see, it's like all these things, I don't want to labor them. It's obvious. But that which I'm identified with is the unconscious. So if I don't see my fear, if the fear is in the unconscious, it's because I'm identified with it. Yes? So the question is one of freeing myself. Yes? You don't want to take what I say just because we've been friendly, or you respect what I say or something. You must examine this. You will be opening up something which is called fear.

So you will be opening up another level, another stratum in my being. This is not going to make life jollier—if it's part of the way towards a more complete life—but you don't need to open it up. If you want to have life on a certain basis—you follow what I mean—you could say, "I'm not going to experience fear; I'm going to recognize, though, that it exists, but I'm going to rely on myself to be identified with it." Now, can you separate yourself from the universal process to that extent? You follow what I mean? Can you plant your flag down and say, "This is what I'm going to be?" Or do you want to open to the full process? This is the question.

QUESTIONER: Yes, I can see that.

LORD PENTLAND: Yes. That's all.

Work is not any particular functioning . . .

QUESTION: Yesterday you spoke about attunement. I found very strong emotional reaction to it all through the day and it stayed with me this morning. I vaguely remember, sometimes, about the possibility of getting things to do that may not be the ones we would be looking for. If we're attuned, we're in a certain environment, what's needed at the moment? And something needed at the moment may not be what I would normally select to participate in or do, but that seeing is what's needed.

LORD PENTLAND: Yes, I think that's right.

QUESTIONER: I had an experience today where I still had this with me, where a demand was made of me that normally I probably would have shaken off and passed it on to somebody else, and I accepted it. I find that I have taken work in a very personal way, digging around inside myself, almost too preoccupied there without letting in what's around me. And, although I want to live and be more impersonal about myself and other things, I have a question here. It's a "how to" question: How to work so as to understand what's needed of me?

LORD PENTLAND: Yes. It's very important to realize that work is a process, that work is not in any particular functioning, that all functioning is up and down, and the work towards the eternal can't be up and down. The work is a process but not an up-and-down process. Growth is not just up and down. Upstairs, downstairs—that's not growth. Functioning, yes, but not growth. So it's very important to connect the experience that we have, as little as it is, of approaching the wish, to this idea of the process. It's very, very important to see that even if I don't grow on the level of my life, there is an experience I can have—in quiet conditions or reading—of the process of growth. Then it's through understanding that, in minute circumstances, that I may hope to, as it were, educate my wishing, educate my approach to work, so that gradually the possibility of a more perma- nent change appears.

So we are all the time faced with this idea that work is a process and what is very, very difficult—even more difficult than one would sup- pose, and that comes even before understanding that it's not just a linear process—is that it always has to begin at the beginning, that every time we take up the work we have to begin at the beginning. It's not possible to go on from where we left it. So in that way I would say it has to begin with the personal. And, of course, it reaches towards something impersonal. But if we start with impersonal, we come up against the fear, the barrier of fear. We are bound to. Therefore, the whole point is this personal relation-ship—we spoke about that at the beginning—it begins there in different parts of myself or between people. It cannot begin from the community. It begins from the family unit, one can say, symbolically and actually.

So, what is that which I call the "family unit," which makes it possible for me to approach the higher, directly—without apologies, without a lot of preparation? That's a good question. Something simple—yes—often can be much the quickest. So we say, when I start to work I try to come into my present situation, directly. You can't begin from the highest, from some highfaluting kind of idea, abstraction. It won't work. You would have a ladder, you would have to begin with the first step, first rung. You understand? But it's a permanent principle—before we begin with the first rung—only when you've mastered the whole ladder, sort of, up and down, then the level of being changes. That's an enormous thing. Yes? But for us it's a question of being able to get up to where we are—from the beginning, every time. That's obligatory.

Real feeling is impersonal . . .

QUESTION: I want to try to understand your use of the terms "personal" and "impersonal." In my own experience, sometimes when I'm here, I'm in the midst of reactions, "considering," particularly toward people who are older in the work, but also toward other people. And sometimes I'm more or less aware of that. Other times those processes are a little weaker in me or there seems to be a little separation. Sometimes, rather rarely, they seem entirely absent. Somewhere between those two extremes just now, there's even a little considering about speaking out, but not so strong as other times that I recall. I wonder if that graduated scale is related at all to the terms "personal" and "impersonal" that you used a little while ago.

LORD PENTLAND: Yes, of course, there's relativity in everything but it takes very extreme positions in this case. We say, for instance, that the highest level of energy that I can experience, and we say that—and you call it God—that That is in me, that That is available to me at any moment. Yes? And we say at the same time that that That is what oper-ates the entire universe. So you can say it's relativity, but according to

Gurdjieff several levels are there in-between. So it's not the sort of relativity that you find on the string of a banjo or something like that. Is that to your point?

QUESTIONER: Not quite, I don't think. I'm wondering if I'm connecting at all with that shift from personal to impersonal that you referred to, or if that's something quite different from the experience that I've related to you.

LORD PENTLAND: Real feeling is impersonal. It comes from very high in the scale and it connects everything together. The story which I've several times used the last couple of weeks to illustrate that is the story of Brahma. He's supposed to be the absolute god in India, and he was taking a nap one day when a very high Brahman—it comes from Brahma, Brahman, it's the highest caste—came with a little child, his son that had died, and said, "Look, Lord Brahma, this first-born son has died. There's something gone wrong down on the earth. You shouldn't have allowed that. Would you look into it?" So Brahma had to get up and dress and so forth and went down to earth and discovered that there was this temple. And a Sudra—that means the lowest caste, untouchable caste—had been affected by some very deep wish and had found his way into the temple. Appalling thing to happen. So Brahma took one look at the Sudra and he immediately died. One look at Brahma was enough to kill the Sudra. However, this had the effect of fulfilling the Sudra's wish because he died in the temple. So he was saved. At the same time, the little infant immediately was again breathing. You understand?

Well, that is an impersonal story, if you like. Yes? But that's rather strong meat for some of us. That's why I say, although there's relativity, you would have to a little bit expand your horizon to try and get the two ends of the scale. Yes?

Part Three

1977–1984

twenty

The appearance in us of what is really true, our nature,
is not a comfortable experience . . .

QUESTION: I have a question that has been running as a thread through my life, and that is, what is natural for man? I've taken different approaches to it but I've just realized that I make an absolute out of the word natural. I've tried to relate mankind to the way other species live. For instance, I've learned that there is an education among birds. Remove a bird from its flock and it won't learn the same song. So in a sense education is sort of natural. But when I turn to myself, I feel that I have tensions in my body that perhaps are related to the whole education I've had—I attach the word unnatural to them.

LORD PENTLAND: Yes, I think I feel the direction that you're asking about. You're questioning whether you have a prejudice in favor of the natural, or would it be right to be prejudiced in favor of what seems natural. Is that the question?

QUESTIONER: Well, it's part of it, yes. But I don't know what the natural is.

LORD PENTLAND: No. I understand that. But of course for one thing, we don't know very much. But for another, when you say "I don't know

235

what the natural is," in a way we do have other means, extra means of perception so that we do have quite a bit of feel for what is natural. Although at the same time it can't be relied on. We're not an animal that knows naturally what it can eat and so forth. Quite the contrary.

But going back to this prejudice that seems to exist for natural foods and natural birth and so forth, I think there's something we need to recognize and that is that we are upside down, educated in such a way that the appearance in us of what is really true, our nature, is not a comfortable experience. In fact, it's an experience that makes us uneasy.

So, if we are trying to put ourselves together, as it were, to understand a thread in my life that connects me with nature, through the laws and ideas that Gurdjieff has given, at the same time as I am connected with all sorts of the knowledge and artifacts of man, then the appearance of this line in me connected with nature will be something that disturbs me. It will not come upon me as something, at first, that relieves me. It will come upon me as something that disturbs me. Is this touching your question?

QUESTIONER: Yes, it is very much.

LORD PENTLAND: I think so. This is the point. You might expect that these ideas would put us all in touch with our natural environment and so on, and they are being used, in a way, with that in mind—which is all right. But I find, and I think most of us find, that if we're seekers of truth, it's not a comfortable truth. We've got to recognize that, if we're going further. We have to put up with the degree, which is perhaps not a major degree, to which opening ourselves to these impressions, which we call self-observation, may a little bit disorient me in my life. Could you understand me—what I am trying to say, or not? Yes? Is it true?

QUESTIONER: It seems that we can be so comfortable at seeing nature as outside us. But once we include it, then what are we doing? I just feel a large responsibility when I am in touch with that question.

LORD PENTLAND: Well, let's choose our words very, very carefully since we're sitting together so seriously. You say you feel a large responsibility. Is it very true?

QUESTIONER: Well, I am not right about choosing the words. It isn't responsibility.

LORD PENTLAND: It isn't really true. If we speak of a large responsibility, that could only be if we were able to respond. And is there such a response to the truth? Or is this something that's more conditioned, suggested in us?

QUESTIONER: There's a reaction.

LORD PENTLAND: Reaction. What do you do when you're washing in the morning and you find a caterpillar in the basin and you feel this response? What do you do?

QUESTIONER: Well, I've never had a caterpillar in a basin.

LORD PENTLAND: Well, assume a life, a live animal—you've never had that?

QUESTIONER: Yes.

LORD PENTLAND: What do you do? How do you feel response?

QUESTIONER: Well, I've often carried them outside because they're inside.

LORD PENTLAND: Yes. What are you doing when you carry it outside? It's worth investigating. We won't take the time now but do you have the right to carry it outside, so to speak? What is my relationship with this life of a little caterpillar? Could you just smush it out or what?

QUESTIONER: Well, I've thought of that when my cat brings home a bird.

LORD PENTLAND: All right.

QUESTIONER: Should I let the cat eat it? Should I take it away? And then my reactions to it have varied.

LORD PENTLAND: Yes.

QUESTIONER: Because I don't know. Is it natural for me to take the bird away? Have I been conditioned? Is it natural for the cat to catch a bird? It seems natural.

LORD PENTLAND: But in a way are there times when you don't respect your own brains as much as you're now respecting the dead bird? Well, anyway, it's a good, fine inquiry.

To feel a great responsibility—it's better to leave that for the moment until one understands better the difference between a reaction and this actual coming together of oneself which takes place, which is the first response that we can feel, and the first thing that we're responsible for. In order to come together, for example, we have to understand the laws of relationship in a way that's quite merciless—laws of life and death and so forth, in a way that's quite merciless. So just a kind of associative response, one life to another, is not enough to go by.

Please don't misunderstand me. I am not saying that we should cut trees down or deal stupidly with the life even of a caterpillar. But the work that we've started of trying to put ourselves together again, so to speak, of turning to myself, is of an order that requires a different kind of responsibility. Well, I sort of try and be in love with everything that is alive.

The study of relationships is the study of the missing link . . .

QUESTION: I have a question about relationships because I love being with people. There's something about it that gives me energy. Yet I can see myself just kind of grabbing energy—especially in family relationships, it seems. But in other sorts, too, when things get very close. I can see that's not enough. It doesn't work after a while and . . .

LORD PENTLAND: You see nothing. You must understand that where you are you're very lucky that you're in a group where relationships mean something much bigger than all that stuff. We're very lucky we happen to fall in a sort of ocean instead of the fishpond. So all this that you're talking about that belongs in the fishpond is not the whole truth.

Relationship, by the way, means between two entities, not necessarily two people. You see what I mean? For instance, the relationship that exists between my two hands. You have your two hands together. Do you know which is which? You don't know which is which. You don't feel your left hand quite different from your right hand?

QUESTIONER: Now I do.

LORD PENTLAND: Well, now I do; you begin there. Begin to study the relationship of your right hand to your left hand. For instance, when you clap, which makes the noise? You know they're absolutely different. Do you realize that? Yes? What's the difference?

QUESTIONER: My right hand feels lighter than my left, it feels. . .

LORD PENTLAND: Well, yes. But there wasn't much risk in making that statement. You know, you try to make really a true statement. And you'll see that in fact if you take the trouble to study your two hands— spend a week or two—you'll see they're quite different. You'll see the joints are different, even the physical size of them is different. And then you'll see they're connected to different sides of your body and so forth. So that what we know, for instance, of a difference between men and women is probably nothing to what you'll find in the difference between your right and left hand. Then you'll be into the subject of relationships.

So we're interested in the idea that where two things come together, there's a possibility of a third thing, making all three things into unity, particularly when these two things are on different levels. So we're not so interested in the two hands or two people or even different sexes. We're interested in things at two different levels coming together—that relationship.

But you've plenty of time. You can come to that. First of all the study of relationships is the study of the missing link, literally. What was the missing link? You understand, this is the basic work we do.

Consciousness is more than a comparison.
It is a relationship that is very direct . . .

QUESTION: Today I tried to actively ponder my situation to see the pattern that appears in my life. The Buddhist image of Samsara appeared to me with its various states and inside the symbols representing greed and desire. In a way it seems like this—a kind of turning around and around and never getting anywhere, having to repeat experiences. The same pattern has appeared here in the house, but in a different way, a much more acute way. There is a false belief in my own strength and a lot of motivation to comfort others, which I can ill afford to do and which seems to contradict the reason I come here.

LORD PENTLAND: It's not so much coming here we need to think about; it's the ideas of Gurdjieff, of people trying to follow the ideas of Gurdjieff, and you coming among those ideas, those people. The fundamental for us is the proposition or conception that the escape from Samsara, the way of going beyond the greed, is through conscious awareness and the changes of our state that take place as a result of an increasing quality of consciousness. Now, in coming here, or also in life, what experiences have you had which you connect with the idea of a change of consciousness, a change of awareness? I don't put too much importance on the awareness that comes when you ponder. You see that in some way you're able to make some similarity between patterns in your life and patterns you've felt here. When we speak of consciousness, it's more than that comparison. It is a relationship that is very direct. It's seeing, a look that is something in which one takes in a situation all at once. In pondering, one fills in little by little.

We speak of confronting ourselves. The moment of an impression of myself is a glancing snapshot. What would you say you have experienced in that sense? For instance, one tries to work alone in the morning. Do you notice how at first your attention is very scattered? Some days more than others, but when you sit down it's very striking. The attention has the personality of an hysterical woman, going in all directions. That goes with a very high degree of seriousness and pomposity. I'm sitting down to my exercise. The phone rings. I'm very surprised people would intrude. Yet parallel with that is a state of attention like some little canary looking in all directions. Don't you find as you sit that, instead of being jumpy, curious, nervous, you come in touch with a more continuous way of perceiving the outer and inner world? Gradually something more continuous appears, as if life were a process. Yes? Do you come to that? At the same time, almost by the way, I begin to be connecting all the inattention, the mistakes I've made, so I'm not taking myself nearly so seriously. The two things go together.

You mustn't be surprised if you find the state of better attention is accompanied by the realization of the paucity of my accomplishment. Yes? Now, in saying that, we've touched on what affects you more than the actual pattern. That may not affect you so much, or it may, but once I am rid of the pomposity, the particular characteristics of my way of being begin to be felt less critically. And, whatever my characteristics are, there is a certain value in them because of their identity with me. Do you understand? It's not so much whether they're good or bad, but they're mine. It's true. It's not a very multi-tiered splendor, but it begins to emerge that this represents my participation in life. After coming to a better state of attention, this is more important than that it has such and such a pattern.

So I'm suggesting that the question you raised, in the form you raised it, shows that you're not paying enough attention to the ideas of Gurdjieff—the escape through awareness, through the collecting of our attention, which at the same time undercuts our ego and transforms the neuroses, the nervous way of looking at things. This is what brings us all together to connect with each other, which is so important. I think this process of coming together, and it means not only innerly but in the sense of as a society, is going on there. It's right to value your time here, but it is for this process of coming together, of opening to more unity, that you should value it.

Somehow the wish and the resistance came together at that point,
and what appeared was you . . .

QUESTION: This morning when I was working in the yard, I tried to take the morning theme of being more aware of myself and more present to my task. And I kept seeing that I couldn't get connected with what I was doing. I was clearing a piece of the yard away—weeding and cleaning up—and it was a lovely day and the sun was hot. I kept trying, I suppose from not the right place, but I tried to somehow connect with the earth and with the flowers, and it just didn't work. I just couldn't sense myself. Then I was asked to sweep the patio with someone else and I began with a great deal of energy and desire to do a good job. Pretty soon I could feel this tension in my back, my neck started to ache, and all kinds of thoughts and boredom—I guess you could call it annoyance—came up. I kept sweeping and watching the movement in my head and in my back. And pretty soon, I was just sweeping. I don't know what my question is. But I don't really understand the process. I don't know how to connect that to earlier when nothing happened.

LORD PENTLAND: Yes. But without taking away from the extraordinariness of the experience, which is what helps us—your experience described in just that simple way—what we would like to add is that somehow the wish and the resistance came together at that point, and what appeared was you. There was a sweeper, so to speak, instead of a side that wanted to sweep, and a side that resisted that. You understand me? This is what we like to say in explanation, that something happens when we go beyond ourselves, we transcend the two parts that wish and don't wish. And what appears, although perhaps only very little, is the whole of myself—the higher, which is the whole of myself—which feels like just sweeping. Yes? But that means there was just a sweeper, or rather a sweeper was just sweeping. Yes?

This way in which the division of my life needs to be transcended is something which I need to experience. But perhaps, also, I need to understand it in some simple way because it is useful as a prototype. Prototype means sort of advance, it means like the first experiment, what goes before the manifestation. Do you follow? The prototype—it's what goes before the manifestation. The protocosmos goes before the cosmos. So the prototype, this understanding, can help you, when you come to insoluble divisions, to see that the solution lies beyond logic, in going beyond what caution or logic, science, or whatever may tell you is possible or advisable.

Without the tennis game there is no watcher . . .

QUESTION: I feel like I've been watching a tennis match all morning in myself and it seems like the ball is going back and forth between the desire for the possession of attention and a movement into things that I'm interested in, things that I feel responsible for, things that I care for. I'm not sure what my question is about it. I've been trying to watch it in a relaxed way but I can feel myself getting anxious.

LORD PENTLAND: Yes. That's what you've had of watching. Without the tennis game, there's no watcher. And the idea is, if we can bear that enough, we come to a particular experience of inner freedom and suddenly realize for the first time that I am a human being. So you see without the tennis game there is no watching. When there is no tennis game, there's no watcher. So the price you pay for the watcher existing is this discomfort, because you want some resolution of the contest, some way of stopping the contest—but as soon as it stops, the watcher disappears. It's what I find. What do you find?

QUESTIONER: I understand what you meant about the necessity of the game, but I don't know the steps towards inner freedom that you were talking about.

LORD PENTLAND: No. But it comes that way. This is why you're asking the question. So I'll tell you that's the way it comes. You're on the way to it as long as you can bear to be in front of this tennis game, looking one way, then the other way, then the other way, without deciding to fold up.

QUESTIONER: Without deciding to—what was that last word?

LORD PENTLAND: To fold up. To go home and enjoy your slippers by the fire. As long as you're watching this game, you exist. The game requires this audience of you. When there's no game, you're not there.

QUESTIONER: I keep on thinking there should be some relaxed way to watch it. Because I . . .

LORD PENTLAND: No. It's not necessary to think so subjectively. The purpose is to find the watcher. For the moment, the watcher only exists when the contest is there. And the purpose is to give up contests and to be the watcher. Then something much bigger can develop.

You've heard the idea that everything is in us. But you're stuck with the idea of tennis. Do you only want to have tennis all your life? The tennis is in order that an inner life could begin. It's not the end of it. You have these different plants—they're all in you. You don't need them outside.

They're all in you, you know. There's a fern in you, but you can't feel it yet. And there are bees and honey, but you don't know what it is. All you know is the contest. Until you suddenly feel "Now, I'm here," and the inner life begins to grow, you depend on the contest for approaching it. You understand me?

QUESTIONER: Yes, I do.

LORD PENTLAND: The only thing you have is tennis, but it's such a little bit of the whole thing to have. It's a beautiful game, tennis, but think of all there is in the world. All the different animals, all the different plants, all the different traditions and philosophies—all of that is inside. You understand? And all you want to do is watch tennis all day. And then you find that it isn't all day. You can only watch it as long as there is tennis. And you don't have that very much. You see what I mean? So you try to bear this contest, even if you react to it. You say, "I wish one side would go away." It's all right if you say it lightly because it doesn't go away. It's much better to say it lightly than to repress saying that. Otherwise you'll find that you explode; then it's no longer there. You follow?

QUESTIONER: Yes.

When too many labels are given, there's no
confrontation of forces . . .

QUESTION: I had the question this morning before we got together sitting. I was sitting with my eyes closed, and I sort of wanted to try for an inner direction. Then I opened my eyes and in an instant there was the perception that opening my eyes and closing my eyes doesn't really change anything all that much. Except it does change something, but what it changes seems to be within the kind of narrow perspective that you were just talking about. I mean it's easier to come to a sort of more relaxed state when I don't look at anything. But what I was hoping to try to understand in a sense was how to become more objective in an attitude towards outer and inner—because outer in a certain sense is just as much a part of inner as what I think inner is in relationship to the scale.

244

LORD PENTLAND: Yes. But of course we want to know how to become this or that. But, as I was trying to show, it isn't quite like that. The inner life at a certain level appears as a result of the action of forces on a lower level. Do you understand that?

QUESTIONER: That's what I would hope to understand.

LORD PENTLAND: Now in order that these forces at the lower level should exist, a certain separation, a certain differentiation of the forces has to take place. And it's a question how far somebody else's words and answers can help in that.

It gives tremendous confidence to know that somebody else has made this differentiation. And when we read in Gurdjieff's books before we came here about these different ideas that he gives, this gives us tremendous confidence because things are named. And until they've been named, we don't feel secure. You follow what I mean? When something is named, the secret question I have, "Is that different from that?" is kind of answered—when it's named. And so little by little we build up enough to come to questions of our own.

Now, whether you need more labels, more names, or just more work is for you to say. Probably you need just more work to open it up because when too many names are given we begin to shuffle them like a set of chessmen or a set of cards. And there's no confrontation of forces in front of the unknown anymore.

QUESTIONER: It's just that level which at times I've tasted over the past few days, that. . . .

LORD PENTLAND: I think this must be why Gurdjieff asked us to not go back to the traditions. Of course we do; we read these books and out of them make more books. But it's questionable whether that really is the best way. He gave us fragments of a teaching, and there are certain energies and certain items of knowledge which he gave names to. And then there are certain things which he didn't give names to. And of course little by little we shall give names to them. Or people hunt them up in the Buddhist doctrine or the Sufi doctrine and say, "Oh, this is that."

QUESTIONER: That's why I've been reluctant to talk about anything like this. But at the same time, it seems necessary to try somehow to find a way of seeking. I mean, like today is different than when I was at the movie theater last night. And the possibility for as much search did not exist then for me at that time as it does now.

LORD PENTLAND: The possibility for what? To be misled?

QUESTIONER: I don't know.

LORD PENTLAND: I would say there is more danger now. In the movie theater it's a sort of one-storied kind of house you're in. But here, one could be misled. Yes? There can be impressions received here that would be useful and impressions that could be very harmful. Yes?

QUESTIONER: Harmful for. . . .

LORD PENTLAND: In a movie theater what can happen? It's all on the same level. Yes? Although it's true sometimes one wonders what will happen next.

QUESTION: What I try and possess in some way is a materialization of something in myself with which I am not in touch. I guess it seems necessary at times to realize that and somehow see that in that space there is an energy which is needed. That by participating in a situation, in my trying to move toward something, which is in fact in myself, energy appears which otherwise would not be around. So I do feel that everything here is in me somewhere. I feel that.

LORD PENTLAND: So. Name ten things that you feel are in you. You can't name more than about two. You say everything's in you. It's ridiculous. Who could name fifty things that they can actually experience in themselves? Do you know what I mean? A python? Can you experience that in yourself, for instance? Choose a dragon or something. The idea is that in order to avoid this sense of grasping outside, I could have it in front of me inside also. Somebody said it moved from the inside to outside; closing the eyes doesn't matter too much. Of course not, if you can feel the python in you—it wants to hide in everything—as well as see it outside—.

Now, how many things like that can you feel in you? Very few, no? So the first step is to have this sense of existing for that, or being here for that. And then after that—and you will know when you come to that—you'll feel a tremendous longing to go back to this state, which is not a negative state, to be in touch with everybody. You follow? And that way you'll lose it all.

Everything has a price. You can't just pick out something you want. There is a certain order in which things are experienced, which as far as we know, is unbreakable. And as each thing is experienced, you have to pay the admission. So it goes like that. And it's a good long time before any irreversible changes take place. So you can always leave your seat in the middle of the performance, but then you have to pay to get in again. I mean pay again to get in.

QUESTION: Once one begins to sense something inside which has a great deal of power in one's life but which appears in a very disguised form, I wonder how to—I don't know quite how to put this. I'm beginning to see something and I see that it's quite central to my life, a certain desire to have a great deal of control and a lot of wanting—a kind of devouring quality, which I see coming at me from the outside world as though other people are going to devour me. I see some of the effects, but I don't know how to see it more directly. It seems to have so much power and yet I see it so indistinctly and so vaguely that I'll never experience the reality of it.

LORD PENTLAND: Well, can you see it now? Can you deal with it now? Without losing yourself, without losing the knowledge that you're sitting here with us. You understand what I mean? Is this power working to cause you to be thinking about or preparing for some big event in your life? Or can you say that for the moment it is under control, at this moment?

QUESTIONER: Well . . .

LORD PENTLAND: Are you afraid of it now? Or not?

QUESTIONER: At this moment I am.

LORD PENTLAND: At this moment you're not. You would know if you were. So that's the way to deal with it. At least that's my opinion. There are other ways, as I was just saying. For instance there's a story about St. George and the Dragon, which is the power, and the lady with a silken thread who leads the dragon because St. George has got his spear point at the neck of the dragon. And this is a well-known story, that if we always have our attention, that's the spear point, on the dragon, then the dragon can be led. Not by myself, because the power would then go to my ego, but by the beautiful lady, which is the soul or higher principle in me and in you. Now this story does not come from our teaching. Do you understand me?

QUESTIONER: Yes.

LORD PENTLAND: And it sort of illustrates what I was trying to say. It gives recognizable labels to these different things. And I think everybody, or nearly everybody, has this question that you've asked, and so already this whole area is a little bit more known. It exists. It's known, so to speak.

Now, I'm not sure, but my idea and what I'm trying to do myself, and for you too, is not bring you so many names like that, because I think the way to deal with the power is just the way you're dealing with it now. How is that? You don't know, but it's not bothering you. Do you understand me?

QUESTIONER: Yes, I think so.

LORD PENTLAND: Now suppose you knew, and now you know, so to speak, up to a point. You can judge for yourself—maybe it will bother you more—when you feel this power coming over you, you know, the dragon, and you want to be angry with yourself or with somebody else, and now you'll remember about the lady with the silken thread and St. George and his spear. We'll see if it helps. You follow?

QUESTIONER: Yes.

What is the truest moment you've had today? . . .

QUESTION: I feel there's something I'd like to ask about. I'm not sure how. It's about the question of right food for emotions. I see that a lot of my emotions are negative and it seems like there's something that could come from me to my emotions, maybe, that would be more right.

LORD PENTLAND: If I may say, where is the problem? Take for instance, what is the very truest moment you've had today? Perhaps it's been in your emotions. What would you say—and everybody could be trying—what was the truest impression of myself that I had today? And I might answer, "Well, I felt sad" or something like that—whatever it is. One doesn't have that many really creative moments of knowing myself each day. Now, did you have one? Did you experience this is what being sad is? That's an emotion; that was the truth. We needn't say it's a negative emotion. I don't know what it was. Could you say what it was, in that sense?

QUESTIONER: Well, I can't pin it to just one.

LORD PENTLAND: You can't find a word for it—it's difficult to find a word for it—but if you had an impression, one puts a word to it usually, very soon.

QUESTIONER: I felt I couldn't bring anything today—to work. I couldn't work at all. I just didn't. I didn't and I couldn't and it was really disturbing. I was really saddened and also shocked that I couldn't.

LORD PENTLAND: So you were shaken by this experience of being in darkness. Yes? All right, so we start from that. But each person has something, probably. And you had that. Now, what has getting food for your emotions got to do with that? You see, in speaking about getting food for your emotions and thinking about it, the truth slipped away. You follow? It would only take a couple of us to answer your question and you'd feel you were on the way again. Do you follow?

Where is the problem? The problem is that I forget the truth so easily— it slips away. The idea of negative emotions that seems to have been given by Gurdjieff—and, as it were, formulated and given greater currency by Mr. Ouspensky—is that becoming negative is one of the things that makes me forget. Forget what? Do you follow what I mean?

QUESTIONER: Yes.

LORD PENTLAND: Was it intended that we shouldn't try directly, that one had to try by working away at these obstacles, because there's no direct way of not forgetting? In a certain sense, yes, but not in the sense that when we're together we can come to our real question through something that's not really a question. Your real question today was something quite other than the question you put.

QUESTIONER: Yes.

LORD PENTLAND: You see? And you see that in putting your real question that even this experience of being separated from the work, if I can actually be free enough to tell it, even that experience is one that connects me with the work. It fills my tank again, or whatever you like. Yes?

I think the obstacles have to be discovered, in a way, all over again since they were read about. The psychological lectures of Ouspensky give general indications, but now each of us has to discover all over again what, for us, gets in the way of remembering, if you see what I mean. We would like to think that some different impressions would enable me to remember better. What obscures the truth that I've discovered, the truth which is me for today, me for this minute? It's very changeable. If, in fact, I'm feeling full of doubt at this minute, what prevents me from expressing that and pretending to a sense of certainty, and so forth, which is not really mine? We have to discover those obstacles all over again by ourselves.

Can we differentiate between what's been put into us
and what's essentially there? . . .

QUESTION: An impression I had yesterday raised a very big question for me. Today, right at this moment, I don't seem to be as much in contact with the question but because it's an almost overwhelming influence, I wanted to bring it.

LORD PENTLAND: Could you say first what you mean by very big? Because there are qualities of questions. What are you speaking about—a very high quality of question or one that exercises a very strong fascination for you? Do you know? There could be a moment when my whole horizon is filled with a desire to touch somebody, for instance, but you wouldn't say that this is necessarily a very high-quality form of wish. Do you follow me?

QUESTIONER: Yes.

LORD PENTLAND: So what I'm trying to say is that we can't ignore the fact that the truth is constantly being forgotten. It slips away and then, all right, you say it's because of identification or something. But how do you connect this bigness of the question with the fact that there are qualities—that not every question is of the same quality? You follow? We're speaking about a tremendous problem. We're speaking about everything. Because the truth is what matters. The truth is what will feed people, what will stop wars, what will get the U.S. government going again, and so forth. It will solve everything.

We've got to have some conviction of that kind about our work. If we think that this is just a little work for a little circle of people—which it is—and that in fact the really big questions are what we graduate to when we've finished with this, then this group is not for us. We're speaking about the truth. It's the question. All the misery and everything in the world is connected with the inability to experience truth. Yes?

So then, starting from there, what is a big question? What does it mean when the real question arises? Does it have to be big or little? I have to be quiet. Maybe it has to be expressed in a whisper. Maybe not. Which is it?

QUESTIONER: My feeling about my question was that it seemed to have something bigger behind it.

LORD PENTLAND: Yes, but I again say, what do you mean something bigger behind it?

QUESTIONER: Because it seemed to relate to the whole question of my nonexistence—of what I am, and why I think I exist, and whether I do in that sense exist or not. And I think that's an important question.

LORD PENTLAND: You think so?

QUESTIONER: I know it's an important question.

LORD PENTLAND: When you say, "I know it's an important question," do you mean "know" in the sense of the perception of what is, or do you mean "know" in the sense of what we've been, from a very early age, educated to "know"?

QUESTIONER: I mean certainly in the sense of perception.

LORD PENTLAND: And do we know the difference? Can we differentiate between what's been put into us and what's essentially there, except when we come to an emotional crisis? When we come to a very, very emotional crisis in life, we see not only that we forget all the time but maybe we see that we don't have that with which to respond, morally, except through educated ideas. It may be in some spheres we do have it, but in many other spheres life brings us to a certain crisis and, if we're honest and have come to that point before and have seen that to put it off doesn't help, we see we want advice, so we ask, we read, we look in the books, but we see we simply do not have that which is called conscience. We do not have that from which I can respond without a feeling of self-contradiction, without a feeling of paranoia, without a feeling of cop-out, without a feeling of cover-up of some kind. You know what I mean?

Well, knowledge—self-knowledge—would mean that from a state of complete unity I could deal with this situation. That would be complete serenity, if you like. Now life brings us, as I see it, into such situations and we feel kind of grateful to God, grateful to life, if you like, for testing us that way, because somehow we manage to come out of it, not with flying colors, but something is kept of our integrity, of our being not completely divided. Because it's a special crisis, it reaches down into us and we feel that this was not a noble moment, but it was my noblest moment—the way I responded. Yes?

And the basis of this house is that, since we have the help of Gurdjieff's system and so forth, we can create situations here which, although not as anguishing as these situations in life are similar and can, in a sense, bring us again before this moment when I don't know how to respond. That's the idea of it, isn't it? So, by knowledge I mean something where we have differentiated between what is intuitive, instinctive morality and some kind of educated morality, which in a crisis like that sometimes one can differentiate because one is speeded up.

QUESTIONER: It doesn't do any good really to keep looking for crises, does it? I mean, isn't there some hope that . . . .

LORD PENTLAND: You're in a crisis right now. What does good is to be in the present instant, not the present moment but the present fraction of a moment. And because one can't be that, one thinks that one has to wait for a crisis. But to be sincere, to be honest, to be true right now is the problem, always the problem. All the crisis does is bring one to that.

Listening is interesting because it is a very active
way of being passive . . .

QUESTION: I can see how things become clear to me when I do have a real outer struggle. I can feel the gathering up of the energy and movement towards something. Today I didn't have a real obvious crisis—it didn't seem like I did—but my life really is always in some sort of crisis. I'm always, almost always, asleep and I don't listen. I am pretty much in a fog most of the time and things are just going by me. For instance, relating to my children, I think I'm relating to them but I don't. I'm not really getting down there and looking at them and listening to what they're saying.

LORD PENTLAND: This is very interesting what you're saying, because it gives me an orientation. Do you see, in what you're saying, there's a whole orientation to your life? Do you see that?

You say, "listening." Have you been deeply into the question of listening and how to be able to listen and what listening has to do with remembering? Have you been into that? Have you seen that when we hear something—like that motorcycle out there—we feel we can shut it out as a distraction, without realizing that the motorcycle instantaneously brings to life in me that "I," if you like to put it that way, that either likes riding motorcycles, or had an accident on a motorcycle, or dislikes motorcycles, or something. I'm dealing with a whole personage as soon as that motorcycle starts up.

Now, one has to go into this whole process. I don't know whether I can evoke it at all for anybody else but, you see, listening can be a one-dimensional, two-dimensional kind of flat thing and when you hear a motorcycle, you just blank it out and you sort of say, that doesn't exist. In other words, you or I allow a buffer to come between that side of me which likes or dislikes motorcycles and myself. Do you follow what I mean? Do you follow what happens? You're there listening and this noise comes up. You think you can order yourself in a moment like this to blank out motorcycles in order to listen better. But that's not listening; that's taking the initiative. That's a completely different mode of action.

Listening is interesting because it can be a way of opening up to awareness, to consciousness. It's a very active way of being passive, of saying let God's will be done. Whatever happens, I'm just going to observe myself. In order to help myself remember to observe myself, I'll listen to everything that comes up. Even if somebody slaps me on the face, I'll just observe and so forth. Do you follow?

But you only start listening. You hear a motorcycle and you say, "Oh, I must blank that out." But that's not listening, that's not self-observation, that's not following. That's taking the initiative. Do you understand what I mean? So I've moved into a completely different side of myself—the one that I need for making trips from New York to San Francisco, or something where I have to take some initiative. But that side can never lead me very far. It can help me to, let's say, buy a house or paint a house, but not to live in a house. Yes? And it comes as soon as that; it comes as soon as I hear even a distant noise and say, "No, that's external, I must look inside." Yes? Just to follow would mean opening that up. I'm dealing there with the possibility of observing something that was laid down when I was very young. Do you understand what I mean?

twenty-one

*Understanding a kind of process which connects
"I can do" with "I am" . . .*

QUESTION: I've had a question for quite a while and I formulated it like this: "The difficulty of putting into practice what I know or what I think I know." Yesterday I had an experience that seemed to point in a completely new direction. Somebody asked me the name of someone I know. I couldn't remember, and not being able to remember put me in front of an experience of being unencumbered by what I think I know. And today I had an idea about how to find out more about that. I was setting type in the printing and tried simply to be active so that all the thoughts and all the ideas about the work couldn't enter into what I was trying to do. I felt that somehow out of this, anything that I might really know would have a chance of being expressed in that typesetting. And yet I couldn't see. I felt that what I needed was somebody to watch me trying that and then they would say, "That's what happens." But I couldn't prove anything. I really feel caught in between wanting to let go of what I think I know, and a fear that I won't be able to carry on. There were other people there but at the critical moment when I felt it was possible to see something about this relationship between what I knew and what I was practicing, there didn't seem to be any help.

LORD PENTLAND: You have put the whole problem in a psychological setting. And this is only part of our problem. It is a very big problem to understand our functions, but it is only part of our destiny.

For instance, as long as I can remain even-tempered inside, I can have a conversation with you that seems quite satisfactory even though I'm double. I may think inside, "What a stupid question" and so forth, but as long as I remain even-tempered, I can remember to say what a beautiful question it is and start to invent something that will pacify you and so forth. But as soon as I become negative, that is to say, as soon as the outside begins to control me instead of my staying free inside and inventing something outside, as soon as the outside begins to take me over, then psychology doesn't work because I just haven't anything. I've never heard anybody explain a negative emotion. The whole of psychology and psychiatry goes up the spout as soon as there is a negative emotion, because I feel that something is wrong there, like transcendentally or something. So psychology works as long as I'm double—as long as there's me and then the instruments through which I convey what I want to protect or what I want to say or what I want to pretend, and so forth. As long as there's this double situation, psychology serves quite well. But it's all based on the idea that my body and its functions are an instrument for transmitting what I want to do or communicate.

Transcendentally that is not so. I am my body. I can't use my body. I am my functions. I can't use my functions. My functions are part of what I am. And the least attempt to divide them off leads to the misunderstanding that I can do. And therefore the whole thing has to start from understanding a kind of process which connects "I can do" with "I am."

In this way we can transcend negative emotions by understanding that process and recognizing that for a moment or longer I can be entirely free of it. But it's going to have to return, and that this is part of the actuality of living. And "help" then becomes something that will enable me to live this process, to understand the laws of this process, to, if you like, identify with this process, to be constantly and dynamically in touch with this process so that there could be a sort of conscious relationship with the various parts of myself which are far more complicated than I ever recognize. There are all these different facets, most of which are blacked out in order to satisfy some theory I have in my head based on "I can do."

So that much of the time when we are here, as I see, as I listen, much of the time we are really trying to fulfill our wishes. We're in a sort of wish fulfillment mode of manifestation based on what we have understood, or think we've understood. And the real question comes when one sees that that leads nowhere, that to come here just to get the results, which are bound to come if one wishes for them, is not what here is for. When the dynamic nature of the process begins to be apparent, then my questions have to do with how to stay in time with this process, how to understand the laws of this process and so forth. I never can hear enough about that. Do you follow?

QUESTIONER: Yes.

LORD PENTLAND: This is the process of reality which includes what you'd call its more passive side where I'm in a state of wishing to have my wishes fulfilled. But it includes an active side where I'm more in touch with a pure kind of attempt to understand, suppose you call it philosophy, to understand something that's not psychology at all, to understand what are principles that hold up not only for a man, but for a woman, for animals, for the stars, for everything. Philosophy that would be. You needn't call it metaphysics, just call it philosophy. And the philosophy has to be something that's psychologically possible. So I would add that there has to be a certain simplicity.

So where to begin? To begin one has to recognize that I'm hopelessly centered in this idea that I can do, that I can direct my functions. So first of all that has to be shaken, that has to be undermined by impressions—what we call self-observation. And then when that's been sufficiently worked over, we need to come, as we were attempting to this morning, to know the process of moving from doing to being. Wouldn't you agree?

QUESTIONER: Yes.

Deep recognition of my nonexistence as an individual could activate some substances in me so I could exist as an individual . . .

QUESTION: A long time ago I asked you what Gurdjieff was saying. You said I should ask what is he saying to me. I couldn't answer then or now what he is saying to me, but I have found that question helpful in the readings here. I try to listen and then I go home and reread.

In this work there is so much expected of one. Sometimes I feel so useless, ordinary, because I can't live up to all these ideals like faith, hope, love. I feel these are so far beyond anything I can touch. Why is the kingdom of heaven so hard to find?

LORD PENTLAND: I was reading today about what is being understood about the movements of fishes and how, when shoals of fishes moved down the river, the movements of each individual fish are all the time made as if in the dark. All the time each fish is losing its way but somehow the shoal moves as a whole in a certain direction. It has been discovered that if the forebrains of the fishes are taken out, the individual fishes are able to find a more intentional direction. They don't go off to the side, but at the same time, they get more lost because they are cut off from the consciousness which exists for fishes in the mass. Somehow your question reminded me of that.

We don't know what Gurdjieff is saying to us because what he is saying is that I don't exist as an individual. So how could I know? Yet he is not saying something totally depressing, because he is speaking about how deep recognition of my nonexistence as an individual could activate some substances in me so I could exist as an individual.

It is the same in reading as in listening. The step we are trying to take at this time in this group is the understanding of what it means to recognize that I don't exist as an individual, what that means in my living experience. For instance, whether you are sitting reading or listening to a reading from *Beelzebub's Tales* there may be an experience that I am in my skin and am aware that something is constantly interrupting my attempt to listen to what is being said and that these interruptions are from me and come out of reactions to what is listened to. In my skin, present to the physical body, through that I can be aware of not listening, that my listening is being interrupted by reactions and one of the reactions is that I wish to listen better. There needs to be a kind of inner work so that all of me could wish to be there, so that I could feel there is nowhere I would rather be than here and nothing I would rather do than speak about this. This I would wish.

I have limits there. Very little actual work is done. I hardly notice—maybe later—that this kind of experience of my body, which is between me and what is being read, has disappeared altogether. I sit down and read without any awareness that I am reading.

You see, something can exist for us that is between what I am in touch with outside and myself. When that is there, there is never any question of the kind you put at the end, because there are always those two things: first, my lack, I am not here, listening, understanding; and secondly, I wish to understand better. So the feeling of impossibility is not there. These are the potential elements of making an individual.

We don't really take in how nearly
the forces are balanced . . .

QUESTION: I feel I am not quite sure how to proceed with your suggestion to use reason to struggle against negative emotions, because a part of my mind starts chewing away at the emotion with the right words. What I find happens is that I start moving away from myself with my mind. On the other hand, a couple of times here, when I have just kept the emotion to myself, a separation between me and myself appeared in a new way. But later it didn't seem possible.

LORD PENTLAND: You can look at it in *Views from the Real World*. It is said clearly there. It is not what you have been trying. You see that it's not a question of not expressing, but, for the sake of an aim, giving up the pleasure of thinking of one's hurt in the old habitual way. It is possible, if you try to think about it in the way suggested, to think in a more objective way.

It is true, for many of us the question of negative emotions has become something understood in a very automatic way: I ought not to have them; I ought not to express them. This absolutely blocks the way of looking at them given by Gurdjieff. I am constantly being hurt and it seems to be more open with myself to say I am constantly being hurt rather than saying it happened a couple of times and I didn't express it. The fact is that I don't see myself as I am, so what is hurt is my self-image. There is a very big gap between my self-image and my actual significance, and so there is this large area for being hurt. And if this gap is ever to be reduced, it is going to be painful—useful. Yes?

In all probability, we don't really take in how nearly the forces are balanced, that one little effort by you or by me may change everything. We don't look at it that way, that one little effort makes all the difference. In a discussion of Peter denying Christ three times, it was said that this denial by Peter could have caused the crucifixion. Apparently things socially and politically were such that if Peter had said, "He's an all right fellow," it could have changed everything, might have changed the whole of history. You see what I am talking about? But we read about that denial in a way which is a reflection of how we are, and say, "One more lie, theft, won't matter; I'll put it right tomorrow." We read that from a sort of thinking that he had to report it at a group meeting and say, "I betrayed you last week." But it could have actually caused the crucifixion. That is what I mean that every moment counts, is symbolic, in the unseen war which is a very balanced thing. I am sure you have seen that. You have impressions which lead you to that point of view.

Being between two relationships . . .

QUESTION: The reading this morning reminded me of an experience I just had in which I saw that the very symbol of what I wanted help from was also what I was afraid of. Not only had I set up in my mind a place where I wanted to get help from, or a person I wanted help from, but also that person or place represented the "correct" way to do things, or what was right or wrong.

And so I see myself going from that very ordinary kind of approach over to another very ordinary approach of just saying, "Well, then I won't do anything. I won't, you know, it's nothing but the same thing." I guess that what it comes down to is what I heard this morning agreed with the way I felt when I read the ideas for the first time. I don't want to just say, "I don't know what my responsibility is," that sounds too heavy. But there's a question there about the whole . . .

LORD PENTLAND: Yes. It's a question about the whole. Gurdjieff said again and again to me "You're between two stools." And then, Madam Ouspensky always used to say, "You must know what you want." Now, is it possible for us, for you, for instance, to put that together? Do you recognize that when you say you wish "to know myself as I am now," that that means I am between two stools? So when it's put to you very personally by somebody—like Madam Ouspensky could put things to you very personally, "What do you want?"—can you say "I want to be between two stools?" And what does that mean?

Of course, even I can make a speech about acceptance of my situation and how self-study begins from that, but what we're trying to communicate is these two sides: that there is a more personal experience which I'm having and then there's what I'm apt sometimes to call the work or the establishment or the ideas. Yes? How to bring them together?

Well, you know, I've told this before but it happened again yesterday. I came out on United Airlines, you know, and so I did it as I did before, when there was this girl coming towards me, I said "Are you United?" and exactly the same thing happened. She said, "No, I'm between two relationships."

Now what does it mean to be wishing to be between two relationships? I didn't say that to her but that immediately occurred to me. What does it mean to accept this position of being called to a very high calling, that of an intermediary between two relationships, between two levels? As Gurdjieff used to put it, there's the chair of the angel and the chair of the devil. So what does it mean to be between these two levels? And then, again, because all the time we're speaking of a chain of triads, that's just an idea. So what does that mean personally? I'm asking you to see if you can make the tracing of your personal experience just exactly over the drawing of the idea, if the two images can be brought together, like the focusing of a camera. You know, you try to bring the whole thing into distinct focus, into sync, if you like, into the same vibration.

So what does it mean to be between? You used an interesting phrase there, not the only one that I think you used, quite unconsciously, "What does it come down to?" You just said, "Now what does it all come down to?" And what we're speaking about is that, in between two relationships, I find there's a block that prevents it coming down. It's like a ladder. You can call the steps "chakras," if you want to associate with the sensation of your spine. And you see, at a certain point corresponding to your throat, or this or that other part—I don't want to get into the anatomical parts question—but at a certain point it sticks, it won't come down. You understand? And therefore you can't speak of being between two relationships—that's the relation with my head and the relation with my whole body. And there's a tremendous system of emotions set up, which are all correctly labeled probably, but I don't know the labels—the Oedipus complex, the fear of being caught with one relationship—by the other one, tremendously strong, which could perhaps only be evoked by using the word "nightmarish" questions, all hinging upon the fact that I don't have a direct channel for moving up and down and therefore at a certain place it gets blocked.

And you can understand how, with fear on both sides and with a little bit of an opening to both sides, I'm really scared that, for instance, the body should discover that I'm going to bed with my mind. You understand what I mean because there can be very high energies seeping through there. And that would be a terrible thing if this relationship is taking place and a stranger came. So this, of course, is acted out in what I call a nightmarish manner, and therefore you only experience it in its full creativity in dreams at night.

But it's not an exaggeration, I think, to say that in the daytime, although we don't see the dreams in their plot and in their color, something of the same emotion, something of the same emotions are evoked. And through the work on the crafts that we do, we touch the various points along this axis and we, little by little in our work, you in your work—I don't know about the others—you've come little by little to relax the resistance, and you touch sometimes the experience of this idea that was spoken about in the reading this morning.

CHAPTER TWENTY-ONE

Until my attention is divided, there is no work . . .

QUESTION: I really feel between something right now. You speak about being useful and I've had recently some very vivid and deep impressions of not knowing what my place is, of seeing that what I sometimes consider to be most useful is often self-important; the very thing that sort of carries me through my job and so forth is the very thing that isn't really very useful. And it's brought a big question, seeing this split between a real wish and this other very self-important side.

LORD PENTLAND: Yes, all right. But the very important thing is how to begin. You see? Until my attention is divided, there is no work. You understand that now. As long as I'm—whatever we call it—in my ego, as long as I think that just following one idea or applying one idea to myself is work, is practice, if you like, nothing can come. Now, very often that is how I begin to work. And then at a certain point the attention divides. Who divides it? It isn't clear to you yet, that at a certain point I feel a relaxation, you know. You understand?

I begin to be aware of a current, a movement of relaxation. Yes? Now do you suddenly switch to putting all your attention on the relaxation? That wouldn't be consciousness. To be aware, part of it remains, part of the tension attracts my attention. Partly the tension attracts my attention and partly I feel myself relaxing. Do you understand?

QUESTIONER: Yes. I do.

LORD PENTLAND: So the attention has suddenly divided. Yes? Well then of course I can really say I'm between; it's not a thought then. That's not something of an image or something; the attention is divided. It's very insecure. You know? It's so brief, it's so insecure I can hardly say that I experience it. Then I experience it again, maybe. Maybe another moment of relaxation, where partly the attention is taken by this current towards relaxation, towards going down in myself, but some of the attention remains behind on the tension. And so, again, for a moment I'm between. Do you understand?

You said you were between. But are you speaking from memory or are you speaking from experience? If you're speaking from experience, you see it's very insecure, a very insecure thing. Sometimes in movements you feel in between. You know something with the head a little bit and with the leg a little bit and somehow when both are going you feel insecure. You feel the attention divided. Yes? It's the same thing. Of course one needs to say to oneself "I need confidence," but in a way there is a confidence in that. Actually one knows that this situation with the attention divided is quite a different situation than when the attention is distracted. Do you understand what I mean?

QUESTIONER: Yes. Yes I do.

LORD PENTLAND: You can tell from most cases, not always, when somebody's attention is distracted. It's different. When my attention is divided, there's a sort of balance. And there's a place in between, but it's not a place that's secure, that's permanent, that's like a place on an organization chart. That would be an image. Do you follow what I mean?

QUESTIONER: Yes, exactly.

LORD PENTLAND: And the fact is that I'm very easily emotional about this insecurity. It just takes one image for me to fall into some kind of self-pity. It just takes one thought. If somebody gives me any grounds, whether intentionally or unintentionally, I begin to pity myself. If there's a letter that I don't like, or a telephone call, or any grounds which touch the thought—grounds, that means logic or thought—then around about that image, the emotion develops and as soon as it develops, it makes the divided attention impossible. I become unified into this self-pity. Yes?

The direct application of awareness without
anything being changed . . .

QUESTION: Recently at times I've felt or seen that I've got things upside down. I do want to maintain some independent perspective from which I can judge the work, or anything except myself. I see the fears I have had about righting it, turning it back the way it should be, but once in a while it comes up against another kind of fear more powerful than that. I know it is going to cost me something to turn it around. Not that I can; it just gets turned around.

Today the direction I felt was to see myself in more obviously homely instances like "What about having that second cup of coffee?" How was I just then? How am I in the middle of the afternoon, when I'm tired and my body wants to lie down and I do and then when I get up I'm angry at myself for having done it? Along with this I felt a kind of emotion about— I don't know what to say it is—a sense of being a little more ready to take a risk which is a lot smaller than I used to think of taking. When I read *Meetings with Remarkable Men*, there's a sense of daring to do something that is seen as ridiculous or not important by ourselves ordinarily. It was also in the music; I felt very much the sense of what was required—a real boldness. I don't want to put it in heroic terms. The feeling of quality about things that have gone on is humbling—when I see someone put their foot on the floor in a certain way that I can't. But I am beginning to see that the possibility of something in this direction is the way I wish to go.

LORD PENTLAND: What you say raises a great many questions for anyone who was really listening. There are various lines of approach to being which were suggested by what you said. In a way the straight idea of consciousness strikes one as being a clue. All the time entering into my vision is this idea about what would be good or bad in the work to be present, which epitomizes what you said. It keeps on coming to "Wouldn't it be good if I could think?" If one ponders that, one sees that the ability would have to turn on and off. Everything is like that. It would be there sometimes and not at other times.

What does it mean to be free, able to observe or regulate the degree of togetherness and consciousness and at the same time going on with outer life? For example, take the case of someone speaking, such as myself— maybe it will be you at another time. In the middle of speaking, you find you're speaking entirely from the persona and what you're saying doesn't have behind it the presence, the core of being. Yes?

QUESTIONER: Yes.

LORD PENTLAND: How to be free from something that comments on that, and simply go on being aware that it's coming from a hollow being?

This is the approach which Gurdjieff gives to the work, an example of the direct application of awareness without anything being changed. It may help you if you started with a turned-upside-down path, an intellectual way of approaching the work. Everything has to be perceived. Then I'm in touch with the truth and with myself, in a certain way.

QUESTIONER: Yes. When I think about the work too much, other things come up.

LORD PENTLAND: What does it mean to think on one's feet?

QUESTIONER: I don't know.

LORD PENTLAND: It includes the ability to be aware I'm not thinking. Once you can be aware, the thinking comes. The difficulty is to get rid of the idea that I ought to think.

twenty-two

We interfere with our fate, which all the same rules us . . .

QUESTION: I have been trying to think about what it would mean to be true to myself because lately I have been feeling the weightiness behind decisions that are made in me about life. Even with all the turning around that goes on in the mind, or with the lack of sincerity, there is something underneath that seems more serious and there seems to be something that cares about that. And yet the whole way I am just prevents a contact from being made.

I am not sure I understand what it means to see, in the way it is used in this system. The way it seemed to my mind was that some people are able to practice living in such a way that seeing becomes more possible, whether it is not being so taken by events, like some people say, or whatever.

LORD PENTLAND: The way I heard you put the question was very mixed. If we take the work as a work to be free from identification, it's quite enough. So for the moment it is quite enough to be able to struggle, with all the force we can find, to be able to be free at certain moments—if you like, four times a day. Right?

Now who said we make decisions? Where did this come from, this idea that we are swept along through life by our own decisions? It's an impossibility. We have a fate, and then that is very much interfered with by our ego and the way we interfere with our fate, but which all the same rules us. And

267

all of that is, like, sweeping me along. So where do you find any place for decisions except in regard to deciding to work to be free? To work not to be identified. That means not to think that I am choosing, not to imagine that.

So every now and then we come to a place where a big change in my life takes place. Are we going to resist that? All right. Are we going to go with it? All right. The question is, can I be free—can I fulfill the requirements of my life, even when there is a strong wish either that the new period I'm going into could be avoided or that it is desirable?

I feel there is a tendency, in this regard, to mix up the social or, if you like, the anthropological requirements of my life, with the work—this sort of superstition that if I work I would have a better fate. But that applies to people who are much further along than we, surely. Wouldn't you agree?

If you were born without the thirty-two marks of Buddhahood, it is unlikely that you will achieve Buddhahood. It doesn't mean it's not a good idea to work to be free and not so identified. Yes? When you see yourself about to do the wrong thing, sometimes you can't avoid it, but you don't need to be guilty. You just have to try to accept that you are not a saint but possibly a sinner. Have you ever awakened to yourself as a sinner without feeling guilty—somebody who gives a bad example, for instance, somebody who doesn't live according to what you know is a good understanding? And yet you see, in spite of it all, there you are doing something that you are not proud of. Yes? But you are not guilty, you just know that you are that.

The emotions are not indicating the direction towards my presence . . .

QUESTION: I feel that the question of identification is an important question. I feel that I need to understand something about that in a practical way and yet it seems that what I've been doing is what you just mentioned, confusing in my mind anthropological activities with the work activities. I have duties that I have to perform and sometimes I don't want to do them. Yet sometimes, like you say, just at a moment when I feel I have to walk my dogs because they have been locked up all day and I don't really want to do that, something happens and I feel that this is not so bad to be walking my dogs.

LORD PENTLAND: Yes. Well, what we are speaking of is including more of the impressions that come to us in the moving center and in the instinctive center, as well as the thoughts and the impressions that come to us through the intellectual and emotional centers. So we are speaking of something that has become possible through our adherence to the work and through efforts to come to sensation, be more relaxed, and of a kind of ability to be present, to be in touch with all these parts together in an experience that I discover goes completely contrary to this worrying. And of course we've seen this before, as Gurdjieff puts it, that we see things upside down. So that for moments we've already seen that worrying about work, about being at the meeting on time, about not missing any of the movements classes, and so forth, we've seen that all of that is something that has to go through a sort of hundred-eighty-degree revolution when we wake up, in order that I understand myself.

But now we are seeing that really the struggle to be present can exist as a struggle against the worry about being present, against the duty of walking the dog, and against the duty of being on time for the class. We are actually coming to the point—can you follow that? No? Yes? You see, it's like something that I'm suddenly aware of, that sort of revolution, that all this worrying about something is unconnected with the work. And I see that I'm only aware of that because of having a little bit of this presence that is the aim of the work—the wish to be present. And when I suddenly see that, I get the idea: I become quiet and the worrying is seen. And you don't know very well what is seen; you don't because it happens very suddenly, like that.

To be not identified is to suddenly feel that I'm seeing that I was going in the wrong direction, that all this energy was going towards worrying, and that is not the direction. The emotions are not indicating the direction towards my presence. And in the same moment, I become aware of my presence. I may even feel something about the scale that appears when I'm present, as if I become present not just to myself, but to myself under the stars, under the existence of a scale of life and higher energies, and so forth.

QUESTIONER: I'm wondering if what you say also applies to all the other worries about my life's activities—how I feel about myself and so on.

Am I understanding you correctly about that? In other words, I don't worry so much about getting to the meeting on time, but I worry about everything else in my life. That is how I understood confusing anthropological activities with the work.

LORD PENTLAND: Yes, but it's the same thing there because if you are sensitive you know that you have to resist, for instance, worrying about whether you'll get your breakfast on time. If you're sensitive, something tells you that it would be more aesthetic, if breakfast is late, to say that I won't have breakfast today, thank you very much—and to say it nicely. And you take that in instinctively. If somebody has made breakfast for you and you want to correct them for bringing it late, that would be the only way—and you know instinctively, even if they bring it on time, that something wants to refuse being served by that person, sort of. But if you're not sensitive to the instinct you don't even say thank you; you start to gobble up what is put in front of you. Something much more sensitive in you wants all the time to push away the things that people give you and to give to them. Don't you find that? Yes or no?

QUESTIONER: With one person I'm a pig and with another person I want to give everything of myself.

LORD PENTLAND: Yes. But the question is, can you trust these instincts? Can you trust life? This is the same question about one's fate. You see that, say one person comes and they want to give you something and you want to refuse it; why do you then say, "Oh, thank you very much; yes, I'd like it"? You don't mean that. Why don't you refuse it? It is in that way that we compound our difficulty with life, I think. I don't know what conscience is. I'm not bringing that into it. But something comes and is it really such a big work to accept all this from them? No. You say to yourself, "Oh, I ought to accept this. It will offend if I don't." It doesn't at all. Say, "Take it away, I don't want it." If they really want to give you something, they will bring it back again. That is what I mean by taking in the impressions with your instinct.

CHAPTER TWENTY-TWO

Because the past exists, it supports my
work in the present . . .

QUESTION: Since Gurdjieff's earthly body died twenty-nine years ago today, it seems important I should understand something about that, and not just with my mind. I think the reading today helped me to understand a little bit with my emotions, but I think I need more to understand it in my body.

LORD PENTLAND: I don't know quite what you mean by understanding it in my body. But I do think that there is an understanding that helps very much, of belonging to a tradition which comes from the past. And I think that understanding begins with recognizing, accepting, that what took place cannot be altogether understood by me now because it did take place in the past. And its importance is not so much in trying to repeat it or imitate it—whatever took place in the past—but in recognizing that because this past exists, it supports my work in the present. I don't think we see that by trying to project this greatness into the future, into my own terms, and even into my own future—ridiculous as it sounds—I take away its usefulness, which is that existing there in the past it is a support to me in the present. It's something which, as long as I don't project it into the future, it gives me help in having a sensation of my body or whatever you like, an understanding in my mind. I don't know whether anybody can follow that, but if one person can pick that up, it will be good. Impressions from the past are so often an excuse for projecting something fantastic onto my present or future, instead of being what they are, a big support.

The appearance of perception as fact is very, very light and
doesn't go with any kind of rigid sense of duty . . .

QUESTION: It was such a marvelous reading this morning and I thought that what you said was so appropriate then. I felt so good that I really just forgot about working—not quite forgot about it, but somehow it just seemed I was happy to be here but I wasn't working.

LORD PENTLAND: Maybe it could be a beginning for you, a sort of arousing of thoughts about what this place is really for, if you see what I mean. One's idea of duty or work is so heavy usually that the understanding of the work and of the purposes of the work place is rather ordinary. And in this state of feeling happy or filled with impressions from that reading, in that state, you see more. Maybe one doesn't become aware of it very easily but one sees more—how very flimsy and light the work of consciousness is—how the appearance of perception as fact is very, very light and doesn't go with any kind of rigid sense of duty or work at all. The perceptions are popping up like little things all over. Maybe even now somebody's eyes are just opening to whom they're sitting next to or what they've eaten, for instance, which one hardly realizes, you know. This is what this place is for and one needs this kind of support that the reading gave. But progressively we should be trying all the time to do with less support and more work—whatever the work is: some kind of work of relaxation, some kind of work of looking for where the perceptions come from—a sort of reconciliation with myself, which is a kind of exercising of myself of a very much lighter kind than the relationship with myself that I call work, or duty. What I can bring to my particular team today is what really is mine today, not just my strength or my formatory understanding, but something that probably I alone can bring to the team.

QUESTION: If what you say is true, how come there's so little expression of that here—that lightness?

LORD PENTLAND: Well, one answer is if that lightness were within our grasp, this place wouldn't be necessary. It's a question of the direction. What's constantly being forgotten is the direction. I have to understand what is the cause, where my tension comes from, where my fears come from. What do you find? You see that if you meet somebody very ugly, you're afraid of them. And you see if you meet somebody very pretty, you're afraid of them. Who aren't you afraid of? Tell me that. You meet somebody pretty, somebody ugly, you're afraid of them both. Who are you not afraid of? I can't see you. I don't know you. Yes? Are you afraid of pretty people?

QUESTIONER: Sir?

272

LORD PENTLAND: Are you afraid of pretty women?

QUESTIONER: No.

LORD PENTLAND: You're afraid of everybody. You know? And this tension, it gets in the way of that lightness. You see, you take in images the whole time—that's what I'm trying to say—and as long as there are images, the whole question of aim and distraction doesn't exist. If you are working through images, you're already lost as far as remembering yourself is concerned. And if you stick to the images that seem to be down the straight and narrow path, that is not what this place is for. Do you see what I'm talking about? If you think at the beginning of the day that the meaning can be grasped in terms of meaning, then if you try and hold on to that, "I must remember this meaning," and you get distracted, "I must come back to the meaning," and so on, you're not doing the work that's asked for here.

QUESTIONER: When I ask if there's happiness here, if there's a person that feels happiness, and if they're not the only person here that feels happiness, why is there so little that seems to be manifested or expressed here?

LORD PENTLAND: You see how tied you are to meaning. What's necessary is to be in touch with myself. And when for a moment you feel that, you want to know why, you want to know the meaning of it. That's a distraction. That's what I'm trying to say. You understand that? You were sitting there and suddenly from something that was exchanged, you felt more yourself but you couldn't stay with it more than an instant without asking for some thought to stick with. Do you see what I mean, some answer. Right? So, I tell you: you're afraid of pretty people, you're afraid of ugly people. You always want to come in to the image. Do you see what I mean? And just to be there is more difficult. Have you ever experienced just being there?

QUESTIONER: Yes.

LORD PENTLAND: You're waiting for somebody to come. You know. You're trying to occupy yourself without getting caught in any particular meaning because you want to be there when this person comes. Do you see what I mean? You're trying to keep a little bit occupied with this and that and not get caught in any project, any particular thing and then sure enough you get caught. Then the bell rings and you don't ever meet this person at all, except through your tension, through your fear. Or maybe if you're fortunate, you've learned how to be occupied in each of the three parts and a little bit sucking a little from this, from that, from another, you can stay yourself.

And then the person comes and you meet for a little while before some project gets decided on or not decided on and one becomes tense and related through meaning. Do you see what I mean? It's probably impossible to make it out. So the reason we're all so heavy is that we're not able to be free from all these tensions. And the idea is to start with something small, something particular, specific and start to work with that.

Everybody has a mind of their own. Everybody in this room has their own problem, their own character to work with. So it's not necessary always to be suggesting something that everybody would follow like sheep. But each person has the opportunity to try something towards being more light because what he said is what we all agree with, that there's not enough of this kind of lightness. I'm all the time being distracted from myself and after a while it gets so confused that there's no way back until tomorrow. My mind is confused, my whole psyche is so mixed up that there's no way back until tomorrow.

There is a tendency towards thinking and towards imagining that what I think can be manifested . . .

QUESTION: I keep finding in myself traces of early experiences from the past, certain moments that I had when I was very young, for example. Something in those moments was very alive and seems to come back to me now in flashes, sometimes, and more and more recently. This may be off on a tangent, which is why I bring it up, but it seems to me that this question of where does it come from, where does my attention come from, is related to this. It seems that in some way, both my problems and my best states come from a kind of fractionation that took place at this certain moment that I experienced once, very long ago.

For example, my inability to meet people face-to-face seems to come from something that happened then—a certain way of taking this moment inside and making myself invulnerable, superior to people. But also locked up in that moment there seems to be something that is calling to me from a very deep place. I want to know how to understand that. For example, is it possible to trace back the sequence of states to that one from the present time?

LORD PENTLAND: I think there are other approaches to kind of making use, or making practical help out of this observation you started with than the one that you spoke about at the end. At the end you spoke about a kind of way of using the appearance of these flashes from your childhood towards betterment of being or something. But I don't know that I could pursue it if it's taken that way. It's a question whether any thought like the one you expressed, about having these flashes from your early child-hood, whether any thought can be manifested into life like that.

The idea of the work is that everything happens—the thoughts that we have are not ever expressed, manifested. I'm not sure that there's time to pursue that, but what I'm saying is that your observation is to me an example of another of the ideas, true ideas, about essence and personal-ity—that whereas personality obviously changes and develops as we get older—quite obviously also—essence doesn't, much. If it develops it's through the work—that's the idea—and so, it's a little bit comforting to you, in a way, to feel that the development of essence is taking place at least to the point that you have these flashes, which is like having evidence that there is an essence. Yes?

We could go further to speak about essence, to open up associations about essence—how little we're aware, I'm aware, of my essence, and how little check we put on the formatory way of looking at other people as well as at myself, as if they were just units rather than essences, so that one could come into a room like this and sort of count the people. But of course you can't count essences, if you think about your observation.

But rather than dilate on all that, I would say I wonder if we've recognized how little the ideas have been made use of. There is this idea of essence and personality. It is almost the only idea really that's brought into our group meetings, if you follow what I mean. That idea is brought a good deal—the idea of an original energy of the centers, which is the essence, and of the personality which is a kind of formation of the essential energy. And so often in listening in the group you hear this idea brought. But what about all the other ideas?

One sees that there is a tendency all of the time towards thinking and towards imagining that what I think can be manifested. And perhaps the ideas were given in such profusion so that we could be occupying ourselves with experiencing the ideas as a rest from this imagination. We take an idea, we take a thought, really, and then project it on ourselves or on our future life or on other people, and say, "Now I'll tell them. I'll make it like that." And the first idea in the work is that you can't do that.

twenty-three

For the sake of an inner freedom, I don't go with the reaction . . .

QUESTION: The last few months, a couple of ideas have been important to me. At least they've been ideas that I return to. One of these ideas, that I read in *Views From the Real World*, was that if there is an impulse to do something or a desire to do something, then a contrary desire would arise, what is called a greater unwillingness, and it will stop me. These ideas have just been in my awareness. I don't feel I've learned a lot about them.

LORD PENTLAND: Yes. Of course, ideas are not in themselves enough. They need to be swallowed or digested or somehow experienced. Wouldn't you say?

QUESTIONER: I can feel that very much.

LORD PENTLAND: I don't know whether you understand enough to have examples already, so maybe you have to make examples—make an exercise, so to speak, in order to see how that works. I'm sure that already your life includes a great many experiences of something that is desired, but because there is a more than equal mechanical pull, it doesn't get achieved or it doesn't get found. However, since perhaps your—my, your, our—lives are so fragmented and divided up by buffers that we don't connect things together, we may need to do a special exercise sometimes in order to see something that really would be obvious—will be obvious later—if we could see our lives from a little above and see them more as a whole.

So what we're speaking about is a willingness to be in touch with two things, to see that in fact I'm often in touch with something that's pulling me and something else that's pulling me in a different direction. This is essentially what that idea is about. One has not only to know it, but sense it. Now, for instance, do you have a motor car?

QUESTIONER: Yes.

LORD PENTLAND: What breed? What motor car?

QUESTIONER: Dodge.

LORD PENTLAND: Dodge. Big car?

QUESTIONER: A van.

LORD PENTLAND: A van. What is the average speed that you drive at?

QUESTIONER: Sixty.

LORD PENTLAND: Sixty. Now, have you ever driven it for a long time at twenty?

QUESTIONER: When somebody's in front of me going very slowly.

LORD PENTLAND: No, but when you're in front of somebody and there's nobody in front of you. So you see that even that simple exercise will show you something. You have eight enormous cylinders but you run the car at fifteen, twenty miles an hour. You get into the right-hand lane, out of the way, and you never let the needle go above twenty miles an hour, for instance. So you go towards Palo Alto, twenty, thirty miles from here and you run it like that. You get there nearly as soon, really you do. But you have all the time this feeling of a power which you're not using. Do you see what I mean?

QUESTIONER: The power in the car.

LORD PENTLAND: The power in the car. You sense it in your body. Do you understand what I mean? All you'd have to do is push the accelerator pedal and you would go at your usual speed. So all the time you're driving you sense in your body that you're free. You have energy, but you're not spending it. Why are you driving at twenty miles an hour? Because I said so. Because it's an exercise. So you desire, you wish for the experience of simply obeying to a suggestion that I'm giving, more than you desire to get there. What does it matter if you're five or ten minutes late? You see that? You need to sense that in your body, not just know it up here. Do you know what it's like in your body? No. So you have to do that. Do you follow me?

QUESTIONER: Yes. I think I do.

LORD PENTLAND: And you see that you might live a whole life without ever doing that, and yet you see what an interesting idea it is. I'm speaking about something that's really interesting. It could mean not only the horsepower of the car but my own physical and even psychical energies. To have the energy and not spend it.

Why? Just in order to observe what happens. As soon as I have the energy, I spend it. Now what would happen if, just for the sake of understanding, for the sake of an inner freedom, I don't go with the reaction, with the compulsion? I think this is an illustration of the first idea you spoke of. But you have to work at that, you have to do that many, many times until maybe a new question appears. Your interest in the question you asked comes from somewhere farther away than the actual question. Something is speaking to you through this idea in *Views From the Real World* but from farther back.

QUESTIONER: What you've just said makes me think that the understanding I came with tonight was almost the reverse of that.

LORD PENTLAND: Maybe exactly the reverse.

QUESTION: Can I make up exercises like that for myself?

LORD PENTLAND: No.

QUESTIONER: May I have an exercise like that?

LORD PENTLAND: You have to bring an observation like that. But what I've told just now I don't think could be made up. I didn't make it up. I think what I spoke about is something important. You can try that exercise yourself. Do you have a car? Yes? You can try it yourself.

Anything that makes dreaming alluring
goes against our aim . . .

QUESTION: That confuses me, in terms of intuition. If there is an impulse from intuition and I don't follow it, I lose perhaps the right way for that particular moment. I've been trying to equate your example to something within myself . . .

LORD PENTLAND: No. Say your own question, that's the way. Begin with some information or, if possible, insight that you've had about yourself. Just be simple about it and erase altogether what I said to him. That's something else. That's finished. That's just one thing, now we'll go on to something else.

QUESTIONER: I could give examples of some of the intuitive things within myself but . . .

LORD PENTLAND: Well, like everybody here you have an opportunity to speak. Now what do you most of all want to say?

QUESTIONER: Something altogether different.

LORD PENTLAND: Right. Then try to say it, quietly.

QUESTIONER: I've been very excited this week in reading a book about astrology. I'm not sure yet what to make of it, but I'm wondering if astrology could be a valuable tool or could it become a limitation? I'm very excited and I have a lot of not quite formed questions in terms of the work.

LORD PENTLAND: In terms of what?

QUESTIONER: This work here.

LORD PENTLAND: Which is that?

QUESTIONER: This work on myself.

LORD PENTLAND: Which is the work on yourself that you're doing? Each person speaks for himself, you know. So what work are you doing on yourself?

QUESTIONER: I can think of only cliché phrases like, I'm finding myself, being true to myself.

CHAPTER TWENTY-THREE

LORD PENTLAND: That's the aim. But what do you actually try?

QUESTIONER: I observe myself.

LORD PENTLAND: You do?

QUESTIONER: I listen to myself.

LORD PENTLAND: All right then. Does this excitement that you spoke of coming from the books help you to observe yourself?

QUESTIONER: I'm not sure yet. It's too soon.

LORD PENTLAND: Does the astrology help you to observe yourself? You must think in that way. If you have a question about yourself, perhaps these books and the astrology get in the way of it. Then you have to give them up. Because you can't get started in the work without being able to clear a little space around your work. So, the excitement, the astrology, sort of fills one up with things so that it's difficult to have the question so much, the question of wanting to observe myself, the question of what am I like, who am I? Do you follow me? When you have a lot of material from a book, like you mentioned, you get kind of filled up.

QUESTIONER: That's what I've been doing, filling as much as I can, so that I can . . .

LORD PENTLAND: You can't do very much. You can't change it very much, but there's no point in adding to that excitement, that feeling of being full up with various interesting thoughts, by reading a book that you don't have to read. So if you can manage to put it down in spite of wanting to read it . . .

QUESTIONER: Are you saying that it's . . .

LORD PENTLAND: I'm not saying that it's harmful. I'm just saying that if you have a kind of real search, if you want to find the truth of yourself, you might as well put these books aside. You can do without them.

QUESTIONER: Only if it confuses my search.

LORD PENTLAND: And it does confuse your search. So you might as well put them aside. You don't need to have your foot right down on the pedal of the accelerator. Do you follow? It's the same thing in a way. Why don't you go at ordinary cruising speeds?

QUESTIONER: I feel in a hurry.

LORD PENTLAND: Exactly. But why do you think you'll get there quicker? Maybe you'll get there slower that way.

QUESTIONER: I just feel there's so much to do.

LORD PENTLAND: Are you married?

QUESTIONER: No.

LORD PENTLAND: Well, people will be much more interested in somebody who doesn't know about these books now. You know that's rare.

QUESTIONER: I've been there.

LORD PENTLAND: You follow me? Why don't you strike out on your own and be the one person who doesn't know astrological types? You know, it'd be marvelous. Then you can pick somebody just out of your own intuition instead of doing it out of a stupid book. And finally you read the book and you find you're right, wouldn't that be wonderful?

QUESTIONER: Well, the only time you know when it's right . . .

LORD PENTLAND: Anything that makes you superstitious, anything that makes you use your power to make theories, weave a kind of dream, is only adding to the problem. The aim is to wake up. Anything that makes dreaming alluring—you know, speculation of this kind makes dreaming more interesting—so anything that makes dreaming more interesting goes against our aim. Yes?

QUESTIONER: Yes, but . . .

LORD PENTLAND: It's not for me to persuade you. You can pick it up or not, I don't mind. If you want to spend your life dreaming, what does it matter to me?

QUESTIONER: I agree with you. At this point I'm not certain if that's what it would become . . .

LORD PENTLAND: Well, I tell you, I'm quite certain. You have the choice with Gurdjieff. You can get the books on how to read people's handwriting, and that kind of thing, or you can work on yourself. I don't know the particular books you're speaking about, but do they give you something substantial is the question. Do they really give you something that brings you closer to God or whatever? Something that really makes your life more ordered? That's the point.

You don't need to change anything except
the balance of relationships . . .

QUESTION: My question is why am I in such a hurry? Why am I so impatient? Why do I keep filling myself up? And there's something, probably left over from childhood, that sometimes gets ignited, that excites me and pushes me on to what seems like greater heights, but it still comes down to a sort of garbage in the end. It doesn't really seem to feed me, and yet I find that I am compelled and I wonder why I'm in such a hurry.

LORD PENTLAND: This, after all, is pure speculation. If you knew why you were in such a hurry, do you think that would stop you? So wondering why I'm in a hurry is just adding to the confusion.

QUESTIONER: That's right, but that thought process goes on so much.

LORD PENTLAND: Probably there's an egoistic taste to it. Is there? When something has an egoistic taste, then this gives me a clue for working. If the hurry has a taste of being self-serving, that sort of futile taste of egoism, then it means that there are other sides, other aspects of my existing life which are underdeveloped, and the egoistic point of view is being overdeveloped. For instance, in your career it means that you're apt perhaps to pay less attention to the presence of the people working close to you and more to yourself. And if you could adjust that a little, to be more aware of the people who are working with you and close to you, then you might find this had a measurable effect in balancing out your impatience, this being in a hurry. For instance, have you gotten to know any of the people working with you at your job, in your career?

QUESTIONER: I find the time sometimes to do that at a birthday or some other occasion but I realize how little I know them.

LORD PENTLAND: You see, you realize just a little how little you know each of them. And it's just enough to sort of get by on. But suppose you deliberately took one of them, either because you felt you liked him, or disliked him, or there's something interesting about him, or even if you did it out of a hat, and made a definite effort to get to know that person; you see how upstream a job that would be, that perhaps it would not take very much time or energy actually, but it would interfere with the entire plan of your life. Do you see that? And in that way it would displace this egoism, and therefore it might affect your nervous impatience.

What I'm trying to say is, it's a question, probably, of some kind of imbalance in the total picture of yourself in your environment. You don't need to change anything except the balance of relationships somewhere, probably. Don't you think so?

QUESTIONER: Yes.

LORD PENTLAND: Now, the egoism wouldn't be so bad if it got one anywhere. But it's like I said in speaking about the car driving fast, you only save ten minutes or something. By driving more slowly, you get much more time.

So, in the same way, perhaps there's somebody younger than you in the place where you do business and you could really try to get to know her for a month, see if you could relate to her, see if you could show her something, give her a feeling of caring for her, teach her something. And see what happens, see whether it leads anywhere. We're always afraid to do something like that. Wouldn't you say it's out of fear that we don't do it? Really? Basically?

QUESTIONER: I was thinking of that, yes.

LORD PENTLAND: After all, one is afraid that I'll get committed, I'll get too committed. But why am I afraid of being committed? I don't need to answer the phone when they ring up. You understand? If I take the initiative in getting to know you, as long as I don't steal from you, I can drop it if I want to. Isn't that right?

As long as I don't steal anything from you, then I don't owe you anything. And so, if you're willing to talk to me and see me and let me teach you something, I can always just drop you when I want to, can't I? Do you follow? I am free. So why am I afraid of getting to know you? I'm afraid of getting to know you because I think if I get to know you, I'll steal from you. But why do I steal? Can anybody follow what I'm saying? It's interesting, isn't it?

QUESTIONER: What if they start teaching me something?

LORD PENTLAND: That would be all right. I think you could do with a little teaching.

QUESTIONER: Well, certainly, but if I were the one who initiated the friendship for the purpose of seeing if I could do it and then all of a sudden the person is giving me something, it would be very hard to . . .

LORD PENTLAND: Well, you could stop it then, if you wanted to. That's what I'm saying. I'm saying there's nothing to be afraid of as long as it's started intentionally. You see, we've never started anything intentionally. Do you understand what I'm talking about? It's not a small thing. But, to move into something like that intentionally is something we're afraid of doing. I'm trying to say, why? Why am I afraid? If I'm afraid, of course I won't do it. But suppose you're not afraid? If they start to teach you, she says you get tied to them, but if you see they're teaching you, you just don't need to turn up. Do you follow? If something's started intentionally, maybe it can be followed more consciously.

QUESTION: What about passivity? For months I've felt maybe something was lacking in my thinking. Then I recognized a kind of passivity in myself that seemed to be fertile ground for anything coming into my head.

LORD PENTLAND: I think it's good if things come into my thoughts, but they mustn't stay in my thoughts. They have to come in and go out. It's like a well-run house, my head. It has to be a house with a front door so things can come in, but there has to be a back door so things can be pushed out as well. In a house there has to be a front door and a back door. Then people can come in and when the house gets enough people they can be sort of welcomed out. Understand? That needs an active householder because I leave the door open; it's not locked. Things can come in, but they have to go out. I have to sometimes help them to go out. Yes? When a very poor thought arrives, you know, and I have a lot of very rich thoughts in the house, I'm inclined to say, "Go out!" to the poor thought and have the rich thoughts stay there. It's very unhealthy for the house.

QUESTIONER: Somehow it . . .

LORD PENTLAND: That's very passive. Rich people think passively, yes?

Sometimes you actually see the self-pity and then it doesn't have this sort of described existence . . .

QUESTION: I would like to ask something about listening here tonight. It has to do with rushing on, getting what's said taken down and put in the pocket, a sort of greed. It feels like a pathetic voice, this greedy one. And then there seems to be some other voice that isn't pathetic at all. It's more interested in a kind of dropping away of all this, and is somehow much more open.

LORD PENTLAND: Yes, but you have to actually see. You have to actually be present to these characters and then the question that you're turning around doesn't exist in the same way; it becomes a different question. There's a kind of state that's in between, so to speak; one's not awake, one's not asleep. One's beginning to be aware of the different voices which I'm split up into. And yet there's not a simultaneity, there is not a kind of being there and seeing it in the moment. Do you see what I mean?

QUESTIONER: Yes.

LORD PENTLAND: So, in a way here's the price we pay for our work. In order for it to be effective you have to see it; you have to be aware of it in the moment. I can't all at once express what I see so it takes some time to tell about it, but the seeing has to be in the very moment. It can't be something that I see later, which then begins to be described, which then begins to have a kind of imaginary existence, an existence in the imagination. What I'm seeing are parts that actually exist, and that's the difference.

Now the price for knowing about this work to bring the parts together is that, in order for it to be effective, I have to actually be there in the moment, collected—collected all in the very moment. Otherwise it works against me. Because with the words that I've begun to know and then the books I start to read about it, and so forth, I begin to have a whole set of puppet characters in my mind which are kind of interesting to play with, but which get in the way of this awareness in the moment.

So there's a very poignant situation in a group like us. Everybody can be contributing to the possibility of actually seeing at the time of the meeting and, equally, I, and everybody, can be contributing towards the existence of these sort of shadow characters—sort of shadow, imagined people. And this is where the drama to do with results from my work exists. It's extraordinary we get results, considering how much of this dreaming there is. But we do get results.

So one mustn't exaggerate the obstacle that these kinds of indirect questions pose. But they are an obstacle. The obstacle mustn't be exaggerated because then fear and tension and the possibility of being wrong—guilt, all of that—builds up. We've got to find our way. Do you see what I mean? Can you agree that sometimes you actually see the self-pity or whatever it is you're speaking about and then it doesn't have this sort of described existence?

QUESTIONER: I don't know if I can say that I work that way.

LORD PENTLAND: You see that sometimes from far, far away you're called to be present. It's like something that comes from far away and you're suddenly called to face the fact that you're being sorry for yourself or whatever it is. We have to get experience in what is an obstacle to that moment and what's not. There is a general feeling that a kind of quiet, and an interest in myself, is helpful towards that experience but it may not be so true, because there's so much introspection and dreaming that goes on when I'm quiet.

Really, what we're speaking of is connected with a kind of sincerity, and an active outer life may not be so disadvantageous to this kind of experience, even if it involves tension, and all of that. Where the problem lies is in the moments when I'm not committed, when I'm in between circumstances which call on me for some kind of work, in between times.

twenty-four

There is an octave of quality of perception . . .

QUESTION: There's something about facing a situation with my head that doesn't work, or it's a part of my head that doesn't work. And there is something about facing situations in a different way. I was in a position once where a drain was blocked and I had to crawl down into the drain, actually to poke down in there. And there's a moment of squeamishness and a moment of revulsion when you finally decide, well, someone has to go down in it and reach around and find the hole. Then there's a connection. But in my life nothing pushes me, nothing seems to bring me to the point where I say, "Damn it, I've got to reach down there and muck around in the filth," or whatever, in this unnameable substance.

LORD PENTLAND: Special conditions here.

QUESTIONER: Yes. And I made a connection with that and with another incident that happened here in terms of what was read Friday night about moments of life being symbolic—that every moment can be symbolic. It seems to me that this is also what you're saying in terms of bringing the head and the instinctive center into confrontation. Because then I have energy and now all I have is words.

LORD PENTLAND: Yes, but we don't change. We don't try to do. We try to come to ableness through perception, through seeing and hearing and knowing better. Through cleaning the vessel, coming to different—there are levels of perception—we become able. It isn't that we're avoiding the whole question of doing, but we are saying doing is avoiding the question of being able. Do you follow? The idea of doing means you have an idea and you put all your energy into, behind, this external aim, this external idea.

We're saying we need to be; we need to be able. And for that the only approach is through better perceptions. And we very soon will find that there are levels of perception—that there is an octave of quality of perception. And you have at certain times to stay a long time with a certain best quality of perception and then suddenly you break through to another quality. So don't get weary in your work on listening, work on seeing. One mustn't get emotional about it; one must get to another level of perceiving. For instance, one can perceive things one by one; and then one can perceive things as a whole. And there are levels of wholeness. Whether one can perceive the first series or the second series or the third series, so to speak.

QUESTIONER: Yes, the way I tend to perceive things is that I perceive things with my head.

LORD PENTLAND: With my ordinary outer eyes, my ordinary outer ears, and so on, that's the way I tend to perceive things, most people.

QUESTIONER: Yes. And then there's another level at which I perceive as I'm moving, in the situation, and there's something about that that's very desirable. And it's . . . .

LORD PENTLAND: It's still literal. But then, there's a level . . .

QUESTIONER: It's not static.

LORD PENTLAND: Well, all right, it's not static.

QUESTIONER: Do you see what I'm trying to say? That what you're saying about perception, I perceive or I turn into a static notion. I don't see—in trying to think about it—I don't see it moving. I don't. It's not moving for me.

LORD PENTLAND: You don't see that you don't see it moving. You only think that. This is something you've heard or read or remembered. It's not something you're immediately, directly seeing now.

QUESTIONER: It's true.

LORD PENTLAND: Yes? Memory is not a way of perceiving. It's a way of losing perception. You have to pay for remembering something by taking your attention away from perceiving. You so to speak go to the dictionary. Well, you lose the sensation you had of yourself, or whatever. You go into a part of yourself. You're sitting there, you're in touch with all the parts of yourself. You have a mind that is able to relate the head, feeling, moving part, thinking part, the arms, the legs, and so forth. All of that is clear. And now you get the idea, "I must go and look it up in the dictionary." You see? And as long as you can resist that, you will remain whole. Now as soon as you give in to that, you get up. What is there left of you? Nothing but the head. You follow me?

QUESTIONER: Yes.

LORD PENTLAND: And you may say you're thinking about being in movement or something and that by moving you'll make the sensation more real, but it doesn't. You lose it. It's the same thing if there's some book of Gurdjieff's or some text of a meeting or something you want to remind yourself with. Memory will not help you. You get up to look up that paper and you get all confused. You see that confusion comes from efforts made by the formatory part, by the subjective part. If you'd only just lie back and dream like you do a lot of the time, you wouldn't get confused. But if you make efforts with this subjective part, you start to get confused. You see what I mean? So either you have to get somebody to support you and bring you food and do everything or else you have to learn to make your efforts with an unsubjective side, with a part that recognizes that this is the lot of man and you don't get satisfaction just from going to the office.

It is only when I am helpless that I will be able to find help . . .

QUESTION: I have a question about being lost. I couldn't stand the feeling. It was a panic almost. Like how do you come to look at that lost feeling in a useful way? I was away from the house and also on break from my regular routine. I wanted to find something to do. I tried reading; I was trying to read *Beelzebub's Tales*, trying to find things to do. It was so uncomfortable, that feeling of being lost. I wanted to go see a movie or to go see people. I didn't go see people all week, somewhat intentionally. But I wanted to burst with the uncomfortableness.

LORD PENTLAND: And now?

QUESTIONER: Now I'm not feeling it.

LORD PENTLAND: How not to put the brakes on it? Is there anyone you allowed to hear your hysteria?

QUESTIONER: My husband.

LORD PENTLAND: So, next time you will understand that it is only when I'm helpless that I will be able to find help. And if I'm helpless, where will I find help? The whole point is that I don't know where I'll find help. Are you able to take it out on your husband without feeling ashamed?

QUESTIONER: It took a long time, but I think it reached that.

LORD PENTLAND: I'm not suggesting to find help from outside, but the first step is to recognize that this is the prior requirement to finding help: I have to feel helpless. Little by little I may be able to consider others in a state like that, but the first thing is not to cut myself into little bits by saying that I shouldn't be helpless. Then the next part says, "I'll be helpless later, when I come to the meeting." We begin to understand about the possibility of movement. When I'm looking for something there is no use in sitting still. I must find some way to move, either inner or outer. Were you looking for outer help?

QUESTIONER: Yes, outer help. I didn't really seek outer help; but . . . .

LORD PENTLAND: Often when we seek outer help, we go into the bedroom and lock the door and when we seek inner help, we start calling the dentist or something. But you must know what you are looking for, what kind of help, and then move toward it. It is very important to relax, to be relaxed, to not be resisting.

QUESTION: I sense in myself the inability to turn around and face the part of myself that I wish to be able to face. I insist on turning my back on it and I'm beginning to see the ways that I do that. I want to understand better how to bring into view the moment when my feeling doesn't support the wish to be turned toward the higher in myself.

LORD PENTLAND: That's one kind of understanding you speak about—I want to understand better how to be better than I am. But there's another kind of understanding—an understanding how I am that I'm not put down by it. Yes? This is another kind of knowledge. As long as I'm so possessive that I want to be better than I am, this is the "Fifth Way" or something. You see what I mean?

QUESTIONER: Maybe I could go on, it calls up a question about egoism. You just called it possessiveness now.

LORD PENTLAND: You see my point. In the pottery, you know, if the pots start talking like you do—you know if one pot says to the one next door, "I want to be like you," the potter or the potteress who made that pot says, "Don't insult me. I made you like you are. If you want to be like the one next door, I'll destroy you." Do you understand that?

QUESTIONER: Yes.

LORD PENTLAND: "I made you the way you are. Some energy came through my arms and you turned out like that. Why do you want to be like the one next door? So if I hear any more of that, I'll throw you out." You know, that's what sometimes these people in the pottery are, quite hot-blooded.

QUESTION: One of your earlier responses seemed directed toward listening. But suddenly it seemed to affect a much larger area than just listening. And I feel that I have a question about this, that there's something weak in my attitude; that I feel that there are some vibrations here that are good for me, but at the same time I feel this weakness in my attitude. Maybe it's because I think that I know what I want, but I don't know.

LORD PENTLAND: Well, that's perhaps a certain particular stage of the process. By repeatedly finding this attitude, I shall eventually be able to come past this place when I feel a sort of weakness and I shall be sure of the attitude. But there will still be a weakness. I won't feel it. I'll be sure of the attitude. But then I shall have to see what goes wrong. Do you follow me? We start with doubts about it. We go on to be more sure of it. And we go beyond that to find exactly how my unique attitude is capable and incapable of being a vehicle for this work of transformation. As long as you feel the weakness, you'll have to go on trying. And in time you'll see you become more confident that you can find this attitude. Yes? There are many opportunities for trying. You try not even once a day now. If you want to go quicker, you can do a little more than that. Yes?

The idea of listening is that—you said, "just listening"—the idea of listening is that there is a kind of opening towards the ideal of just listening, of there being nothing going on except listening. And you see something always interferes; some association, some dream, is always interrupting. You were trying to listen to me now but you see you interrupt. Almost everybody is interrupting. You don't just listen. And this interrupting is what is the first step. How to see that we interrupt the whole time? It's such a mockery because outside, outwardly, externally, we're very quiet. And we're sort of like good little kids. But inside there's all the interrupting going on. You know? So just listening is a long way ahead of us.

You see when you start to listen, like now, you see that there are inner noises and outer noises. That's the first thing you heard. Did you hear that just now? Yes. So you see, to start with, you have to make up your mind about that or you'll get giddy, first listening to inner noise, then outer noise. It's all the same thing. But to start with, you have to make up your mind, be absolutely impartial, to give exactly fifty percent of your interest to the inner noise and fifty percent to the outer noise. Do you understand? You start like that. You have to have a more exacting standard. What would be exactly giving the same amount of attention to the inner noise and the outer noise? I think I have that equal, you know. Then, at a certain point, I jump. I say, well, it's all the same anyway, inner, outer, it's all one thing. And you see at that point, if you wait long enough, you cross over to a new level of just listening.

Do you want me to go on further? Well then, ask some questions about it.

Listening is a way of finding what I am—the listener . . .

QUESTION: The wonderful thing about sounds seems to be that they have no duration. Just like in this moment, either I hear them or I don't. Yet they go on forever. Could you say anything about the effort to listen and its relation to a search for some movement which simply corresponds to life? My association about efforts is that the rhythm can't go on, and yet it's clear that there is life here, going on at this moment.

LORD PENTLAND: You see the whole thing is really a kind of catch to create a situation in which we get so interested in sound that we forget what we're really interested to find is the listener. One has to be aware of this movement as a conversation proceeds. We started out to find the listener; this is what it's all about. There's no point in listening. I'm not interested in listening except that it's a way of finding what I am—the listener. And as I listen to the conversation, it has to move out, it has to get farther and farther away from where it's supposed to go. And it eventually gets so far away that it's gone. And then, you know, suddenly you realize that we were talking about nothing. This was a conference, if you like, of caterpillars, one caterpillar saying to another caterpillar, "What is transformation?" And the other, answering in certain terms.

And yet? "I am a listener," we're saying. Not, "I am a camera," this particular time. I am a listener. Not self-observation but, sort of, if you like, self-listening—that's the idea. Everything is vibration. So instead of trying to free myself from all sorts of habits of taking in form and color and speaking as a kind of—out of a sort of sense of—visual freedom and looking around and saying all these particular forms, particular colors, are just a particular arrangement, I'm trying to listen and think of the sounds as being particular. And the point is that, just like suddenly the forms and the colors stand out from the walls and you say, "Oh, that's that, that's what that is," so can the sounds be different when the listener is transformed. Isn't that right?

What helps me is a kind of reduction of myself to size . . .

QUESTION: Lord Pentland, you speak as though there were a quite definite order in terms of the work, in terms of what is possible for men. And yet, at the same time, in trying to make efforts and live my life during the day and during the week, I find myself in a state of disorder. The contact with that order doesn't seem to happen, doesn't seem to come about. And yet it's always like a wish or feeling that yes, there is really an order that I can make contact with that would be intelligent in a way where I could live my life and be in a new way, other than in the way I am now. And yet, constantly, there is this experience of just always falling short, just never quite being able to be there and make the contact.

LORD PENTLAND: Yes. What I was saying is simply that what's obvious is not always seen. And the obvious fact is that I'm one of three or four billion people who are potentially candidates for self-development, and one of so many million people who are seriously giving study to that, one of so many thousands who are working in the Gurdjieff system. But the way I approach the search has a kind of carelessness that doesn't testify to these facts.

In order to be more sincere, I should be more aware of the distractions to my aim. I've found that the only thing that helps me is a kind of reduction of myself to size, which is something that can't be done once and for all, so we work at it every day. Yes? This is what community effort looks like from the point of view of the work. In other traditions it's put differently. In other traditions we're asked to say a little prayer, or something, for all sentient beings. Well, that reduces one to size. See what I mean? I'm only saying the same thing but from our point of view.

We start from saying, "I occupy this space." But somebody was telling me today that at one of our sittings they occupied the whole movements hall. Well, I understand what they mean and, you know, it's not to laugh at it, but unfortunately if we go that way we shall get careless. Our attention won't receive the help it does if we can reduce ourselves to our actual size. We think to borrow some of the power that's in the system—as if we could—but until we have our own power, we have to recognize that that belongs to the work, not to me.

QUESTIONER: It really gets to be a question of what is it that I'm really searching for, what is it that I really want, what is my real aim? Because it seems to change so often. One day it's this, the next day it's that. I don't get really focused in on what it is I should be making efforts for.

LORD PENTLAND: Well, if you can remember not to let your thoughts go more than one meter from yourself, this gives quite a limitation on the changing of one's aims.

The difficulty is to accept the results . . .

QUESTION: I've been attempting to study or examine what motivates me in the work, in my creative endeavors and in almost everything that I do in life. It seems that I'm always trying to satisfy my ego or my feeling of self-importance. My question has to do with what else would be available to me? What is an alternative to my being just centered in my own self-concern?

LORD PENTLAND: When you started this, asking what motivates me, would you say it was an open inquiry and you really wanted to find out?

QUESTIONER: I don't know if it started as an open inquiry, but it became that.

LORD PENTLAND: So you find the answer. So what is the question?

QUESTIONER: Do I have something that motivates me other than my ego?

LORD PENTLAND: But you started to find out in a right way. You found out that your ego motivates you. So what's your question?

QUESTIONER: How do I find another way?

LORD PENTLAND: You started with an open inquiry to ascertain something, to find out if there was anything but your mechanicalness and your ego. You found out that there is nothing. So what's the question?

QUESTIONER: I don't know.

LORD PENTLAND: It seems to be how to accept that. Yes? You got the answer, but you are not willing to accept it. Would you say that is right?

CHAPTER TWENTY-FOUR

QUESTIONER: Yes, that's right. I'm ambitious. I want to be something else.

LORD PENTLAND: What motivates you in that?

QUESTIONER: I think part of it is a dissatisfaction with seeing how small I am, but there's part of me that is genuinely wanting something for myself, but not in a judgmental way.

LORD PENTLAND: So you started to find out what motivates you and you found that there's something non-egoistic that motivates you. What's your question?

QUESTIONER: How can I make this part of me grow?

LORD PENTLAND: That's something else. What is the conversation about? You have doubts and fears. But did you find something out? Is there something you can tell us? Is there something apart from my ego, or not?

QUESTIONER: Yes, there is something apart from my ego.

LORD PENTLAND: Well, now you say you want to make that grow. That is something else. What motivates you in that? Your ego? I'm trying to find out something.

QUESTIONER: Most of the time it is my ego, yes. But not always.

LORD PENTLAND: How do you mean, "not always"? Who is speaking now? The ego, do you mean?

QUESTIONER: No. I feel like it's the other part of me.

LORD PENTLAND: You think it over. You're just talking. It's very marshy ground you're on. You think it over. You're not treading on anything firm. It's a good question to ask, what motivates me. The difficulty is to accept the results. To go further, I must accept the results. You take it to a certain point, that my ego motivates me, that you always seem to be lying. Now, how do you get beyond that?

QUESTIONER: I would have to have a real wish.

LORD PENTLAND: In order to be truthful, it is necessary to accept that I am a liar if I find that I am a liar—not to find a part of myself that is truthful. If I hear myself and find that I am talking lies, I can be truthful only by accepting that. Yes?

QUESTIONER: Yes.

LORD PENTLAND: It is more truthful to say I'm a liar than to say I'm truthful. But you can't say it.

QUESTIONER: I am a liar.

LORD PENTLAND: Sometimes you can say it. Maybe.

Resistance only comes up when I am freed by a moment of observation . . .

QUESTION: I had an impression yesterday which I have had before, although it never quite penetrated me in the same way, of a fundamental delusion that I have. I work and I have moments of being more awake, of more presence, and I am involved in this process that I call my work, which is a cumulative one, and the aim is that at some point I will be more awake than asleep, but it is the familiar me that has these expectations. It is the familiar me that will one day be more awake than asleep. I don't know if I can say that that delusion is shattered or not but it was very clear to me.

LORD PENTLAND: Then it's not.

QUESTIONER: Then it's not? If I can't say it, then it's not? What was clear was the possibility of another being in me. That is my possibility in fact. So how can I work with what is, the familiar me, and somehow support or help this other being to emerge or be more active?

LORD PENTLAND: I think the impressions that you based your question on are very important for you. They represent important experiences. I think the question that came out of you was an imaginary one. The way in which you connected these impressions indicated that you were asleep when you made the question. But the material out of which the question came, on the contrary, was very important. My sense of myself, that you refer to as the ordinary self, could be imagined to be very strong, but, in fact, it is hardly ever there. The ego is always below the conscious level or almost always, so that I manifest in this way that I do out of the most primitive thoughts and emotions without really being aware of it. So that this sort of sense of myself as number one can't be in quite that way opposed to the appearance of my presence. It's like a false struggle. Do you see what I mean?

Even if we had enough time to go on and talk about what you might call imaginary impressions, we could say, I think, that in some groups the idea of self-remembering is taken on that level, so to speak, remembering myself as number one. You follow? This is a natural way to take it, if you haven't got material for coming to deeper impressions. We have never taken it that way here that I remember. But the absence of this sort of sense of self in my ordinary functions is so strong that even the idea of self-remembering is applied there, if you see what I mean. It is not where we apply it, but I am so forgetful of myself that even there it is sometimes applied. So we can't really say the opposition is between that and presence.

There is an interesting thing I could add, but it doesn't directly refer to your impression. You see, when I do observe myself, very often the observation is accompanied or is followed by a big emotional reaction to the observation—a feeling of satisfaction or resentment or something. This is where the ego comes up. This is where what you were describing as an enemy of the presence comes up. But the very fact that it only comes up when I observe myself shows me that this resistance is something that I am not usually conscious of. The resistance to the wish is something that only comes up when I am freed by a moment of observation. Then all my vanity, all my greed, all my everything comes up. Do you see what I mean?

QUESTIONER: All of that is submerged.

LORD PENTLAND: All of that is below the conscious level most of the time. This false sense of "I" only comes up then.

The vision that I need doesn't arrive until I come to myself . . .

QUESTION: I feel that I need to be able to think in a direct kind of way, which I can't do unless there is this element of observation. I feel that the thought that appears, interesting or not, even when relevant or helpful to me—that I need to let go of it in order to think. I have thoughts that are very complicated and I need to let them go. I feel that I have these images as you speak, as if I could be able to think more fully about the work, my work, in a way that would support my work on attention. I have this image that I can work on myself, that I can pay attention, but when I look more closely, I find that I have to question that.

LORD PENTLAND: I need more energy. The thought appears that I could be a thinker, that there could be thinking, and I prematurely grasp it. It's like other thoughts. It is something I meet with at a certain level. But then in order to operate at a level where thinking will turn towards myself, I need to let that thought go, too. There are levels, and the vision that I need in which there is a different kind of thinking, a different kind of feeling, and so forth, doesn't appear until I come to myself. But if I go off, taken by this thought about how to think better, before coming to that level, there never will be the energy to make my thinking turn towards myself.

So, in a way, the appearance of this thought is a promising sign, like a cloud is promising rain, but it isn't rain. Even the thought is a beginning there. Everything appears first of all in glimmerings. Perhaps, even this thought is the beginning of something, as long as I don't take it to be more than it is—just a glimmering, just a pointer to an actual ability, when I am freer from all those hang-ups, to put things together with my thought. There is a different kind of thinking, but first of all I need to open to myself at the moment I am taken by all these external things— thoughts—even the thought about better thinking. I need air. I need impressions. I don't need thoughts about thinking.

I don't feel enough my inattention, my inability to come in touch with the wish. It must be that I don't enough recognize, I don't accept, my poor ability to come in touch with the search for the wish or the wish itself and, therefore, some stray thoughts about this or that or some memory of some experience can take me away. I am not enough clear that it is this wish for coming to a better state of attention that can help me in this aspect of my life connected with the work. I can't expect my recognition of my inattention to help me in making my living or in looking after my family. That's another aspect of my life. But as far as I am taking some special valuation of the work, giving some of the best of my life to that, what helps is to see that I am divided, that I am not able to bring this extra energy because it is going off thinking about something else. So, I need to see that, and seeing that makes me emotional. When I see that, it makes me a little angry, a little irritated, a little annoyed. I can't accept that and I need to see this emotion arising out of that. This emotion comes, has a taste of the personal, and if I am able to see it, then the action of seeing my inattention is to bring more of me together, to make me more attentive, and for a time, it goes better—the search—up to a point where this happens again.

twenty-five

No one is practicing the study of the food diagram . . .

QUESTION: I feel lost, lost in how to see myself and relate with other people in some way that's not critical, constantly criticizing so much that it seems to be the only way I do see and feel, very locked into that way of seeing.

LORD PENTLAND: The point of an exchange has to do with understanding our effort better. What are you trying?

QUESTIONER: I was attempting just to see, just to see myself and others.

LORD PENTLAND: So what's your question?

QUESTIONER: Isn't there another kind of seeing instead of being locked into this way of analysis? I tell myself "So you're seeing that you analyze," but I'm not satisfied.

LORD PENTLAND: Everybody remembers but no one is practicing the study of the food diagram. We study the thought part of it and try to see thought, and we study the physical part of it and see that, but to study it means to study all of it—to experience the food and the digestion of food and the variety of energies all at the same time. You make a separate practice of studying the physical and the psychical, yet it's all one octave. We tend to eat, then to talk. By the time we talk, there's no digestion experienced and when we're eating, there's no thought being observed. It's nonsensical really, isn't it? It's still a mystery that the energy that goes into the body becomes the negative energy another time. So people actually choose not to eat sugar or to eat honey and so forth. What's that got to do with it? Maybe something, but it hasn't all that much to do with it, does it? Or people drink Mu tea. Do you know what Mu tea is? It's all right to study the effects of foods on you, but it's the whole physical-psychical thing all at the same moment. Well, it's just a thought. You know, this Mu refers to a koan; what's the koan?

QUESTIONER: Does a dog have Buddha nature?

LORD PENTLAND: And what's the answer?

QUESTIONER: Mu.

Once I have accepted, then I'm in touch with a big movement . . .

QUESTION: Is acceptance not reacting? I wonder if going toward acceptance is seeing that you are reacting as opposed to being passive, going along with everything. From what I can see, I do react. If there's some emotion attached, I go along with it. I guess I don't see any possibility of my not judging. Instead of going with judging and seeing that I judge, I guess I'm asking how close that would be to accepting.

LORD PENTLAND: Acceptance in itself puts me in touch with a movement which changes what I've accepted. If you try to compress that and say, "That's too complicated so I won't accept it," that doesn't work. Once I have accepted, then I'm in touch with a big movement. But I have to really accept it and give up the idea of changing it. And then I have to give up hope, but that way I come in touch with a movement which is in the same direction as hope. You may say that's too complicated, but it's not. You feel better already about acceptance, don't you? But you couldn't have come to that without having to accept.

Unless I am ready, I won't work . . .

QUESTION: I've had two experiences. One on the bus. Someone sat next to me and I felt a chemical reaction, wanting to get away. There were other seats the person could have sat in. I remembered that it was an opportunity and in that moment it seemed to shift and I tried to experience what I was feeling. And I just felt the wind on my face and the ride of the bus. It seemed so simple at that moment. The question at that time was, "Why does it always seem so hard?"

LORD PENTLAND: Because it is very hard. In order to work with that, I would have to start to work at once, as soon as I experience the chemical feeling. If I delay for an instant, I will never do it. It means that unless I'm ready, I won't work. And that's what life, unfortunately, is made up of— of opportunities for real work which I can't take because I'm not ready.

So I think everybody would agree that we don't work enough. There are two reasons for that. One is when there is an opportunity—I don't know yet what your work is but whatever your work is, when there is an opportunity—it's limited. I come to the limit. You try to work and you soon reach the limit. You get angry, or whatever, and you work with that to try to be quiet, and you find you come that far but you can't come farther. If you want to learn to be farther, there are the other occasions when it occurs to you to work, and you say, "No, it's not especially important today."

Being aware of the movement of my attention . . .

QUESTION: Lately a number of things I have wanted in life seem to be falling into place without any effort on my part. The question that leaves me with revolves around the subject that there are things that I've desired. And I have a question about will, a question of how can I have a taste of knowing it isn't what I thought it was? I'm trying to be more present to what's happening in my conversations with other people, an effort of wanting to be present to that conversation that's taking place, having a sense of myself during the process of it.

LORD PENTLAND: I can't understand will unless I've understood something about the movement of my attention. What do you find? Are you able to prevent your attention going to your emotions? All the attention that goes to the emotions is wasted. In order to understand will, that means putting the three parts together; you have to be able to keep your attention on them together. If any of it goes to the emotions, feeling satis-fied, and so forth, you won't have enough energy to keep the parts together. Insofar as you have said in your question, if we let any attention go into that, we are not able to be present to the parts.

So will isn't quite the point. The point is, what control do you have? Do you have an attention at all? When you go into the movements hall, you find you have very little attention. If you weren't in the movements hall, you might not have noticed it.

Being aware of the movement of my attention—it's for that I come back to myself. It's only when the parts are in a relative degree of balance that I have any freedom of attention at all. One can try listening, looking at things. But really the attention doesn't appear unless there is a degree of presence. And free attention then is very apt to wander into the emotional areas. But there it's quite useless. My self is what exists if I can keep the attention from playing with the emotions at all. Do you understand?

The question of what I want is not yet settled . . .

QUESTION: I was struck with the Far West lectures, with the question about what it is to be living because it was once said to me that I had never lived. I thought off and on about this and never really understood. It seemed to me from the lectures that living is an inner sense of being alive, having that feeling of living. When I am reminded about the idea that I could be alive, it excites me. But the doing is so different. Maybe if some-how I could keep in mind the bigger scope of things it would make the lit-tle things I try seem not so meaningless. They seem so arbitrary, the things I give myself to do for the day, like that I would sense myself. But it seemed empty, and did not seem to have too much to do with living.

LORD PENTLAND: I think it's very good what you're trying. But we know, of course, that the challenge has to do not only with what I'm try-ing, but with the way I'm trying it. In what you said at the end, you were touching on this. It is as if there is always something more immediate or direct. In the task as it is remembered, there is something more indirect. When I first face it, the challenge reminds me, and I can go through the whole task without coming to the more direct way I'm working, which is where work is. In the earlier part of what you said there was something very valuable but not so immediate or direct, because you were speaking about an emotion or an attitude that you didn't have at the time, about a feeling of "I." A more direct way of working is "Who am I now?" If I asked them, many people would say, "I'm an emotional person." But when you look now, you see that "I" must be somewhere.

So we come to this way of working by looking to the very present moment, which is often the contradiction of what I regard as the meaning of the task, which is usually an outer meaning. The question of "Who am I?" is a large question, yet it is a small question, really, of who I am now—what I am now, not what I might be later or tomorrow morning. Something about the food diagram relates to this too, that it is given as an example as well as a particular description. It is an example of any evolutionary octave. So this is going on right now. We are reaching toward a result that is very interesting. You could ask yourself with great benefit, "What is it I want, what is the result I'm working for?" The movement back from the distraction of what I recognize as the task is weak, but this is what leads to the results of working, which means a kind of broadening out of my viewpoint—not a strengthening of the impressions, but a widening of those impressions, seeing the implications of my work, taking in other people's work as well as my own—instead of heading very strongly in a certain direction. So it's very useful in this, to not only be making up my mind to work but to be observing this making up of my mind, to be observing then. You see, the question of what I want is not yet settled. This is why you feel excitement—you move from one desire to another. Yes? It is good that you try to come back, to see that. The intention is so much wider than I can take in; even my intention is something to be observed, and it gets stronger not through will power, but through self-observation and a kind of study.

The ability to control my emotional trolley . . .

QUESTION: I was really interested in what was said last Thursday night about being either too withdrawn or too impulsive, because I thought it was a way of capsulizing two things I think I am that keep me from being in the moment. It seems that the times this week when I tried to be present, thinking about this being too withdrawn or too impulsive was a kind of being filled with myself. It's like when I first came into the room tonight. I wanted to be available to something, and what rose up was a kind of being so habitually in appearances, of wondering what kind of impression I'd make. I can't quite get rid of it even in this moment. Something has been said about self-absorption and not feeding it. I wonder. I'd like some seed in myself that maybe could remind me.

LORD PENTLAND: Yes, we're all very moved by what you say. I don't have the freedom to move forward to you—I don't have it, and I'm too withdrawn. Or I'm too impulsive—I light up, and I'm all over you, without restraint. So I don't have the freedom, the ability to control my emotional trolley away from you or toward you. But that's why we start with self-observation, because all this judgment that I'm too withdrawn or too impulsive makes me tense. I have to remember that I'm alive, and I'm doing my best. I feel drawn to you because of this question. So it doesn't help to put judgment and distance between us. We have to observe, and we'll come to remarkable conclusions. We'll see that this lack of emotional freedom is not so important. It's important, but we'll see that it is not so important as we thought. Something else will be more important than that, and we'll respect one another. You follow?

QUESTIONER: Yes. I think the fear is wanting something. But I think something is coming through in spite of the fear.

LORD PENTLAND: The fear will always be there. Freedom from it is something we have to work for. Be careful of these judgments. They come, if I may say, chiefly from judgments of others, and they are also taking place in myself: "I'm too this" or "I'm too that"—negative judgments, not connected at all with self-observation. Self-observation is a question of seeing myself in a moment like that. I see that I have no emotional freedom. It is something else to say that I'm too impulsive—that's a reaction to seeing that I have no emotional freedom. Be careful about judgments of other people, because we make them of ourselves— if we can see this. Anyone who can invite the judgments of other people is a saint. But that's your suffering; you see your conversation is nothing but these judgments. You score yourself according to how subtle your judgments of your friends are. To do without that is the way of working.

It's more important, the seer end, than what is seen . . .

QUESTION: I started to accumulate a certain number of glimpses, a certain number of observations of myself. Some caused me real anguish. In terms of trying to verify statements of the work, I observe incessant inner talking. I can be negative and go into rages, and I am not able to prevent them. I can see my inability to remember myself. I can see the various statements that the work makes about myself, though sometimes I rationalize them away. My question is, basically, to what use can this fuel be put? Where do these observations lead me?

LORD PENTLAND: Do you feel them as leading you nowhere?

QUESTIONER: There's a sort of helplessness in the sight of some of these. I've probably seen these things about myself since I was very young, and I've excused myself by saying that I evolve as I grow older. But I'm beginning to realize that they are permanent features of me.

LORD PENTLAND: Very good. Then what's important about observing?

QUESTIONER: To learn about myself.

LORD PENTLAND: If these are permanent features, then what is important is that at the moment of observing, I'm seeing them. So it's more important, the seer end, than what is seen. Yes? The big element that we're not conscious of is not just in what is seen, but in the absence most of the time of a seer. Would you agree?

QUESTIONER: Yes.

LORD PENTLAND: So with this understanding, one can return to the work of self-observation with a quieter and a different sense of purpose. One can return to observing with less curiosity, but with more determination, because the seer is rarely there. The idea that the seer is there for more than the brief moment when we see, it is a hopeless question. So the question is if the seer could be there with some duration. Have you asked yourself that question? If not, there is a revolution awaiting you—the emphasis is on the observer.

QUESTIONER: I've sensed that before.

LORD PENTLAND: In a way, the two come together, the outer and the inner life are part of one thing. If we try to separate them too much, if we make too strong a distinction, then we bury the whole thing. If we talk too much about my inner self that has to be discovered, then something becomes too heavy. So I'm beginning to see the need to appreciate more the seeing.

QUESTIONER: I recognize this, because I'm rarely there in the observation. I may observe something, but I have no sense of presence. I'm just observing a function, and often I observe the same thing over and over again because there isn't this presence.

LORD PENTLAND: It's a question if I've really observed the same thing again and again so much, or whether I anticipate it when I'm close to observing it again. To save myself the work of observing it, I just think about it again in my mind. So in observation, I may have the sense of newness about it even if I'm observing the same thing. I can observe it as if for the first time, with that newness. Have you noticed that, too?

QUESTIONER: Yes, because each moment has a newness, if it is being repeated or not.

LORD PENTLAND: For example, lots of people speak to me about how to have compassion for myself, how to accept what I see, that I am that. They ask also how to have compassion for others. But you see, it can't be had. Compassion for others is an empathy for another. I observe myself having compassion for another, but it comes from observing, not from trying. You're on the right road, but there has to be a revolutionary shift from the observed to the observer, and it has to be done lightly—not because someone told you to do it, but because you see that is where the honey is.

The inner life comes to us, not from anything that has been planned . . .

QUESTION: Often I observe myself doing the same thing I've seen before, and I get a new feeling from it. It is as if I had never learned it before. But I thought that was wrong, that it was invalid, and that if I observed something again and it felt new, it was because I never really observed it.

LORD PENTLAND: This inner life you spoke of earlier, you think you can learn to be in touch with that. The difficulty is here: I can't by myself have access to that, just by myself I can't have access to the truth of what I am in this moment. To some extent, I can try—I can try to be attentive, to listen. But by myself I can't. That is why we speak of a search. I can't come to my inner life until I've recognized that I've ignored it, that I've not made room for it so that it could come in. But still something else brings it. So it's why we speak of search. The search is not to go down every blind alley, but it still is a search—it is in the unknown, though not in a mysterious way. The inner life is not mysterious, but the way to it is unknown. If it comes to us, it comes out of the unconscious, not from anything that has been planned or written to do—even in *Beelzebub's Tales*. Does that meet with what you were asking?

QUESTIONER: Yes.

The attention settles on something characteristic of ourselves . . .

QUESTION: I've observed that I spend a lot of time at home, and it is the hardest place for me to observe myself, yet I feel it is an important place for me—my husband and my children are important people in my life. But as soon as I leave my home, I sense myself better; I wake-up. Tonight as I was leaving my house, I turned around and a sadness came over me because I miss so much. I try, but never seem to be able to move forward quickly in my home. I don't understand why that is.

LORD PENTLAND: It's because you are attached to your home, isn't it? What is work for, if not for de-identification? If there is someone—maybe not your husband—whom you are attached to, how can one free oneself from that? That is the question. To be attentive, I have to free my attention. What a work that is. My attention clings to things and maybe for you it clings especially to your husband, to your home, to your nest, how you've arranged things. You've given up something precious to you maybe; you're attached in some way. I don't know—I don't know you. But work is a question of freeing my attention again and again from what it is sitting on and bringing it back to myself. It is related to observation. The attention settles on something characteristic of ourselves. We have to keep bringing it back, to free it. It is obvious that I need that energy to see at the source, and that is the source in myself. If I don't see what is going on in myself, my family won't benefit, even if you arrange everything well for them.

QUESTIONER: Sometimes I see clearly what to do, but then I forget it and go back to how I was before.

LORD PENTLAND: You have to make up your mind. The whole work is responding to a challenge you put to yourself. Do you do movements?

QUESTIONER: I've just started.

LORD PENTLAND: You've just started. So you see something is given to you that is more difficult than you can do. So there is a challenge. Or do you put it off until the next week and say, "Oh, well"? We have to realize that the work is one thing which we are not—it is totally unsentimental, unromantic. Do you follow what I mean?

QUESTIONER: No, I don't know what you mean by that.

LORD PENTLAND: You'll find out. You have to be free from the emotions to be able to make use of them, to be able to move where you want. It's a big order.

QUESTIONER: Sometimes I get an insight into what I need to do, but then I lose it.

LORD PENTLAND: So you see, you have to try more often. You see that you forget. But the first thing is to remember. Yes?

QUESTIONER: Yes. But the insight leaves very quickly, and I am back to where I was before.

LORD PENTLAND: Then you have to make a program to work more often, yes? Then you won't forget so easily. It is the first step. Do you see what I mean?

QUESTIONER: I'll have to try it, I guess. Certain things come and I see that I want to work in a particular way, but then I go back to the way I was before and lose that insight.

LORD PENTLAND: You don't need to remember that insight, but to remember that there is an insight within reach if I try to work now. I have to remember there is a presence I can see if I come in touch with it. It's not that particular insight—that insight applied an hour ago. But there is an insight there. So forget the insight; the "inseer" is the one you want to remember. It's a very big aim, what you are speaking of, to observe oneself in one's home. Can you afford that yet? Are you really willing to do that?

QUESTIONER: I try. But when I leave home, I can work easier.

LORD PENTLAND: Some people who aren't clear about what they really want have this devil in them that sets them to try something that is too difficult, and so they have always an excuse for not working. It sounds very elaborate and subtle, but it is really very common. The work absolutely cuts through that and says, "Why don't I be more logical and work in easier conditions for me, and work up to these conditions where there is a strong identification?" Do you see?

There is this potential energy that can just look . . .

QUESTION: I've been having difficulty feeling sincere about the work. I feel that sincerity toward the work is the only thing that will gain me anything, if I work. Yet when I leave here, the resistance always seems to overtake whatever feeling or achievement, whatever I gain. I know it feels better when I'm here than when I'm away from here. But the resistance is strong. I would like some help in being sincere toward the work. I always have the feeling that I can do, but I don't do anything.

LORD PENTLAND: What is the work? A work of self-observation?

QUESTIONER: Yes.

LORD PENTLAND: So in a way, how can there be any resistance? As soon as the work is placed in the framework of simply being, of self-observation, of simply observing what goes on—if that is the work—what can resist that? It is always possible to look, if I remember that. What I see may not please me, it may not be what I think I ought to see, but that is exactly why the approach to the work is possible, and how a change can be theoretically and practically conceivable, because it simply takes place through awareness of what is. Nothing is changed.

When you go away, one tries to do these things and one tries to do self-observation. But what is the difference? What really is the difference? For example, now, you can look at yourself, just look. Whatever is going on emotionally, whatever your mind is trying to remember and record, you can look. It only takes a flash. You can look at your body, its posture. Do you follow what I mean?

QUESTIONER: Yes.

LORD PENTLAND: It is possible. It is something very light. It is something that still falls within the category of self-observation. You are just looking, but you did it. It connects self-observation and doing. Is that enough of a connection?

QUESTIONER: Yes.

LORD PENTLAND: Why do you have to be heavy about it? What if I said that were you to move even a little finger, it would upset the whole cosmic plan; Venus would start changing its course, and so on? Everything is interconnected, so the idea of doing is out. I'm just a tiny speck, a particle, of that vastness. Isn't it enough recognition of my identity that I can remember just to look? If you go by that, then if I move a little finger, I'm trying to alter a plan made by vastly greater forces than myself. So what is being initiated is enormous changes, but starting from something that is possible and not a change at all. Do you see what I mean?

QUESTIONER: Yes. I think the resistance stems from a desire to do more.

LORD PENTLAND: What is being suggested is the initiation for enormous changes. In a man, or a woman, there is this potential energy that can just look, but can't do more. We don't know what will be the result of starting that process. Each time you start that process, it seems you forget, and forget again. But each time I start, I don't know where I'll forget or whether I'll forget or not. I don't know where it will lead. When I don't know here it will lead, maybe then it will last longer. Maybe then I will be interested when I start. If it starts from some ego that wants to change something, it won't last long. But if it starts from an energy that has awareness, that has the property which light has when it is transforming energy—do you understand what I mean by that?—if it has that property, maybe it will continue. I don't know at the time I initiate this who is looking, whether I am using the right energy. There is a *doing* this and a self-observation.

Maybe I'm cheating and trying to do something. Or maybe I'm drawing on a possibility that exists, something universal, a chink of awareness. Maybe that awareness can ferment in me. I don't know what is the process of that fermentation. But you see that coming to the meetings has changed your life. You see that you didn't know where it would lead. So now where will it lead if you start looking?

QUESTIONER: I don't know.

LORD PENTLAND: Then that is what is interesting, to try to follow it, because you know there is a heavy way of working at it that you say creates a resistance.

QUESTIONER: Yes, a feeling of resistance.

LORD PENTLAND: Yet it doesn't make sense. Why would there be a resistance to looking? There must be some way that more parts of me could be interested in looking, that could be curious about this process that is started by looking. Maybe there is a real resistance somewhere, but not this "feeling of resistance." Maybe some parts would really be threatened by this looking, but it wouldn't just be an emotion I keep coming up against. It is very important to see that. Probably you have come across other explanations or keys to human life, to your life, and I think you wouldn't have come to a study of Gurdjieff's teaching if you thought that it was possible for me, and you, to be completely transformed into light and grace and compassion, so to speak. Do you follow?

CHAPTER TWENTY-FIVE

QUESTIONER: Yes. Well, I'm going along for the ride.

LORD PENTLAND: So maybe there is a resistance somewhere but you haven't found it, the real resistance. Maybe you have a kind of intuition that transformation is not as easy as all that—one doesn't become an angel. There will be some real discoveries that can't be foreseen, that are not uniform. You won't suddenly have compassion for every living being—then you would become a Buddha. So there is a resistance but not what you say, this "feeling of resistance." It is a reaction to a heavy way of observing. I'm sorry to be so long.

QUESTION: I've experienced a sense of unreality for most of my life, for as long as I can remember. It has always been with me to a greater or lesser extent. It is a sense of not understanding why I'm here, of being totally out of contact with both the external and the inner life, of not feeling in touch, in contact, with anything. I'm wondering if you can throw some light on that.

LORD PENTLAND: There is something very healthy, something very positive, about your question, because it is always in trying to face life, to get over what separates me from life, that the thrust of the search needs to be. The very fact that you speak of not being able to face life, to confront it— inner life, outer life, it is the same thing—shows that something is working in a right way in you. Have you ever read René Daumal's *Mount Analogue?*

QUESTIONER: No.

LORD PENTLAND: It can be gotten; it's in the library. He speaks of a search—that when a group finally gets started to climb the mountain, the leader picks up a "peradam." He picks up a moment of truth or of self-observation, so to speak. You see this happen at the base of the mountain which they have to climb, in the middle of a culture which has sprung up around the climbers who made it to the base of the mountain and set up shop, waiting to get up the courage to climb up—as if it is possible to have one or two "peradams"—one or two moments of self-observation—and, based on that, to set up a whole life of introspection, which is one step removed from inner or outer life. It is as if one picks up the one moment of self-observation that is so valuable that one can stop living.

I find what you say is right. You have to go on living and there is the doubt that I am not really facing it, that I'm not really living my life. Yet I have to go climbing the mountain, with that burden, so to speak, or else the alternative is to stay at the base of the mountain, in Port o' Monkeys, as Daumal calls it, with all these groups, encounter groups, and so on.

Through a feeling of a lack of contact with my life, to find a moment of direct contact with it . . .

QUESTION: It seems that the very thing that gets in the way of my self-observation is trying to do, or else I can get a moment, a short moment, of observation of myself and then I try to do. For example, seeing tension in my body and reacting by not just seeing the tension but relaxing it, or trying to relax it. It is a very automatic thing. The most I can get from that is to see that is what I do. I would like to be able to not react so quickly to that but to see that tension, or other things in my life, without trying to do.

LORD PENTLAND: You speak of something which is even bigger than we generally imagine. I will explain. When I say, "I'm trying to do," I may be accepting or admitting to the fact that there is an ego, a subjective, very often emotional person which is trying to get what it wants out of things. I'm comparing that with some kind of energy of awareness that has kind of magical properties which I don't understand. So I'm saying that I must try to give up this doing, because I prefer to have that awareness. But of course, the motive behind that is still egoistic, if you see. So that isn't going to work.

When we speak of awareness, we aren't just speaking of a kind of light that has photoelectric properties, if you like. Do you understand what I mean by that—that has alchemical properties, a light that can transform—do you follow? But we are not just speaking of that but of an awareness of myself in the universal environment. It would be very egoistic to think I can grab hold of the stuff and that way get ahead. But that is how we often work. Right? That is why I say it is a bigger thing than maybe has dawned on you.

Fortunately for us, Gurdjieff discovered a technique for approaching those vast changes in a way that is possible. That's what is being said.

We're trying to inform, to encourage, to make the rediscovery come alive for you. But you must find your way. We can't hold your hand.

So, is there a possibility of an attention which is not "doing"? That's the question, that is what your question was. Yes? Is there an energy in life, in the inner life or outer life—it is the same thing—which is not tainted by egoism in any way? That's the question being put. If there is, is it possible to make contact with that?

What is really the opposite to doing is that life which exists, and goes on existing, which has properties that go beyond logic, beyond everything I thought. When I speak of doing, when I think that I'm thinking, what does it mean to be in touch, to be out of touch, with life? It communicates to me, one's life—getting up in the morning, taking the ferry. But what is it? Is it possible to be in touch with life? If there is a way, if there is an attention that is not subjective, introspective—that is not ego—it is an attention in touch with life energy. You spoke of sensation, didn't you? Didn't you speak earlier about sensation?

QUESTIONER: I don't know if I used that word. I was speaking of the centers.

LORD PENTLAND: I see. Well, if I am a part of organic life, is there the possibility of being in touch with organic life energy in myself? It is something quite special. As we read in *In Search of the Miraculous*, it is overlaid with all the layers of education, of conditioning, so it's not easy. But is it possible, through a feeling of a lack of contact with my life, to find a moment of direct contact with it? Is it possible to put an infant in a jungle, full of lions and tigers, and so on, and that infant not be harmed? Is there an organic life we are talking about and, if so, is it possible to be part of it?

Gurdjieff said in one of his lesser known sayings—though it was known enough to probably have been printed, so you might have heard it—he said, "I don't like to give you techniques, but take a sponge full of cold water and put it on your wrist, and what you experience then will be the sensation of life—pure of thoughts, not tainted with introspection, with desires." This is what we are speaking about. Is it possible to distinguish, to separate, that kind of energy from the energy with which we think, and analyze, and which eventually causes us to have this layer of subjective conditioning that protects us and perhaps prevents us from contact with this life? Is it understandable, what I'm saying?

QUESTIONER: I can remember moments when I may have had touches of that, something more direct. To see it in that way, a cold sponge on my wrist, I see more now how much I'm not touched by it.

LORD PENTLAND: Of course, you have understood that everything we say is to be taken both literally and metaphorically. And when we speak of putting a sponge of cold water on your wrist, despite the thousands of people who have probably heard it, even from Gurdjieff, and never done it, we still have the faint hope that you will try it. Everyone imagines what it is, saying, "Yes, yes." It was true in Gurdjieff's time too. But we're talking about real layers of conditioning. We all go on and say, "Yes, yes." But we're speaking of such enormous changes that everything has to be taken literally—of coming to these "peradams," of coming to these moments of truth, when I see which center, which energy, predominates—sensation, thinking, or feeling energy. It is very difficult. You can't just go into the bathroom and now you have it. As you say, you may have experienced it. But to differentiate, really to know now I'm in contact with my life, not with the forms of it—how I get out of bed in the morning—but with the energy of it, that is the point.

We do come to higher perceptions than the function of the senses . . .

QUESTION: As part of this process we're working with, will we experience perceptual changes as well as other changes? Will we experience changes in our senses?

LORD PENTLAND: It depends on what you mean. I would say that all the changes will be beyond the level of what we ordinarily call the senses. The ability to perceive life-energy is beyond the level of hearing, seeing, tasting, touching, as they are ordinarily understood. Is that in touch with your question?

QUESTIONER: Well, the form of our visual perception, for example, is limited to a certain band of light. Is it possible to increase this?

LORD PENTLAND: It depends on what you call seeing. In our latest edition of *Material for Thought*, it speaks of "eyes of flesh" and "eyes of fire." Are you speaking of "eyes of flesh?"

QUESTIONER: Yes.

LORD PENTLAND: You see, what is possible is to develop eyes of fire. What is possible is to hear different things than are heard by ears of flesh. But what that means in terms of physical changes in the brain is something we can't speak of, because how can you investigate that? So whether there are new perceptions in the ordinary sense, through a change in the brain, I would say is doubtful. Is that answering what you were asking?

QUESTIONER: Yes.

LORD PENTLAND: I think people who are deaf, relatively, and people who are blind, relatively, can have this kind of perception. So I don't think it is directly connected to ordinary hearing and ordinary seeing. It is not bad to have stated it, because I don't think sensation should be confused with the sense of touch. We come to sensation through a movement of removal or withdrawal from the ordinary senses, through a movement beyond that. So if I'm occupied with thinking about how to have other perceptions of touch, taste, and so on, nothing will happen.

We do come to higher perceptions than the function of the senses, but they are different. That follows, in a way, from the differentiating, the distinguishing of sense energy from thought energy. I think all ordinary senses feed through the front brain, through thought. We're speaking of something more at the back of the head.

The force of intention is as necessary at a certain point
as the tentacles of search . . .

QUESTION: I had an experience this evening that made me question again that part of me that does not wish to work. When that question was originally posed and I tried to search for that part which managed to work, I found a laziness in my body, a feeling that the wish not to work was a wish just to stay put, not to do anything. This evening I experienced something different, which was a very strong feeling saying no, a feeling of being identified in some anger. But it had a quality that was quite different from the usual state which I had experienced and which I thought was preventing me from watching myself, that state of laziness. On the one hand I was overwhelmed by the strength of it. On the other hand it gave me something real to struggle against. It was an enemy that I could see very clearly. There were times when I could try to stand up to it, to try and observe myself, to have a sensation of my body in spite of it—those were very alive moments. It gives me a question about emotions and what part they can play in increasing this struggle.

LORD PENTLAND: I would like to take advantage of your question and say something about the work on intention, which doesn't seem to have been brought into the work of the groups enough here, in my opinion. I think the work on self-observation is the best starting point and has been more or less received by all of you as the starting point for this work, and although there's a lot further to go in order that the idea of studying myself and observing myself might become fixed in me as an attitude, and although it's probably still not apparent to all of you how this idea of self-observation underlies the whole of the work as presented in *In Search of the Miraculous,* and even is constantly being referred to, both literally and metaphorically, in *Beelzebub's Tales,* still the work of self-observation and, beyond that, of receiving impressions of ourselves, hasn't been adequately brought into view.

However, when I look back, this is not the first thing that was brought to me. When I look back, the first strong impressions of work were around a question which was put very much to us by Madam Ouspensky. Madam—she was always called Madam—used to say, "What do you want?" and she practically embodied the question in the way she faced people—What do you want? She was somebody who studied minutely all the aspects of the manifestations of the passive force; and she had all the majesty, all the width of vision of the mountain. And besides her skills of an active kind in the kitchen and so forth, and besides her humor and the laughter which was always around her, there was always this way in which she just sat there, so to speak. And even when she was ill, which lasted over twenty years, she just stayed in her bedroom. In that sense she manifested literally a sort of passive force because the house, and quite a lot of the work around the world, revolved around her bed. And she kept saying to me, "What do you want?" and I didn't understand. What I understood much better, although of course very inadequately, was Gurdjieff's picture of myself as a hackney carriage or taxi into which one passenger after another would get and drive me to different locations. So that I was stumped by this question, "What do you want?"

Nevertheless, the question was brought in a way it needs to be brought, because this idea or force of intention is as necessary, or more necessary at a certain point, as the tentacles of search. And where they come together is where the riddle is solved—that is to say, in the movement of intention, in the fact that intention is not fixed, but intention can bring me in touch with a movement. It's there that I begin to understand the necessity for shocks for the octave to go further. And for the octave of self-observation to go further, for octaves to go further inside us, shocks are just as necessary as they are outside us. And so when you are trying to follow me now and you say to me, "I understand what it means, 'What do you want?' It means nothing to do with outer life, it means the inner." And I say to you, "All the same, how do you keep your intention moving, how do you keep it moving past the shock?" Even if you understand that what you want is to reach myself, presence, the question still arises—how do you move past the shock where you get diverted? What is the inner shock? Have you ever thought about that? If there's an inner work, it can't depend on an outer shock.

I'm supposed to be answering your question. How do you understand the possibility of an inner shock that can bring you back to the line of your intention, your wish to work, your wish to come in touch with your presence, myself? How do you understand that? Did I go on too long? Have you forgotten what you asked?

QUESTIONER: No. I don't quite understand the term, inner shock.

LORD PENTLAND: Well, if there's going to be an intention, it's going to be something that comes eventually in the scale—*do, re, mi*—to a place where it can't get any further. There's an interval. And in order to get further, there needs to be a shock. What do you understand is the shock?

QUESTIONER: A form of energy.

LORD PENTLAND: The shock was being continually given by Gurdjieff, and of course he gave it externally also. When he gave it externally, he said—and he repeatedly did this to all of us, including myself—"I've put you in old Jewish galoshes, up to here." And sometimes he made it even higher. And he refers to the shock repeatedly in *Beelzebub's Tales*, and there he calls it by a very difficult word, suffering.

And what I'm trying to say is that this action of Madam Ouspensky on me in continually saying "What do you want?"—and, of course, you can understand she was not only a much respected, but a much loved figure amongst us—and then she'd keep saying this thing. And you're told that you're not to do anything you don't understand. And you don't understand her. You follow? This is a kind of suffering. She keeps coming back to it, and you feel an idiot, you feel stripped, you know, stripped down like a chicken when it's had its skin taken off, its feathers taken off. So that's what the shock is.

So this explains why we need to understand something by that in order to get further here. We are starting on an inner work. The inner work, ninety percent of it, is in the intention, the wish, understanding the wish and the wish to not work. And this can't get any further because it comes to the interval. And at the intervals a shock is needed. And an outer shock doesn't help when it's an inner work.

I think it's more or less clear what I'm saying, yes? The shock is the recognition that I don't wish observed in the light of wishing, observed in the remnants of an intention. This is a very important thing to take into account. However, it's not easy to come to that. Even to be put externally into galoshes is quite difficult. This is because of the care with which we've all been trained to be responsible. That is to say, we don't understand conscience, "partkdolg duty," or suffering, or intention, inside; it's been educated into us from outside—how to behave, how to keep one's chin up, all the different forms that responsibility takes, how to not acknowledge one's faults; this outer education is largely an education in what one might call responsibility. And in order to allow the falsenesses to show themselves to me inside, instead of always suppressing them due to education and canons of behavior, I have to shed some of this educated coating of responsibility.

And some of you have gone some way to do that. You remember in *Beelzebub's Tales*, Hassein is advised not to try to be responsible yet. We have to watch ourselves closely here; we have to be careful to make the house at St. Elmo available as a place where these various lessons can be learned, because I'm sure you've seen how coming here helps me to expose myself to myself and therefore to see how I have no intention, or not enough; how I have no attention—the carelessness which I manifest here is really more evident than it is at home. And yet, you see, people have to take a certain responsibility in all the various activities; and in taking that, if I take it in the wrong way or too soon, I begin to hide this carelessness from myself; I begin to behave just like people do in life—I'm too busy to work—I've got to get this or that done.

And so gradually, if we're not careful, the house, which is the main theater where we can learn the lesson of the various forms taken by my false passivity, can cease to be useful. That's why we try to get together to plan things and don't succeed completely or not very much. But we try not to make you, when you're too young in the work, subject to the same kind of demands to be responsible, the same voices, so to speak, that were put into us by our educators. And it's also why we try to emphasize the need to study inner considering, which in effect is studying the results of this wrong education in politeness and so on. I don't know if that's apropos; I was trying to bring some of the things together that have been discussed during these days. Did you understand more or less what I'm saying?

twenty-six

There is no sensation except in joining the head and the heart . . .

QUESTION: I want to ask what does sensation mean. It's difficult. We're given exercises, ideas, direction. In a way, sensation is the bottom line. It seems so far away from some of these great ideas, but the grand structure implied in the books about the work and the vain way I aspire seem to be distant from sensation. How to find a practical relationship to sensation and the ideas on a scale bigger than life? I feel attracted to that way of looking at things: it's wonderful, amazing, to think there might be correctly functioning higher centers in me, but how to find a practical relation between sensation and the ideas, relative to the scale of the ideas.

LORD PENTLAND: The point is, the head, which takes in ideas, and the feeling, which takes in scale, can never meet. Sensation is the relating element. How to feel what you think or to think what you feel is through sensation. We practice sensation in a way unrelated; for the head and feeling to meet is . . . only in the body. My head feels all over my body. With the sensation of the body, the head and feeling can come together, and that is the basis for so-called inner life. How to call feeling back. How to call the head back to meet with the feeling is only through sensation, where feeling and thought can come together.

QUESTIONER: It is difficult to sort out. I'm trying to understand before thinking, before categorizing things. What is the difference between emotion and impulse? Also the thought process located in the head is different. What seems to be asked for now is something more difficult to know.

LORD PENTLAND: How can you feel the scale of what you say? How to connect what you say with the importance, with the scale of it? Only through sensation. It's very difficult. It is only possible by letting go of the thought. You don't have a way to locate the work of sensation as something that can reconcile thoughts and feelings.

QUESTIONER: I want to believe what you're saying.

LORD PENTLAND: So it will never be built, the bridge. Sensation is an extraordinary contrivance.

QUESTIONER: It really works?

LORD PENTLAND: Yes. Your head and heart are separate anatomically. There is no circulation connecting them. That is what sensation can do. Like two different bodies. Sensation relates these two, even from the point of view of physical equipment. Sometimes this difference can cause illness. And many exercises have the virtue of relaxing this. It is not a work ever done, ever finished. Sensation may come through the words spoken, but there is no sensation except in joining the head and heart. Excuse me, I'm boring you now, but you see what I'm saying.

The sensation we can reach now is not enough . . .

QUESTION: Assuming the head and heart are both sick, both going crazy, then when sensation appears, what is the value of bringing them together?

LORD PENTLAND: That's like saying, "What's the value of bringing fire and pan and a raw potato together when separately they are useless?" In fact their only real usefulness is in their being related. Thought goes out and in this annoying way returns, and that's how it goes. Feeling is apt to go everywhere, except back on itself. So everything is related. So the body to be healthy does all these things to produce illness. To relate them means they come simultaneously together; to relate the attention of the head to the attention in the body is to take the wish in the head related to the resistance of the body. The feeling of the importance of my body as a sacred place of work begins to appear—my body including the head; we are not trying without the head.

QUESTIONER: Sensation comes when I try to avoid unpleasant emotions. With a group of friends talking about movies, my toes felt cold but sensation of the rest of the body had disappeared and I did not hear anything until there came the awareness of a woman talking about her illness. Then I was just aware of breathing, listening, comprehension. I didn't try to do anything. It was all done for me.

LORD PENTLAND: I think there are a number of things that are interesting in what you are saying. First, the way you felt that it has all been done for you. There are different levels of sensation. The sensation we can reach now is not enough, so we have to work towards having sensation of all parts at one time, to have relationship between the head and heart and body. We have to have that registering all at the same time, not successively. For that, it needs a better level, a better quality of sensation, the wish of sensation, not through doing it but through the work of awareness. The wish also comes about with this kind of sensation of the whole body. We talk endlessly about it but it is a physical body. But go out and try it; sensation is not only provided when we sit. Do physical things—scrub floors, and so forth. It is very interesting if done with attention. That means remembering I'm doing it plainly, just to get things clean. Practice it.

QUESTION: I can't face a feeling until I've classified it. I suppose I think I'll recognize it even though I don't know it's there. I'm not sure I'm seeing the feeling at all.

LORD PENTLAND: That's very good to start. One needs a completely different approach. One needs a different relationship to the body where these questions can be answered. You see there how the case for classification feels through awareness. The case for classification is presented according to whether or not it helps awareness. A devil says, "Instead of facing this inability to feelings, I'll classify them." It's this indirect way of approach that leads to abstraction. It is very close to the point to classify so that I'll be aware. This indirect approach is very striking in some of Ouspensky's early books.

CHAPTER TWENTY-SIX

Becoming aware of the passive, I can become aware
of the wish, the active . . .

QUESTION: As I was sitting here waiting for you to come out, I asked myself what I was doing here. I was wanting something but I don't know what. I want to ask you something but I don't know what. Wish is a small part of my life. I don't seem to find it often. When I do, it's very big. But seldom. I don't know where it is or what it is.

LORD PENTLAND: How are you going to find out? Can I tell you what it is or where it is?

QUESTIONER: I don't know.

LORD PENTLAND: Would you believe it if I told you?

QUESTIONER: If I experienced it, maybe.

LORD PENTLAND: If I say, for instance, "You don't exist." Do you believe that?

QUESTIONER: No.

LORD PENTLAND: How did that take place? Did you observe that electrical movement in your brain? What exists?

QUESTIONER: To feel my body?

LORD PENTLAND: That's what you wish to understand. That's your wish. So I did find it for you. Do you understand?

QUESTIONER: Yes.

LORD PENTLAND: Some valuable advice we give is to study wish in relation to attention and the three centers. And what seems to me also very important is to study the resistance, also in relation to the three centers. To study what it means to be aware, what study is, and what resistance is, is where we get stuck. And in relation to studying what's aware in me, how in a passive movement, very quickly, when looking at something, I get stuck in it. They are parallel. Otherwise, I will have peak experiences, big highs, but they will be unbalanced. So study the wish to come in touch with this big movement in myself, and study the resistance. There is a movement in me towards evolution and towards unity and differentiation, and also the side that doesn't want to come in touch with this movement, with the natural, universal order. Gurdjieff called it the struggle between Yes and No. We must know the ideas. Later we have to let go of them. But unless I can study the psychological work and the cosmic, spiritual work, work gets subjective. All right, it's your work. It's not for me to tell you what to do.

All the same, I will tell you what to do. You need to get more stuck. The wish to be free isn't strong enough, that's why you don't feel it. Do you understand? The nonexistence isn't strong enough for wish to exist. I don't need to tell stories about it. You need to study and see your fear of life and not accept the limits that you seem to feel are put to what you can relate to. It can only lead to getting stuck. But, becoming aware of that, the need to escape is strengthened. I can't do anything but become more aware, so I need to be less afraid. I don't need to put barriers between these animals in me, so they can relate. So, becoming aware of the passive, I can become aware of the wish, the active. Then you become aware of both at the same time. That's the idea. The struggle between Yes and No—a struggle for awareness. It has to be clearer than the head can do it. Only in quiet conditions, otherwise the head pushes. So for now it's possible only in quiet conditions. Little by little let life in until the moment you get caught. And then I come back. For example, you were out there listening to me, then came back to yourself. I always have the opportunity to come back, from passive to active. If we see it. If we're aware.

Self-respect comes from the struggle between Yes and No . . .

QUESTION: I have a question about respect. I wonder if you could clarify it. I wish to understand respect in terms of the work and respect in my usual worldly ideas and associations with that.

LORD PENTLAND: Yes, I think that's a fair question. But why do you want to know that? Do you lack respect for yourself? Do you abuse yourself?

QUESTIONER: No.

LORD PENTLAND: Then why?

QUESTIONER: It's not myself. Someone made a remark to me about wanting my respect. I didn't know how to respond to that.

LORD PENTLAND: Why respond to that? Is it on a biological level or what? What does it mean? Do you want them to like you, or what?

QUESTIONER: My response was, "Why do you want my respect?"

LORD PENTLAND: That's indirect. Why respond? Everyone calls the same thing respect.

QUESTIONER: I'm confused.

LORD PENTLAND: Certainly. That's not the point. We think respect is very important. But self-respect is coming to us only when I struggle between Yes and No. Since I don't make it, I deserve it, I deserve no respect. So when asked for respect, I respond only on a physical level. Maybe I want to borrow money or something, from someone, so of course you respect them more. I remember once very long ago—I feel it is my duty at my age to tell anecdotes—fifty-three years ago I was with a man named R.B. Bennett of the Conservative Party—he later became Prime Minister—in Calgary. It was a Sunday morning and he was wearing a black coat and a top hat. It was the time of the Calgary Stampede. As we walked across the railroad yard, a stoker looked out and said, "Hi, R.B.!" And Mr. Bennett lifted his hat to him to get a vote. He gave him his respect. It's alright, but it's on that level. Self-respect comes from the struggle between Yes and No. And results come indirectly, from being in touch with big forces, intermittently or only for moments.

QUESTION: I keep looking for this quiet spot within me, and when I find this spot, there seems to be a force that takes over that insists on quiet. Then a vibration or sensation takes place. It doesn't seem correct. That approach to quietness doesn't seem to be the way.

LORD PENTLAND: So in the very moment when the brain says, "That's not the way," it says at the moment, "I am sensitive enough to know the way." At the same time, if someone said, "There is no way," it would say, "Yes, there is a way." You see?

QUESTIONER: But at that moment?

LORD PENTLAND: Electricity. It's very fast. We can't be sure if it's that moment or the one after. You realize that. They are complicated currents for this electricity that goes along. So, until next time, or Friday morning for many of you. Thank you.

twenty-seven

*There can be consciousness without functions and
functions without consciousness . . .*

QUESTION: I have a question deep inside. I don't think it's quite come
to my consciousness yet, but I feel very much the need to ask it right now.
Then maybe in asking, the question will come up.

Something in me knows that I'm not what I think I am and this something also knows more than I know. I see that I contain a being inside me
and I really don't know what it is. I feel it more strongly when there's a
gap in my day between two activities, and my attention is not yet focused
on anything. At that moment when I look out at the world and meet
myself, I feel nothing and I feel like I am nothing. And I really don't know
why I'm alive. I look for God and I find nothing and I can't find meaning
in that moment. Yet I don't lose hope. I just realize that at that time I
have nothing. Then when I look at the things around me—I look at the
walls and the table and the chairs and my body—it feels like everything is
only half true. Everything that I believed in throughout my life is only
partially true and I don't feel as much at home in my ordinary life. Yet I
have nowhere to go.

LORD PENTLAND: You've heard the idea already that we have two
parts—the consciousness and functions. Yes? And that there can be consciousness without functions and functions without consciousness. What

you've just said is true. It's not so common that one of us can experience this division in our lives. There are moments when I feel I am nothing—I have no consciousness, and these are mainly between periods of activity when there has been functioning but no memory whatever that there's no consciousness.

So how to work in these moments? What does it mean, "work"? Work is towards unity. How do you see the work of having an awareness of my nothing-consciousness while functioning? That means getting rid of or letting go, giving up, all the misunderstanding I have that I am someone, somebody, and the fear I have of giving up that I'm something—and at the same time functioning as a service, not with ambition, but as a service. Simply functioning and at the same time having the experience of nothing-consciousness. Yes?

QUESTIONER: At that time I look for motivation.

LORD PENTLAND: The motivation is to be whole. Any other motivation is subjective, egoistic. You follow? Motivation comes from nothing because I have no consciousness. So the motivation is to have at least some consciousness or to keep this experience of nothing-consciousness while functioning. There is no other motivation. I wish to be whole because that is the next level. Working that way I can serve as if on the level that corresponds to my wholeness. The serving is by the functions and nothing-consciousness is the consciousness. The whole work is there. A good starting point. You understand what I said?

QUESTIONER: Yes.

LORD PENTLAND: Gives you a direction, yes? In other words, the work begins from seeing, becoming aware, becoming conscious that I am nothing but my functioning, that time is going on, my life is going on and the only result is the result of my functioning. There is no inner growth. Information is being accumulated enabling me to function more efficiently, but compromises are being made all the time so that I don't see that I'm nothing but my functioning. Seeing that creates a movement of the two towards each other, creates by itself the beginnings of a relationship between consciousness and functioning. Just seeing that starts a movement which could go on if I didn't interfere with it all the time and let other people interfere with it all the time.

The idea that helps more often than not is to stop the head . . .

QUESTION: People were calling me, saying that the fountain was a mess and that something had to be done about this for you. The first call I sort of said I would do something about it, and I didn't. The second call this morning I had an appointment somewhere else and I thought, "Well, maybe I should clean the fountain because no one else seems to know how." So I came here and I realized while on my way that I was so filled with doing it for you that I wasn't there, and that idea really helped me be there while I was cleaning it out because, I would be cleaning it, doing one thing or another, losing all sense of doing it for myself, but doing it for you. It's really interesting because of that idea of who am I working for? Who am I working for? Is it to build something in myself so someone else will think I'm "conscious man" doing a responsible thing, or is it something else? And there's a play there that seems to go back and forth, and one reminds the other. I saw that in this project.

LORD PENTLAND: In other words, this particular idea of working for yourself, or working to serve the group rather than a particular person, created a sort of play, a relationship between your hands and feelings, and it is an exceptional thing that this idea continued to have an effect on you because usually a true idea like that just lights me up for one moment, like the light of a firefly or something, and then I'm back where I was. I find myself looking for another true idea.

In order to have a durable experience of this life, some other parts of the body have to take part in the work and you find that took place. There was a relationship between the idea and the head, and the hands, and the feeling, in some way. But that's not usually so. In fact, it's so little so that sometimes having found an idea that lights up, instead of telling the other parts, being open to the body and the feelings, trying to come inside, instead of that I try to find a different idea. Yes? And that only lasts a second, and then another idea. And in that way I am overlaying the possible relationship between the idea and the other parts. Yes? Just like when I'm looking for a question or trying to make an answer, there's a tendency to keep waiting until some question or answer gives some sort of lighting-up. Do you follow? It seems to come from myself more, seems to be more true. And I turn over years and years, and keep hunting for something that is more true. But maybe what is more true is to look for the relationship between the head and body.

So, the idea I need to begin with is to empty the head, to quiet the head. Not to start hunting with the head, in spite of what you found. The idea that helps more often than not is to stop the head. Is that what you've tried?

QUESTIONER: Yes. Sitting here, waiting for you, I was in my head . . . questions. What I asked isn't what I was thinking of. Then I quieted down.

LORD PENTLAND: So there are two good examples.

QUESTION: I've been working with the listening exercise you left us this last time and I see that an experience like that leaves me with rather a negative response to my condition, and I discovered by talking to my group leader and getting the support of people near me that that can change and I can find something positive. I don't have that experience when I'm alone, and I feel like I'm wasting an opportunity. If I could, perhaps, find a different kind of attitude or less harsh way of reacting to this.

LORD PENTLAND: When you speak to someone more experienced in the work, you see, they can be a support in your work, not a support of your personal emotions. They could reflect you, if they can. In that way I have the benefit of being here, alive, but at the same time they may reflect the emotional state I was in. It's something we're not always ready for. We're not always ready for the result of a conversation with somebody, you understand. We expect them to connive with our emotional state, to support the emotional state. Do you follow me?

QUESTIONER: I'm not sure I follow that.

LORD PENTLAND: We do in a way, but we can't acknowledge that. We expect some affirmation of myself. We're not ready yet to be told I'm nothing, but in conversing with somebody who's working, sometimes I can have this reflection of my bad emotional state at the same time I have the all-important experience to be alive, here. It makes a right separation between my life energy and the emotions.

A wider sample of my functioning . . .

QUESTION: I had the experience shortly after you left, with the exercise of saying, "Good morning," to my boss, and he answered by saying, "Good morning," back. The moment was just as you described where he left me alone. You could tell he was surprised with how I said "Good morning," and, yet, at the same time, there was something very natural in the way he said it right back to me, and that was the end of our conversation. I was impressed but not overwhelmed. He didn't intimidate me. I did not feel I had to affirm myself. Mostly in my job I seethe over everything.

LORD PENTLAND: Yes. You see, I don't want to interrupt, but everybody who heard the exercise given perhaps didn't hear the conversation was supposed to be related to some necessary communication I needed to make to the person. This is a fundamental part of the exercise and so you should try again.

You're quite right. You had the feeling the conversation was too short, out of too narrow a spectrum of my functioning to enable you to have this extraordinary moment of relationship of a natural kind with your boss, because of the fears that exist, no doubt on both sides, when it's that kind of power. But the exercise only begins there. The exercise has to do with longer conversations. As well as being present, being able to face the unknown—not all the time being interfered with by preconceived conversations and so on—as well as that, I'm supposed to be able at some point to ask the person about something necessary. You understand? "Can you please lend me your car tomorrow?" or something like that. The attention that's necessary to be present as well as to make this necessary communication is what we're interested in, a wider sample of my functioning. I hope everybody who knows about the exercise and wishes to try it will take that in. It's not easy, but that's the exercise. Yes?

The truth is very powerful if it really is a
movement of the attention . . .

QUESTION: You touched on something of great interest to me about relationship to others supporting our emotions, and about reflections of our nothingness when our emotions are not supported as we expect them to be. I see that if I don't have affirmation or support of my emotions I'm confronted with seeing my nothingness. At that moment I see that my resistance is much greater than anything that is there to work but, at the same time, there is this great insight in seeing this new step towards a very difficult work, the possibility of a new relationship.

LORD PENTLAND: What we're trying to say is that truth is very powerful even when it's very small. Now, what can I say which is true about myself? I'm able when I sit alone sometimes to come to be present to all the parts, yes? But the moment I get up I lose it. The only truth I can say about myself whole, including the functions, is that I'm nothing. The sense of truth that I feel when I'm here is lost when I get up even to walk across the room. Is that what you find? Yes?

I don't want to go on talking about nothingness because it's even bigger than that but, in fact, I am nothing. That's the only truth that is true within my presence. Yes? So, as I get up or go to the front door, how to keep this truth that I'm nothing? Then I can keep it until the resistance appears. It's a movement. Suddenly, the movement stops. Is that what you're saying? No, but it is the question.

The truth is very powerful if it really is a movement of the attention. Then, why do I turn away when it stops? Why do I try to understand everything except the one thing that could help, which is to stay with this movement? Not to go away from the action, to stay there, instead of interrupting this movement of consciousness by wanting explanations. If only I could see beside, behind, in front, yes? I need to stay with that movement—that's what we're talking about—not go away from the movement of truth.

Sometimes this movement is heard just like a call from the other side of the resistance. Like a call. Yes? Like a call of return to myself. So why don't I just keep it simply a call instead of all the time I'm tempted by every sort of distraction? You hear it spoken of as the call at first. Yes? Or how do you speak of it here? The call comes not from the distraction which is often emotional; the call comes from within the emotions. Is it possible to understand my language? Or not? The call comes from way inside. It doesn't come from the emotions. No? So it brings us back to the work on listening.

Staying in front of the resistance . . .

QUESTION: It seems to me that the only thing that would stop that point of becoming distracted would be to have a degree of will that comes to one's aid at that moment.

LORD PENTLAND: What is will?

QUESTIONER: As I understand it, it is the ability to do what one wishes.

LORD PENTLAND: What I wish. Because it's not for one, any one, of the many I's. So, we don't understand what will exists. I'm not sure how much it helps to bring another word into it. So here it is some kind of work to be understood. Is it persistence that's needed? Not exactly. Persistence can be very stupid, can be just stubborn. What is staying in front of the resistance? What counts for will? What is will? Is it a form of the attention itself that is listening, has been called back from the dark towards myself? It certainly is some kind of aspect of that attention which enables me to stay with it instead of interfering or being distracted. Whatever it is I don't have it because if I had it I would stay there in front of the resistance. Even if there was no movement I would be coming back again and again—instead of losing heart and coming right outside myself—and begin from the beginning.

Is it something to do with a kind of interval in an octave, this work on the emotions? Has it got something to do with the second conscious shock? If so, is the lack of will something to do with the tendency to start to work before I've really understood what I'm trying, to start with the right kind of *do*? [Referring to the first note in the octave]. Is will something that can be developed in us? This seems a more fruitful question because if it can be developed, it's only, I suppose, by becoming aware of our lack of will, by experiencing the disadvantages of not having will. Is that right, do you think?

All these are possible questions, but it seems to me they all add up to one answer which is, I need to not go away; I need to stay there. What's the use of bringing in another concept? I need to stay. Bringing this concept is, in fact, bringing us into the kind of distraction that I was speaking of. Yes? And instead of staying there, you start to ask about "What is will?" You follow what I mean?

QUESTIONER: Yes.

LORD PENTLAND: Yes. Maybe there are various aspects of attention. There's an aspect of faith which makes me obedient to the call. That must cover the question of will. If I was obedient that would cover it, wouldn't it? It's enough if I can stay in front of that. I don't think we need to get into the ethics of it or all these questions and various concepts.

Gurdjieff says in order to be born, I must die. What has to die are all these questions which really are avoiding the point. The point is to stay in front of it. Yes? Something has to give up.

My work is to be available to a conscious force . . .

QUESTION: You were saying that will is a physical feeling that you have being here and now?

LORD PENTLAND: No, I wasn't quite saying that. I'm sorry, you heard it wrong. If you all understood it that way I'm afraid what I'm saying is not clear. I was saying there is no way in which speaking about will is going to help us. It's just a word. What we need is to stay there with a certain feeling of my insignificance, a certain feeling of my real insignificance, which is the truth, in the face of this block, resistance, and that because that's true and, of course, there is a kind of movement toward the truth which we call "a call," that is the only way to come through this block, this resistance.

Is that clearer for you? Does it correspond with what you've been hearing when you have readings? Is what I'm saying off in another direction? Is what I'm saying, insofar as it reaches you, corresponding with what you understand are Gurdjieff's ideas? That's the main thing. It can't be just the ideas. We're trying to go beyond the ideas, but as long as it corresponds, then we can try that all together.

QUESTIONER: My question is related to the feeling that I had in these rare moments when I am in the here and now, a feeling of being in touch, being related. In these moments of relatedness the question of life—nothingness, life and death—they don't seem to come up as issues. It seems in my work I have to be more of a conduit for something deep within me that wants to live in the here and now.

LORD PENTLAND: I think what is up to me, my work, is to be available, to be in touch with a higher level, higher force, a conscious force. I can't expect from below to control that energy in any way, but I can make myself available so that that energy enters me, enters you, enters us. In that way we feel related as a result of each of us being related to a higher level of energy. Is that what you're saying?

QUESTIONER: I was saying both higher or lower.

LORD PENTLAND: How are we related to the lower? That has to be understood very clearly. What I want to say about that is that I need to understand that if I can accept the distorted and ugly manifestations which I make, and you make, and we all make—to accept them is also possible thanks to the action of this conscious force that enters me. You understand that?

QUESTIONER: What does it mean to accept that?

LORD PENTLAND: But why do you ask that? It means to accept it. Again, that's another roundabout conversation and leads nowhere. The point I'm making is that I'm not only an intermediary between the higher and the lower. It's only through a kind of grace from the higher that I'm in touch with it, and through grace from the higher that I'm in touch with the lower—that I'm able to accept that I'm nothing. Yes? You see what I mean? I think it will help you to look at it that way.

So you said, "What does it mean to accept?" I say it means a conscious acceptance. Something I can't do by myself. A great deal is up to me, but I can't go that far.

QUESTIONER: I was told that I should be a conscious container.

LORD PENTLAND: A lot of people like me have been trying to tell you things. That's the problem. You need to make order of it, sort it out. That takes conscious contact too. Try not to mix them together too much.

twenty-eight

A question that is with me all the time . . .

QUESTION: Since the last work period, I've been able to work occasionally with something that I haven't worked with before, which is when I'm agitated it can serve as a reminder through a long period of time, through a day or maybe two days—if I've done something that's embarrassing, or if I've gotten angry over something. Today I told myself I wanted to speak tonight. And it kept reminding me to come back, to try to be with that sensation, that agitation. It helped in that way.

I guess the question is how to keep that a right effort. Because the agitation can be consuming in a way. I mean, I get too nervous and then don't speak.

LORD PENTLAND: An important question. So as things are with you, is it a matter of luck whenever you're caught in the agitation? Or as far as you can see, as little as you can see, sometimes you're free. Sometimes you're caught. How do you understand that? Maybe it's something to do with your aim. But what sort of aim?

QUESTIONER: It seems maybe there's a taste of something that's available.

LORD PENTLAND: Something's available. A very special energy is available. Maybe Gurdjieff calls it "okidanokh." Well, let's just call it oki-danokh. We don't know what it is, and it's everywhere. But it's not something I'm able to draw on. Sometimes it comes in and I move away from the agitation. Yes? Other times not. And no explanation satisfies me—that when I've been good it comes, or when I've been bad it doesn't come. What do you think it is? Luck? What sort of aim would correspond?

First of all, what's interesting is that you find this important. Because of course what you are saying is that just a little detail of life is important. This isn't like you're facing a big crisis. You're speaking about something that you face every day. Or more. And this is what interests us. If we can understand that, it would be much more use than being able to deal with the big crises, because they would get included. Mostly we refer our questions to some specially difficult moments. But this is a question that's with me all the time, and it's the whole question of work.

How do you regard your "successes" and your "failures" in regard to that? What kind of a world scheme have you got to deal with that?

QUESTIONER: I would really have to say I'm not sure.

LORD PENTLAND: I'm not sure. This is, in a way, what we find is the main reason for coming to the work—in reading *Beelzebub's Tales*, we see that Gurdjieff seemed to understand something about that. And now, I wish to understand, you wish to understand something.

It seems to be a matter of luck. What is luck? You follow what I mean? Luck. A word of the Celtic religion, the Druid tradition. Very important. It can't be just what we say, luck. What is it? Are there ethics? It must be a kind of law, not ordinary ethics.

Nobody will be able to answer your question. It's one of the main questions for me. Certainly there needs to be some aim, but what? In any case, you see, and many of us can be helped by that, that it's a very small thing that can swing the balance. It could go either way. This sort of naked psychological situation shows me that it's often coming up and each time it can go either way. Either I can contain the various distractions, or I react, and that makes them more and more various in form and in the end more seductive. How can we help each other until we understand a little better.

It's late. We can try. We have a little more time.

The wish, the real wish, is I . . .

QUESTION: Lately it seems there is a real sporacity to my efforts and I've been trying to see what it is that takes me away. In the last couple of weeks it seems like there's a kind of negative attitude in me that makes little judgments about things I surrender to; and seeing helps. But it's really there. It's part of me. And it seems as if it takes the place of a kind of wish, some kind of real flame or something of being present.

My question is, what can be done there? I even noticed it in trying to phrase this question, in a way. It's a kind of snapping at myself when I'm afraid. This morning at work I didn't put something away properly and I turned away from that because something in me didn't like that, didn't want to see that. It seems it's like that. It's something negative that comes in there that puts me to sleep.

LORD PENTLAND: Yes. Are you sure that you're awake when you wish to be whatever it is, conscientious, in putting things away? Are you sure you're awake? That you do that voluntarily? Or is that something sort of "good boy," that you learned?

QUESTION: I think the reaction to want to put it right is something I've been taught.

LORD PENTLAND: I think it's something like learned, but I think this kind of disorder that you felt guilty of this morning is something that you didn't learn. But that comes perhaps as much from you as the other. Yes? I won't dare to say it comes even more from you, but it's possible.

Now the idea that we are trying to understand, which Gurdjieff gave, is that "I" don't exist. I'm somewhere between these two. The wish, the real wish, is I. The wish to sometimes leave things for other people to clear up and to sometimes clear up to myself, according to what is most intelligent. You understand?

QUESTIONER: Right.

LORD PENTLAND: It isn't always the same thing. Sometimes other people can clear up much better than me, and I can do something much better than them at the same time. It depends. On the other hand, if I'm living alone or something, it's more intelligent to clean things up. Yes? So, what's proposed by Gurdjieff is that these two, what he calls the struggles between Yes and No, have to be allowed to come closer to each other. And it is out of tolerating that, that I can be reached. That a central voluntary wish, I wish, can be reached. You follow? Does that help? Is that idea any help?

QUESTIONER: So you are saying that I need to find a way to allow this negativity to exist.

LORD PENTLAND: Yes. You can't avoid it. You see it exists a lot. You see that on the other side of it is something that is no more than another aspect of yourself, and that both have a right to existence. So you let them struggle with each other.

QUESTIONER: I just don't seem to go along for the ride very often.

LORD PENTLAND: No, that's the general situation of man these days. That's what Gurdjieff says. I like to be told or to kind of commit myself to a habit. Isn't that right?

QUESTIONER: Yes.

LORD PENTLAND: And then I kind of smother the most important part of myself. Which is the freedom, very little, but freedom, a little bit, to choose. Of course it isn't perhaps as bad as it sounds because if I come in touch with free energy, freedom to choose, I use it on some ridiculous small thing like, "Shall I go to a movies tonight, or watch television?"

So there is a big work to be done, when we reach this freedom, to connect it to a real call to myself—but first of all to free myself from the misunderstanding that I exist, and let this struggle between Yes and No be the main structure of my day. To see it as it's all the time going on. Yes?

The point is to be this kind of human being that we are . . .

QUESTION: I've noticed that when I'm in front of that kind of agitation, particularly when there's a very strong physical sensation of judgment or negativity, I feel as if I have to do something.

343

LORD PENTLAND: You have to work with it more often. Don't you think so?

QUESTIONER: The question is how do I work with it? How do I stay and just experience what is painful?

LORD PENTLAND: Well, the less you work with it, the longer it'll take. But nobody but me can work with myself. The people in the work are not here, whether they're older or younger than me, for providing a kind of vibration that will—so to speak—evolve me by osmosis. You understand? There is no osmotic evolution. The people are here because it's in the becoming aware of our interaction, and being able to accept it in all its ugliness, that we can take an entirely new view of what it's like to be a human being, as we are. And the point is to be this kind of human being that we are. Instead of all the time dreaming about turning ourselves into something different. Yes?

So you have to really recognize that people are here for that and not for some kind of quietness or tenderness rubbing off on me because people are so quiet and tender. You understand? You have to get that into your head.

Gurdjieff was not wasting time in getting that into our heads, generally. Roses, roses to start with, but then it was thorns, thorns. He moved quite fast into the second period. You understand that. Now, we are none of us Gurdjieff, but we've got to face this interaction between ourselves, from inside—for what it is—instead of trying to color it outwardly for what it isn't. You agree with that? A sort of working principle of community.

QUESTIONER: It's my experience that that's what happens.

LORD PENTLAND: Yes. That's my experience, like the book published on How to Come to Religion Without Being Religious. So the same: how to come to community without community? There is no community, but we come to it by seeing the struggle between Yes and No.

As little as it is, the attention which I have
is very impartial . . .

QUESTION: I find it very difficult to distinguish, in the way I have been working, between what has been described as allowing and pushing. It seems distinct when you describe it, but in experience I begin with the idea of allowing and then I practice pushing. The experience of what I understand by allowing seems to take place by itself. I don't understand why, but my efforts are as a rule efforts of pushing.

LORD PENTLAND: What is the origin of this willfulness? You say, "I push." This means will, subjective desire. Is it impatience or fear? You are responsible to do this or else? What is back of this pushing? I have not really understood why I am working. It has not been a voluntary choice. I haven't really the need to work, so why work? I start out of some kind of responsibility or fear of bad consequences. Is it some kind of superstition that I want to keep on the good side of the big powers? One should read the chapter on "Justice" in *Beelzebub's Tales* where he says there is no truth in all that. These angels and devils seem to exist, but really we can be, at least to the extent of starting to work, able to work voluntarily. We can't altogether understand why. If we could, we would be very different than we are, but we more or less make ourselves take up a suitable posture and take half an hour in which, even if we don't see it at the time, we shall see later that we have been pushing and then I can come back and let it go.

QUESTIONER: When you were speaking about this earlier I was relating it to what I have been trying in regard to the incredible noise of associations that goes on all the time in my head. I guess I am speaking about a reaction to that experience. And every once in a while I have the feeling that this is my condition at this moment and I try to simply experience that.

LORD PENTLAND: You think, "This is my condition at this moment," so you go on with whatever you are doing. You don't let that stop what you are doing. So I don't look into it, I don't investigate it or study it. I see it but pay no attention to it. I keep in my lane. I don't go in that lane. I have to see other lanes, but I don't enter them. So if you feel disturbed by associations while you are shaving . . .

QUESTIONER: Or speaking with somebody.

LORD PENTLAND: You try to remember about the work to be present and you see how small that is, how I am practically nothing, but you go on with being there in a kind of straightforward way without any violence but simply moving forward because as little as it is the attention which I have is very impartial. The mind is very powerful. It creates extraordinary changes, far greater than the Indians ever dreamed of. It is like it pulverizes the various kinds of resistance. It goes straight on. It is simple too. But it is not a hunting for some method.

QUESTIONER: I think I understand.

Our body is exactly what we disappear into almost all the time . . .

QUESTION: Well, the task for this morning was a means of study, and I am sure that needs to be reported on, as a help. I found that I could remember the task quite frequently and, as I feared, as soon as I went upstairs and sat down, I seemed to take a posture that was typical of me, and lost touch with my body. And throughout the morning I tried again and again to be in touch with my body, and really couldn't—not in any way that felt inspiring or hopeful. And, I came downstairs and walked into the patio and spontaneously entered into this state that was suggested in the morning task, without any apparent effort—and remained in it, explored it. It is a puzzle to me. It seems as if my work is uncontrollable. The ordinary will has very little power.

LORD PENTLAND: Of course it's nothing to do with the ordinary will. The trouble is that the first movement experience I have, I give it at once a name without really knowing the language, what are the names that apply to the teaching and to the laws of the forces. You say, for instance, which is extremely misleading, that you wanted to be in touch with your body. Our body is exactly what we disappear into almost all the time. I can't even sit still, without wanting more water, more coffee, without scratching myself, wanting to move my chair—the body is a very big devil for us.

And what I mean by that is in trying to come in touch with the energy of the body, the sensation, the energy of the instinctive, moving, and sex centers, one is trying to understand where it fits in, to a system of awareness. The body is, more or less all the time, the principal reason why I am going to sleep. Yes?

I can't even breathe regularly. I can't even keep my head on my shoulders without raising my chin too much or something, so the body is all the time the devil that's sucking my energy away so that I can't be aware. In that way it seems to me we could understand better how an effort to be in touch with the energy itself can sometimes be a great help in allowing the natural transformation to take place, and this effort, as usually understood, can be almost the greatest hindrance, so that it gets forgotten, so that in all the traditions the rituals have become either unphysical, or if they are physical, mechanical.

Now we're in the process of forgetting them again, forgetting the way in which the life energy enters into the work of transformation again, by talking about sensation and trying to sense with my head. It seems to me that it's difficult to talk about in such a large group, but there will be an opportunity this afternoon and the main danger is that we keep on attributing all our difficulties to the head, as if restlessness came from the head, as if greed was only for more thought, as if self-pity was from the head—all these terrible animals in us are the dogs around the sensation center, aren't they? There were supposed to be villages in a Gurdjieff reading that we once heard. The villages of sensation and so on, and there were supposed to be dogs around them so that we couldn't separate the energy of the head from the energy of sensation from the energy of feeling.

What are the dogs around the sensation? It seems to me that there's the problem. It is possible to speak of it that way, or one can say we must try for a finer quality of sensation. It isn't only by sitting still one comes to sensation.

There is some work, of course, to separate from the thoughts. But the main work is to separate from this continual way I want to stroke my body, or somebody else's body. What is that? What can each find for himself, herself, of the freedom that comes when I am in touch with my space, the space—my presence—which I don't think we understand without sensation—which is suddenly given, like you said. Could you agree with some of what I've said? Somehow, after a time, the idea that tension is the problem doesn't take us far enough. To relax when I am trying to make something only works in a crisis. I don't know how it is when you are playing the piano or something like that—you can't be relaxing all the time, but you need the sensation to your fingertips. And it has to come to your fingertips.

You remember the story we published in *Material for Thought*, do you, called "The Devil Chase"? When this Russian business madman gave a tremendous party, keeping himself under certain control, and then afterwards went to the bath and to the church to pray, and while he was praying he received the contact with some higher energy. But his young nephew who was watching could see that even then, his toes were wiggling. And that to me is an image of work with sensation, of course. There has to be a reason for it and somehow the contact with the energy appears through a struggle for it.

There are two movements of energy . . .

QUESTION: This summer I found that all my work was quantity, not quality. In the exercise I did and the outer work I did, all that was possible for me was quantity. Hopefully there were moments where there was a little glimpse of quality. My question is since I'm so easily discouraged when I do those exercises, can I try something else? Maybe all I'm fit for is just trying to be present and having an occasional slight satisfaction that there is some work that provides me with hope. It wasn't even easy to stay with quantity of efforts, because I'm lazy. I start something and I go to sleep and I forget what it was and that's how it was.

LORD PENTLAND: There are two movements of energy—when we're apart or when we're here. We try to come into touch, but it's very difficult. We try to be aware of, if you follow me, a movement towards more of myself—for instance, to include in this very movement, a movement towards the energy of sensation. Which means letting go of some preconceived thoughts. Yes? We try that and to some extent we come in touch, we actually experience, although intermittently, that movement. But it doesn't go very far. The sensation doesn't have enough of a call, except perhaps sometimes, to put my mind in order, to quiet my thought, to bring me to a state of mind which I can call order. Yes?

Now what of the other movement? You're speaking of the other movement, of quality and quantity in regard to something you make or to your behavior, is that right? Both. Now, that movement has to come from my presence. Where does it come from? You see, you may work, I may work and come to this or that intensity of the sensation of the whole of myself and I may come to a moment or two of being present. Now that movement is very fragile, very difficult. We are at a low place in the universe for finding this return movement to the highest. But we find it. You see, yes? But what of the other movement? That needs to come from my presence, what you might call the creative direction of the ray of creation. That needs to begin in my presence and go down, creating a form. Now what happens? Before I have started to relate to a particular material, or to a person, I've lost the experience of this movement towards myself. So I don't even have normal perception. I don't even see what I'm doing. I may talk to a person and I don't even see what may be so obvious, that they're not listening. I can get so wound up in what I'm talking about that sometimes I sit for an hour while someone is speaking to me and they don't even know that I'm there. So I don't perceive. I'm blind. I simply don't perceive the environment. That's why there's no quality. My mind is not in order, so as soon as I look at the result it reflects the confused condition of my mind. So where is the work?

Or it's the same thing with time. You see you have a certain amount of time, an afternoon, for instance. You work and the mind is in order. Now what happens? You decide to make a visit to someone. Before you have gone a few yards, your mind has lost its state of order. Yes? And on the way to this person, something comes into your mind—I might as well buy something at the drugstore.

Our products, the results of this creative flow, can have quality only when they result from an ordered mind. Those of us who have worked regularly over the years have some sense of what is an ordered mind. However, while we might start from an ordered mind, it quickly disintegrates into disorder, confusion, and associations. Then I don't even know if what I've produced is good or not. I look at it and it's junk, then I come back tomorrow and I think it's okay. Or I might be proofreading a page, and then having another person check it and find ten errors that I missed. Or merrily weeding the garden, when in fact, half of what I'm pulling up is plants. You especially, perhaps.

We need to see the reality of what the second energy flow is like—the tawdriness of our products. This will produce a thirst for more moments of ordered mind, and hence a motive for working more frequently. When our attention moves inward, it is towards order and unity. When our attention goes out, it is towards disorder and confusion. The ray that goes outward comes to nothing because we are not there. When we make up schedules for ourselves we are never there because we always have to be somewhere else next, trying to squeeze in this or that, ending up by being late for our meeting, for example, particularly if it is a clever plan.

I need to see that it is all my time. It's wrong to think in terms of giving a certain amount of time to my job, to my sister, to this house and then this little bit is for myself. You know, sometimes I'm late for a plane, not because I forgot what time it was, but because I didn't arrive at the time the plane was supposed to leave. Well, why shouldn't I? It's my time to do with as I please. We need to be there for each event, each moment as it occurs.

Well, don't listen too much to my words, listen to how I speak to this one, how I speak to that one, the tone.

twenty-nine

Two movements are there in me all the time . . .

QUESTION: My question begins when one "I" in search of a quiet place inside me meets with another "I" that refuses to let go of my mechanical habits. And the second "I" is so strong that I find only reactions. And I wish to have some direction on how I can better study in the face of such a strong part of me that creates a strong reaction. I might add, it seems that in the past I've felt that there's not sufficient understanding of that moment to study it properly and I've just allowed it to be. I feel at a stalemate with that so it's stayed with me for some time.

LORD PENTLAND: Your question is very clear, but of course I don't know what background you have in your mind of the ideas of Gurdjieff, so it's hard to speak in general as if there were something to do that would help you. There are so many different considerations there. But when it's a very strong resistance like that, one could say in general that I mustn't be in a hurry to try to confront it. I know I shall need some freedom, some room, so I don't allow it to attract me earlier than I need. I'm all the time in movement and maybe at this moment I'm not very separate from my automatism, only a little bit in myself. So I don't need to hurry towards confronting this resistance. I find that in a way I can stay in my own lane, instead of being immediately attracted to watch the cars in the next lane and the next lane. Yes?

So I wait until this actually comes in front of me. And then I have to understand I can't be still. I have to move on towards it. I wish. So my wish moves on towards the emotional resistance. And I don't give up. It seems very big, but I find the emotional resistance itself is not fixed; it moves, and I'm more and more trying to stay in touch with the part of me that is watching, that is perhaps a little bit separate. And I study; I watch what happens. Maybe the resistance swallows me up, hypnotizes me, draws me into it. Maybe I'm able to stay longer. Yes? Maybe I lose, but if I can keep quiet in my mind, I come back again. I'm free again to face the resistance. Do you follow?

QUESTIONER: Yes.

LORD PENTLAND: So, there's a great deal more to be said, but I'm participating there in a much bigger process. I'm participating in a little part of a much bigger process of two movements in myself—one which is bound to move out from myself, and one which I'm very insecurely in contact with which moves in towards myself and which gives me the freedom to watch. Have you thought of it like that?

QUESTIONER: Yes, I think so.

LORD PENTLAND: There is this kind of tiny ray of creation in me, and there is both the direction from highest down into manifestation, creation, and the return movement towards the highest in me. I'm not very far up that scale. Just enough to see something. All the time I'm about to go down. It can't be prevented. Your particular difficulty may be at some big interval where there are important forces so that I'm bound to lose. I don't know. It depends. It's different at different times. But the possibility of a study is what's important and therefore relating this to this idea of the two directions helps me because it shows me how these two movements are there in me all the time. And I experience that at a moment like you say, and in experiencing that with the idea, I'm able to get some understanding of my own. I don't think anything somebody tells me is very much help. So you try and understand about these two movements.

QUESTIONER: By attempting to participate in them rather than watching them from another place?

LORD PENTLAND: No. Separately from your work practice, you try and learn about these two movements. And then when you practice—of course your mind has to forget it, but still—something in that will help you. All the time two movements, but I'm never very far towards the source in myself. I never really work to free myself enough. So that when I come in the return movement to face some difficulty, I don't face it with very much consciousness. You work probably in the mornings, yes?

QUESTIONER: Yes.

LORD PENTLAND: But you see that you give up before you've reached real strong sensation. Yes? So you're not very free. So as you come down and meet a resistance and reactions and so forth, the study is very difficult. What's important is to recognize a possibility, even mentally. The way that we are showing here that Gurdjieff left behind is a very, very narrow way, very precise way. It can't be mixed with other teachings without losing. So we're speaking about something that is felt as an extraordinary possibility, and you feel that. I can tell from the way you ask. You're on the right way.

What I'm wishing for is a quality of being, a quality
of how far the parts are related . . .

QUESTION: One idea in this teaching that has always struck me is the idea that we cannot do. And it's always brought about this question in me. I think this comes from forces of resistance in me and says this idea in itself limits me and becomes a self-fulfilling prophecy. And now you mention possibilities. Maybe that's where my real question is: what are my possibilities? What would be a proper attitude in aspirations, strivings in my life?

LORD PENTLAND: Yes, you're right. We cannot do, or maybe that's to say I cannot do. But that has to be put in perspective. Gurdjieff also said, "Man is a being who can do." And in more detail he said, "I am, I wish, I can wish." So you see there is this possibility, this is what we mean. All the three sides have to be touched—the consciousness, the feeling, and the will—and even at the beginning. So I wish, I am—very relatively—I am. You ask yourself. It's very relative—but I can wish to be, more. Yes? And then, if you work with that you'll see the wish disappears as soon as you wish it. But there is this possibility that can enable me to return again and again to the wishing. You can try sometimes to say to yourself, "I wish," and then you say, "I wish, I wish," that's twice. And then three times and four times and so on, up to ten. And then nine times and eight times and so on, down to one, and you'll see how far it's possible to say, "I can wish." You follow what I'm saying?

QUESTIONER: Yes.

LORD PENTLAND: So this is a big possibility; it is a big possibility—that's the whole point. This is an immensely difficult undertaking, particularly for us at this time, in this place, culture and so on. All the more honor to us, if and when we really try. The point is not how difficult. The point is there is no other way that we know. And so how precise can I be in relation to the possibility? What gets in the way of this kind of work? We don't need to ask yet what is beyond it. We're at this stage. Of course there's something beyond this. There's development—a presence that's much greater. But at this point we're simply speaking about the wish to deal with the various attractions that come up, to one part or another part or another part, and how to continue the search, realizing that there's all the time the dangers of being distracted—not only by the more obvious negative resistances, but being distracted by the wish for a particular quality that belongs only in one part: a pure feeling or a quiet mind or a relaxed body, when in fact what I'm wishing for is a quality of being, a quality of how far the parts are related. So the search is not up and up and up. You understand?

QUESTIONER: Yes.

LORD PENTLAND: You understand me or not? The search is towards the center, yes? Towards some relationship between all the parts at the level I am, instead of dreaming about going up tomorrow, being absolutely free or being absolutely calm in the face of difficulty. We're speaking about some thing that's much too urgent to be put off. We're speaking about how to have a quality of being, now.

CHAPTER TWENTY-NINE

*Just to face emotional resistance like a knight in
armor is not the best attitude . . .*

QUESTION: About six months ago, I began to experience my feeling in a
different way while working. And it was almost like I had never felt
before. There were huge areas in myself which were full of sadness and a
lot of negative things. Examining them couldn't be put off any more. And
it didn't seem there was any way to go but through this. I've felt ever since
then that sometimes something so strong, the sensation would be so
strong, that I would have to marshal myself and bring all of myself
together in order to really see it and otherwise my mind would start spin-
ning delightful conversations and fantasies and things like that.

LORD PENTLAND: Yes, you'll see this is true. And you need to observe
that much more closely. I'm looking for the truth of myself. I'm not looking for just the truth. And it's true that there are negative emotions and
that these are in a way obstacles to consciousness. But they are part of
myself. So I need to learn from experience what is the attitude, as somebody just said, with which to face this kind of resistance, emotional resistance. Just to face it like a knight in armor is not the best attitude.

As I am, as you are, maybe we don't see, we're not sensitive enough to
see. Even now there may be some negative emotion. Now, how to be now.
It means in some way to at least not to react, not to identify with and react
with the emotion. That will only make me feel guilty. Now I have another
emotion to deal with. Yes? Not to be afraid of it. What does it mean to
have a particular attitude of attention that recognizes it as an obstacle, but
one that's part of myself.

Thoughts I can be able to let go of and sacrifice more easily than emotions. Yes? I can let the thought go. But the emotion is there. How to
move towards this—as an obstacle, but not exactly as an enemy. That's
why we say to study, at least not to be identified. How to give up my self-
esteem enough to do that? You understand? I'm so pleased with myself
and full of my studies of the Gurdjieff books, and so forth. "Don't express
negative emotions." This isn't an attitude with which to face negative
emotions. In order to include them in my being, I need a very scientific
attitude, very much an attitude of not-knowing, wanting to know how to

include them. And that for most of us is very difficult, because we know so much. It's like a very narrow gate we go through there. The attitudes have to be light and investigative, inquiring.

What is that kind of attention which has a sort
of organic knowledge?. . .

QUESTION: I have a great opposition to being present. It seems like there's something that's stronger in myself that creates this feeling of "Don't be present, don't be present." It seems like my flying around with my imagination is a lot more fun.

LORD PENTLAND: Yes, that's an example of what I was saying earlier. As you were sitting there, you didn't need to speak about this. You let that resistance in too soon. You could have been struggling more to be present. You follow? You had this thought which is based on your memory of past experiences and you could have let the thought go away. But by allowing, by being hypnotized by it, so to speak, it became emotional and you had automatically to speak about it. It's an example of what I mean—the timing is very important. We can't avoid having resistance. The question is, are we relating ourselves to all these parts? And what is that kind of attention which, through becoming connected with myself, has a sort of organic knowledge and knows better than my ordinary mind how to deal with these things? That's what we mean by in search of the miraculous. We mean in search of this kind of attention.

So let's speak about that. You follow? This kind of attention is my possibility, my right. And it knows much better than we do, than I do, in all sorts of ways. When the attention is there it can manifest physically much better than I do. You see when you do movements that you are able to do things that you never can do when you have no attention. It manifests my speaking behavior better. I don't interrupt; I wait until the right moment. I find myself sometimes, I'm sure you do, asking a question of a quality I didn't know existed, coming from somewhere immediately, not preconceived, like this one was. Yes? And even I can manifest a certain thought sometimes. There's nobody here who can't look back on their lives and say, how really—without pretending that the ordinary "I" did it—how did I manage to be so smart on such and such an occasion. You know what I mean? You know it didn't come from you, the ordinary you. Yes?

So what is this attention that can exist? We don't expect to be able to understand it at once, or understand it at all in terms of ordinary thought. But the only point of coming here is to make steps, little by little, towards the appearance of that. The Japanese Zen master, Dogen, sixteenth century I think, said something which I like very much. He said, "Enter here, where everyone may succeed together at once." He's talking about that, I suppose.

Listen to the places where one idea is related to the next . . .

QUESTION: When I first read In *Search of the Miraculous*, my most overwhelming impression, that still remains with me today, is that there's a whole bunch of sensible observations about human behavior and about efforts that people can make, and then in the next paragraph there will be some talk about octaves which I can't understand at all. It's as if I were reading a cookbook which was really understandable to me and then the next recipe was for how to make DNA or something which I couldn't do. And I don't know what the connection is between the ideas that I can't understand and the ones that I can understand. Will I ever be able to learn this?

LORD PENTLAND: Well, that's just what I'm speaking about—that's up to you. You have to repeat. Through repeated readings of *In Search of the Miraculous,* you have to be able to listen to the places where one idea is related to the next one in that book. The whole point is in the relationship, where he's speaking about one idea and then he goes on to the next. It's the juxtaposition of those two ideas which is the central point. And that includes all the tables. And of course it's the same thing, only more so, much more so, in *Beelzebub's Tales.* But in that sense, these books are themselves teachers. Until you can understand the sequence, the relationship between one idea and the next one, you haven't got very far.

QUESTIONER: So I should continue to make more efforts?

LORD PENTLAND: It depends what kind of effort. You're up against something very big. You see that. What does it mean? Again and again you can go on reading but you've lost the meaning. You're not reading with any kind of real understanding? So maybe you have to learn to read. That is to say, to be able to have an attention while reading, instead of having the attention doing several things at the same time as you're reading. Yes? When do you read?

QUESTIONER: Usually when I have time to myself and I know I won't be interrupted.

LORD PENTLAND: Good.

QUESTIONER: Possibly three or four times a week.

LORD PENTLAND: Then you have to watch while you read. You see you are unable to bring all of your attention onto what you're reading. Can you follow that or not? You see that while you are reading you're thinking about something else.

QUESTIONER: I don't know yet because I haven't tried to observe it that way, but I'll try that.

LORD PENTLAND: It's not very difficult. And then you have to try all sorts of things. You have a hot bath and read in bed, or have a cold shower and read in the morning. You have to try all sorts of things; then you may finally find that Gurdjieff was right. He wrote his book in a crowded café in order to have attention. But just to sit here waiting for people to come and talk to you, you won't get very far.

I can't be certain, but I can wish to be
present again, here . . .

QUESTION: There's a moment when attention leaves, and that interests me. It happened pretty clearly today and yesterday. Both times in my job, when I noticed that I had something to do and I had to accomplish a task. In one case, today I was on the telephone and I had to mollify somebody. There was a sense of moving out with the task, and then, when it was successfully completed, that was the end of me and I couldn't return. I didn't return. And the same thing happened in a different set of circumstances the day before when I noticed that I wanted someone to like me. I was talking to a salesperson and I could feel tension and fear grabbing the attention. I could remain with that for a little while, but then that went also. And I guess what interested me about it was that there was a quality of giving up in me.

LORD PENTLAND: Yes, exactly. That's a good observation. You see it is an interesting question, where does the attention go to? It's not such a stupid question as it sounds. In the sense that if I really were sensitive enough, intuitive enough, I had worked enough, wished to have it back enough, I might be able to, so to speak, coax it back from that part of me into which it had disappeared. Yes? You follow that?

QUESTIONER: Yes. It seems that's what's sort of needed. I just don't do it.

LORD PENTLAND: Right, what's needed is the attention, not really to know where it disappeared. And so, although your question is good, in a way, possibly you'd get more from remembering about the times when you did have an attention and, as a result of that, you manifested in a miraculous way. Although it's an interesting question, "Where did the attention disappear?" tends, as you yourself said, to drag me into a kind of negative attitude to the search. On the other hand, are you married?

QUESTIONER: No.

LORD PENTLAND: No. On the other hand, if you keep remembering about the sort of magical manifestations, that might help you to remember about your wish to keep the attention. So as long as we do think a lot about our impressions, one could say that a lot depends on thinking about or remembering about the many miraculous impressions you've had. And a lot of relationships are broken because of not remembering enough about the miraculous relationships, the miraculous part of the relationship, and thinking too much about worrying this will disappear. Do you follow that?

QUESTIONER: But there's . . .

LORD PENTLAND: No. That's enough. Just let it.

QUESTION: I experience such a difference between when I'm here with this group of people and when I leave. It has to do with your question about what am I responsible for when I'm in a moment of relative freedom, and when I'm alone.

LORD PENTLAND: You mean you have some energy then which you feel should be useful in some way, or what?

QUESTIONER: Yes. I have the energy but I also feel torn. I feel like here I am, what am I responsible for? I'm here with myself. It's a question.

LORD PENTLAND: It's very short, this moment, "Here I am." It's what we call an impression of myself, a moment of real observation of myself. I am here. It's that, yes? So I need many of those moments in all sorts of different inner situations. So now already my situation is quite different because before I was kind of feeling helpless and very insecure in front of the unknown. And suddenly I was able to receive this impression of myself— I am here. And this is so true that I became filled with energy, but very much colored by a sense of personal satisfaction. So now there's an entirely different inner situation and I'm responsible for trying to be here. What's up to me? I can't do. I can't be certain, but I can wish to be present again, here. And certainly I need all sorts of inner conditions in which to try before I can have anything like a permanent I, a permanent center of gravity. Yes?

The search for truth—it begins with a question . . .

QUESTION: It seems that it's possible to work more for the work or for other people and sometimes through that I'll find something out about working for myself. But in my daily life, I see that work on myself isn't clear. It seems to be something that serves my daily life in a way and yet, when I've come to whatever I come to through work directed more from the idea of working for something else or other people, or with other people in the work, when I've come to something that seems more right or more pure, it seems that I'm a very small part of something big, and it somehow seems more right. I find in my day to day life that there's certainly something quite practical about this idea of work on myself, but somehow the point of view doesn't seem to be quite right. Maybe I'm missing the point. Maybe it's all right to work with relaxation so that I'll be comfortable. I think something always seems a little off about that. It always seems more right the other way. I just don't really believe that I'm asleep.

LORD PENTLAND: I think that's a good starting point for work and for a meeting. The search for truth—it begins with a question. In a very general way, there's both a certain acceptance of something that's being passed to me and a certain revolt. Always. And these are the facts. But even further the question is about myself. In a way the work is to remember myself but not the ordinary "I," and therefore, it is exactly what you found; the work to be in touch with other people is often better than a work that's too narrow toward myself. The question is about "I" and the whole work begins from looking at myself, not in order to have sensation or something, but simply the question, "Who is there?" And if the one who's there is the one who is trying to follow something that was said, then that represents only a very small part of me. I don't exist through this part that is following some teaching. Or at least if I exist, it's a very thin existence. So I begin with questioning myself. And it can be only in relation to something, and it can well be in relation to the other people. There are many ways towards remembering myself. The way you're going is a good start.

There are so many of you. I would like to go on with that but we'd better let it move. The work is about people and it's about myself, so better relate to other people than to some very narrow aspect, some teaching, that's supposed to bring me to myself. Are you following me?

QUESTIONER: Yes.

LORD PENTLAND: It's splendid. Yes. Don't tell anybody I said that.

What it means to have a work to make it all my time . . .

QUESTION: I really need to open up. What I find in my head are these questions that tell you how my work is or describe some detail. I suspect that I am not available to what is possible in either of those places. The ideas tell me to attempt to include them both, which I believe possible, so that I come to a real strong taste of the fact that I settle for so little. I feel really good about myself if I can sense my feet or something, as a beginning. I stop; usually it seems I stop too soon. This work I've been trying to do with the ideas of late has seemed to make some kind of a connection with higher images and the impressions that I have.

LORD PENTLAND: So I take an idea, any idea, but maybe one of the more central ideas—that I am not one. Man is a plural being. I'm many. So you start. You try to find sensation, which is a relationship with the body which is so far from being the same as the relationship with the head, that it's like zero to infinity. It's a whole other world. Yes? So you try and find sensation but you have to go on. When we speak of man as a plural being, it means what it says. It means there are many parts, many aspects, not just the emotions and sensations and the head. For instance, are you sensing the right foot or the left foot more? It's quite different. If you start to sense the feet, it leads in a very short time to show me that it's quite a different thing. If I'm in the right foot, maybe it's more of an indication that I'm lost in a particular part, in the head. In the moment you sense the right foot more. You feel it?

QUESTIONER: I feel the left foot more.

LORD PENTLAND: The left is tense. When you're in the left foot more, you're in the body. It's quite different. In any case you see the difference, yes? If I'm sensitive, it's possible. But the point isn't that. I'm not trying to lead you into some kind of complexity. I'm simply saying that the only point in sensing is to help me to come to the impression of myself as a whole, yes? And that means to come out of wherever I'm lost in the head. Sometimes I'm lost more in the body, in the instincts. Then it's not complex to become aware of that. It's only when I'm aware of the sensation of the whole of myself that there's a sense of this being—my body calling. But I am. This is the aim of the work of sensation, to come to the experience, which is unmistakable, that I exist.

When there's more sensation in one part, in another part, the hand, it's not possible to have the experience of being present, here, now. So, for instance, you could change now and try to be aware of the sensation of your hand. You could make an exercise two or three times a day to look at your hand, look at my hand, at certain times that you set for yourself. Alternately, the right hand and the next time the left hand. And you'll see that it takes a little time and a certain degree of freedom, relaxation; freedom from the preoccupation with surroundings and with your own inner emotions to reach the experience that this is my hand, not a hand. You follow me? That it belongs with what we call my body. It's more difficult than that.

I have to give something for a real effort; there is something I have to give which we're very reluctant to give, to pay. Even if I remember, "Now I'll look at the right hand," I can be looking at it a very long time and nothing happens. I have to give something. There has to be a certain activity, whatever is needed for a search—to try something, not just wait there. I try making the arm very tense. Then I try making it very relaxed, letting the tension go. Maybe that helps. Maybe it doesn't help. I try letting the whole experience like that be part of something greater.

And then I have to give time. I see I haven't really confronted what it means to give time. My time isn't my time. It's all the time compartmentalized. This is the time for special business out of which I give this time to the work, all pasteurized, or I'll give this time to talk to the family, and I have this time for writing letters. This has got to be my time for speaking. And I don't know what it means to have a work to make it all my time. Whatever I'm doing, it's my time. It's only then that I can make a voluntary work.

QUESTIONER: I have a real sense of that, of the compartment.

LORD PENTLAND: You see you have an appointment book and as soon as things begin to go wrong, you lose this sense that it's all one life—it's all my time. And out of my time I'm going to give some time to work. Without that the work won't go. That's why some of us look back and say, you people say, "You know, I've been in the work five years," or something. Sometimes even longer. But how much of that time was given, so to speak? You understand what I'm saying? A voluntary work. Somebody perhaps says to you, "Will you wash the dishes?" Yes? Now what's the difference between giving time to washing the dishes or watching the television? I mean there's no difference as long as you give the time. You understand what I mean?

QUESTIONER: Somewhat.

LORD PENTLAND: Washing dishes is for washing dishes. It's not for anything else. Here the work is to simply wash the dishes. With television it's the same thing. If you work, you simply watch the television.

QUESTION: That sort of strikes me because I'm really starting to see that there's, maybe I'm seeing wrong, but it seems to me that certain things draw me, and that everything doesn't seem to be as equal as you're saying. Certain aspects of my life seem to be able to exist only in sleep and I don't know how to really see them, really be there for them. I know how to judge them afterwards and I see them coming on before. I see that it's possible to arrive in the middle and see something about myself and the relation I have to them.

LORD PENTLAND: Yes, that's quite true, but it's also true that in order to work effectively we need each other and we need a certain wish to adopt new categories, new values with new categories. Instead of valuing this that I'm attracted to more and that that I dislike less, we have to take our stand upon—as if we value the wish for Being more, yes? And everything that comes in the way of that—less. In that sense the work is artificial and in that sense the work begins from trying to free myself from these habitual patterns, yes? And we're all doing that. We're all watching television less and washing up more. Yes? But that's no help just to put different categories like that. I'm suggesting no categories of that kind. We need inner categories; the wish to be and the resistance to it, which as of now, we could say, is partly my attachment to certain things. Do you follow?

QUESTIONER: Yes.

LORD PENTLAND: It's not a very big difference between watching television and washing up. It only takes a short time to see that the habit of washing up is just as bad a habit as watching television. What we wish when we wash up is to be there washing up and not talking or thinking about something else or being sorry for ourselves.

My problem is my opportunity . . .

QUESTION: My life has entered a phase of very much conflict in that . . .

LORD PENTLAND: Good. Your life is . . .

QUESTIONER: My life is in a phase of very intense conflict.

LORD PENTLAND: Your life is . . .

QUESTIONER: A phase of conflict.

LORD PENTLAND: Yes.

QUESTIONER: The problem that I have is that on one hand I understand that what speaks does not exist. The work has proven that there is something in me that can exist, and I have to finally face the situation here and now. And yet even knowing this, I'm still drawn back into the intoxication of my suffering like a drunk. I don't see my way clear of breaking from this dichotomy, this, so to say, springing on myself.

LORD PENTLAND: In a general way, following the point of view that I have been projecting in this meeting, my problem is my opportunity. Do you agree with that? You see that afterwards whenever you've had a problem in the past you wish that you had confronted it in a different way than you did. It was like an opportunity and you were never able to take it enough like an opportunity to have a free attitude to it. Yes?

QUESTIONER: Yes.

LORD PENTLAND: So we must start there. Whatever it is, this dichotomy, in some way it touches two different aspects of the same life, my life. So it's not so much a question of which is right or more important. It's a question of how to bring them together, to relate them. Yes?

QUESTIONER: Because there is no relation.

LORD PENTLAND: There's no relation between them and that's the artificial work that's up to me. And that means being concerned. It can't be possible to just, through a little bit of conversation—we hardly know each other—to change my whole point of view like that towards big things. So it depends on me, on you, how far you can have, through perhaps sitting quietly with yourself, a beginning of a real feeling of concern about your whole life.

QUESTIONER: That's precisely the point.

LORD PENTLAND: Not about one side or the other, but a feeling that your life is going on the rocks or something, a feeling of real concern that the whole of your life needs to be turned around. And only then can you try to see it as a whole instead of as before, always getting caught in one aspect. How to include both? And that usually means the difficult work of simply going on as one is, without taking any strong initiative in either direction. You understand. So it means living with this question, living with this question until it begins to be less urgent and then finding another question as I did before. You understand? We're all the time, as we look back—and we need to look back sometime—all the time exactly missing the emotional opportunity when there's two sides. My life quiets down and is all right, then I ring up here and come spend long periods here. Quite useless. It's when I'm involved that I need the work. Do you see what I mean? It's very important. I wish you luck.

QUESTIONER: I could use some luck.

LORD PENTLAND: You will have luck. Do you understand a little what luck is? It's what comes to people who work like that.

You don't struggle against your subjectivity—
you struggle for seeing . . .

QUESTION: I commonly experience what I call my ego rubbing up against that of somebody else's and that seems to usually bring about a tension that takes away my energy for the task at hand. I do try to work with it when I'm here on Sundays and in my group meetings yet my attempts here seem more of a camouflage, sort of a quiet passivity, just dropping it rather than having anything genuine take place. I'd like to try to work with that in some way where I would actually be using that rather than just screening it.

LORD PENTLAND: What is the work together? You'd certainly do better not to come than to come and not be able to make use of the work. To spend the day at home would be a better work than to come here without knowing how to make use of the work. So the question is "How to make use of the work together?" You're not the only person who's asked to understand that. You see, the work together theoretically, and I have to say theoretically because I haven't been here on Sundays very much, but the work together is very much what could be regarded as the nearest we've come to a school here. Something goes on between the people on Sunday. Whatever it means, self-development needs a school. It depends on how we understand the work together. Gurdjieff himself, speaking of course about different people at a different time than us now, said about his work at the Prieuré, "Here I can't help; I can only give conditions and direct conditions." So the help was in between the people, in the relationships. If you don't understand that, of course you can't be interested.

The idea is that by starting with a question, I begin to be able to see myself, I question myself. That only lasts an instant, but in returning again and again to the question, I begin to see what goes on in me. And certainly a lot goes on in me in my relationships with other people, where there are a lot of people working in the same room, yes? So we're speaking about questioning and then as I work, the wish to see myself—that's a relative consciousness—the wish to be aware, but of my subjectivity, my automatic side, functioning. Yes? You follow that? And you see that when we come together, each wishing to be aware of his or her subjectivity, it creates an entirely new possibility of being present to myself because as long as I'm wishing to see myself—let's say as long as I'm, relatively speaking, seeing myself, seeing what's going on inside, taken only sometimes by impulses—then it's the same with the others. I'm seeing them also as wishing to be present and taken only sometimes by tantrums, something ridiculous. So there's no judgment when I'm all the time with others and I'm seeing myself and them. We're not conscious people but by making this step of questioning ourselves, we begin to see ourselves, see what goes on in myself when I receive the interaction with you. That's what we mean by the work on Sundays, yes? You follow me?

QUESTIONER: I'm getting a glimmer of a path to follow.

LORD PENTLAND: Well, you'll have to see if you can use the work for that. Otherwise, it's better not to come. Do you follow? Sometimes you can't avoid it—you make a judgment of someone. But mostly you are trying to be free from these judgments. And even as was just said, seeking opportunities to be with especially subjective people to see how far you can be quiet. If there are any subjective people.

Doesn't that interest you? It's maybe a risky thing but if you really wish to use the work and use it for that, you will get something. You have to work very hard. All day. Then in the evening you go out, you forget the work. Do you follow? Really have the will.

QUESTIONER: Are you suggesting that it might be better to try to see my subjectivity and struggle against it?

LORD PENTLAND: No. You struggle for seeing. You don't struggle against your subjectivity. You struggle for seeing. Yes? That's what we were speaking about too. Right?

Once I'm lost in the automatism, it's better to let the reaction take place . . .

QUESTION: A long time ago when I was meeting with a woman in the work, just before I was invited to the work here, and this woman asked me if I was angry and in that second I knew what she meant. And now all that's been aroused again. I'm sitting here and I'm angry. There's no two ways about it. But that's normally where I'm lost, normally where I go away or what I go to when I begin to see. So what do I give to that, you know? What can I possibly give to that that's as pertinent as the ideas that you're making right now are to me? In other words, the ideas that you're suggesting right now all only hit me in a place of submission. In other words, because my supposed anger is so obviously out of hand that if I submit to whoever's in front of me or with me, there's at least a chance for another second of sight and control, or sight and lessening of the anger. Is that risky? Is that how simple it is?

LORD PENTLAND: I think there's a point in your question which you need to be careful about as far as it relates to some things I said this evening. But you see, the point is that once I'm lost in the automatism, it's really better for the whole of myself to let the reaction take place in order, as soon as possible, to come back to the wish to be. To hang on for a little moment longer through some mental kind of tense struggle only means it will be longer, much longer sometimes, before I'm really balanced enough to come back to myself. So I'm saying it's better to let the impulse manifest itself in order as soon as possible to begin my wish for being. So that when a group of people work together there's bound to be some of this impulsive behavior, and the question is not a matter of whether there's complete quiet, but the question is when certain people manifest impulsively, whether I'm able to not judge it because I'm doing the same work. It's the judgments that make for the problems between people.

This may be quite new to you but I don't think so. You have Hollywood; you have lots of friends in that. Some of the most gifted actors and actresses understand this and they behave very subjectively, you know. But then they're back making these wonderful films. Do you follow the idea that I'm giving? That's what I was giving. For a lot of people intensely trying to be quiet, this is a worse condition than occasional outburst. That's what I mean. I hope I've made that clear. It's quite important. It's a new idea for some of you.

The knowledge that helps self-observation is communicated
by self-observation . . .

QUESTION: I'm disappointed that work isn't more central in my life. I feel there's a kind of stubbornness that comes up which says, "That's enough," or "Stop," while sitting. It seems when the possibility is greatest something comes in and says, "Stop, that's enough." Yet I find I need help and understanding for how to make it more central.

LORD PENTLAND: One needs help staying on the way. The way is a way of self-observation, self-study, self-consciousness. And it means self-study, self-knowledge. So when things stop or go on, that's to be observed.

And when I begin to be hostile to myself or to the way, that means I have to observe this hostility. It's the only way back to the way. The temptation is not whatever it is thought to be—power, money, sex—the temptation is that I love myself and don't observe myself when the power or whatever comes. Do you follow?

So you may say, how do I keep on observing myself? You have to observe that you don't observe, and gradually you discover things about the way to live with this idea of self-observation. You sit in a tidy room and it helps, or you lose the idea when trying this way. That's how it all comes, little by little. The knowledge that helps self-observation is communicated by self-observation. It's very difficult but as I've tried to say, it's simple.

QUESTIONER: Does the observation come from the mind or another part of myself?

LORD PENTLAND: It's an observation of the mind and all the parts of myself and comes from a moment when the higher energy enters me. It enters me relatively, so it makes of me for a moment one or another of different levels of attention, and according to these levels I see more or less while the energy is passing through me. And it needs a certain level to communicate that kind of knowledge. At first I have the observation of two or three—but usually two—centers without the higher energy, so I have an observation of myself as a paradox. Don't you find that? But when the higher energy comes in, I have observations which give me a kind of knowledge if I can be sensitive enough to take it and not react to it, saying that's not me or whatever. They give a kind of knowledge of what to avoid, what helps. Having many of these observations in the midst of my life enables me to avoid some of these temptations or to go right in the direction of my weaknesses. Which may be what I need. But in moving like that or connecting things, there isn't the faintest affirmation of doing something, so this makes it possible to keep in mind that it's a work of self-consciousness. Self-development takes place through self-consciousness, if it takes place. It isn't taking place because I don't feel bad enough, in principle, seeing myself.

CHAPTER TWENTY-NINE

*You see that's where the work on
emotions fits in . . .*

QUESTION: I have a wish for an awareness of something higher in my work. And that experience seems very rare, happening in sittings sometimes, in movements. It was mentioned in the reading yesterday, and I'd like to find a way to begin with that. I feel the need for that and don't know how to approach it.

LORD PENTLAND: If you mean by something higher, something you don't know, obviously you don't know how to approach it. It has no real meaning to think of it as above me. The higher energy we need, that can pass into us, is all around me. What is higher? Look up. What is higher? The level of energy is higher.

So I make myself available as far as I can by being more sensitive and by making a more stable wish to come in touch with this higher energy. You see that's where the work on emotions fits in. To observe emotions is interesting and very valuable in the sense of observation, for then more energy is taken from the emotion to observe. Do you follow? In observing the emotion there is more energy being used for observing that would otherwise go into the emotion. By the accumulation of many observations, I could free myself from emotions.

You don't feel emotional, true, but sensation enables me to observe, to control, the emotion. And when I'm not emotional, the sensation can connect me with emotion. I need to be free regarding the emotions, and that's possible by observing myself only. Why do I need to be free in relation to emotions? There are two reasons and they don't conflict with each other but they often get mixed up. The first is because my ordinary relationships with other human beings are important to me and the first collision always takes place in the emotional area. The more I can find emotion when I have none, and control them when I have emotions, the more my human relationships are possible.

But your question deals with another area, which includes human relationships, which is how to relate to the higher emotions, and it's useful to separate that from the first kind. The work with emotions, as understood

by the human potential movements and others, can improve my relationships. But it's only through a relationship with the higher energies that we
can really have a stable relationship with humans because that's the only
thing we have in common—higher energies enter me and higher energies
enter you. We each have a number of centers but even my essential material of centers is different from yours and all the information depends on
being brought up differently and so forth.

How to be able, to be open, to have room enough for this higher energy
to enter? That's what the work is chiefly concerned about. Yes, it's necessary to be free of the fear because I can't work without concepts though
they can hold up the flow of energy, particularly emotions about concepts,
like "I'm right about this concept." The main thing is the higher has to be
unknown. I am lower. It is higher. I don't know it. So there's probably fear
in approaching it.

You call it higher but that's all you can say. It's a level where some
things take place analogously but I can't know that except by an observation of myself with that energy. I have to be ready, to prepare myself, to be
available to this energy because it's too convenient when it comes to go
away. I have to try to have contact intentionally even though I can't know.
I have to try to let it be received. That's why we emphasize the somewhat
ceremonial aspects of our meetings, even at the expense of it being rather
stiff.

It really is useful to study this alone, sitting in the morning. And there
again it helps to be rather careful and ceremonial about it. I choose carefully the place I put the cushion. I make sure there's going to be enough
time for how long I want to sit. I don't sit in bed or in a mess. I get out of
bed and tidy the bed. But why speak, you may ask, of such absurd details?
It's a good question.